FEAR
OF
INE

FEAR

OF

WINE

AN INTRODUCTORY GUIDE TO THE GRAPE

Text by Leslie Brenner

Illustrations by Lettie Teague

BANTAM BOOKS

New York   Toronto   London   Sydney   Auckland

FEAR OF WINE

A Bantam Book/November 1995

All rights reserved.

Text copyright © 1995 by Leslie Brenner.

Illustrations copyright © 1995 by Lettie Teague.

The Wine Aroma Wheel copyright by A.C. Noble

BOOK DESIGN BY GLEN M. EDELSTEIN.

For information address: Bantam Books

Library of Congress Cataloging-in-Publication Data

Brenner, Leslie.

Fear of wine : an introductory guide to the grape / text by Leslie Brenner; illustrations by Lettie Teague.

p.   cm.

ISBN 0–553–37464–8

1. Wine and wine making.   I. Title.

TP548.B817   1995

641.2'2—dc20   95-15038

CIP

Published simultaneously in the United States and Canada

Bantam Books are published by Bantam Books, a division of Bantam Doubleday Dell Publishing Group, Inc. Its trademark, consisting of the words "Bantam Books" and the portrayal of a rooster, is Registered in U.S. Patent and Trademark Office and in other countries. Marca Registrada. Bantam Books, 1540 Broadway, New York, New York 10036.

PRINTED IN THE UNITED STATES OF AMERICA

FFG   10 9 8 7 6 5

ACKNOWLEDGMENTS

Deepest gratitude to our editor Jennifer Hershey, for her vision, patience, good judgment, and good faith; my swell agent, Jennifer Rudolph Walsh; Dan Sullivan, for his generosity in sharing his remarkable collection; Kimberly Charles, for flaming the vinous fire; Dawn Ann Drzal, for warm, enthusiastic support; Joan and Warren Winston, my favorite mom and stepfather; Chris and Ron Bass for their generous hospitality in Napa and elsewhere; Randy Dunn, who was kind enough to take me up in his plane for the best valley tour. Thank you, too, to Mike and Elena Clark, Sue Jamison and Richard Sykes, Ronn Wiegand, Lisa Bishop, Bob Spitz, Sally Gordon, Pam Hunter, Janet Kafka, Jan Stuebing, Katrin Naelapa and Wines from Spain, Carol Sullivan and the German Wine Information Bureau. Special thanks to Lettie Teague for her warmth, good humor, and wonderful cartoons, and to Alan Richman for his invaluable tips on matching wines with tongue and other deli sandwiches.

And most of all, thank you to Thierry Pérémarti, the best thing ever to come out of Bordeaux.

L.B.

Thank you to our editor Jennifer Hershey for her unerring taste, enthusiasm, and support; to our designer Glen Edelstein for his patience and good humor; and to our agent Jennifer Rudolph Walsh. Thank you to my parents, Edward and Patricia, whose library has always held not just the Harvard Classics but classic cartoon works as well. Thank you to my co-author, Leslie Brenner, a swell partner and friend. Thank you to Amy Levin

Cooper for "Breadloaf." Special thanks to Suzanne Ausnit, Linda Amicangioli, Ben Boltin, the late Lee Boltin, Victoria Kent, Kathy Levy, Willie Norkin, Lynn Schwartz, and Nola Tully. And finally thank you to my husband, Alan Richman, who was always there with kind words and badly stored wines.

L.T.

CONTENTS

THE ROOTS OF FEAR OF WINE AND WHY IT'S WELL WORTH OVERCOMING

How in the world did we manage to get so far in life and still wind up so terribly afraid of something that's just—dare we say it—a *beverage*?

Wine is a thing of fear and dread to most Americans. We're cowed by descriptions of it, fearful that we won't have what it takes (whatever *that* is) to taste whatever wine professionals have found in it. We're intimidated by unknown bottles, fearful that we cannot predict whether what's inside will be delicious or depressing. We're scared of French labels, since we can't pronounce them properly, and scared of German labels, since they look like gothic horror movies. We're scared of California labels, since we feel that we *should* know every single California wine, but of course we don't. We're afraid of corks, fearful that we won't be able to remove them without embarrassing ourselves. We're afraid of ordering wines in restaurants, fearful that we won't know how to talk to the wine steward; and scared to send it back if it's a bad bottle, fearful that we don't *really* know how to tell a bad one from one that's okay. And we're afraid to bring a bottle to a

dinner party, fearful that our choice will be perceived as unsophisticated.

All of this boils down to the same thing: We're afraid of wine because we sense that somehow wine will make us look dumb.

Sadly, we're also afraid of attempting to learn anything at all about it because we're put off by the pompous tone of wine magazines and the overblown or overtechnical language of wine books. Not to mention the glib remarks made by salespeople in wineshops who inform us, without even trying to figure out what we *like,* that Château Dégoûtant has a marvelous roasted blackcurrant and cedar nose, lots of ripe fruit, and plenty of depth, with hints of hazelnut and mint in the middle palate, and a lingering licorice finish.

What if we hate blackcurrants? What if we don't even know what they are? What if licorice makes us retch? What if cedar reminds us of our grandmother's hall closet? Is that good or bad? Of course on the other side of the retailer coin are those who will tell you, "This is an excellent wine: Robert Parker rated it a 94." That tells you nothing about it, except that one expert happened to like it. (Robert Parker is a very well-respected wine writer and author who assigns numerical ratings to wines as they're released in his incredibly influential newsletter, the *Wine Advocate*.) Far too many people believe that unlike any other beverage, wine requires someone else's opinion before it's drinkable. The truth is that no one particular wine will appeal to everybody, no matter what Robert Parker or the *Wine Spectator* or anyone else rated it, and the single most important thing to know is that it's what *you* like that matters.

How did we come to the point where we trust someone else's opinion more than our own?

The question is best attacked in a roundabout way. In most wine-drinking cultures around the world, people are not afraid of wine. You don't see French people running around Paris bistros, wringing their hands and crying, "Oh, *mon Dieu*, would a Côtes du Rhône go with my *gigot d'agneau*?" You don't see Italians waltzing into trattorias only to slink out without ordering, embarrassed to ask whether the Chianti is a Classico or a Rufina.

Is this because the Italians and the French know so much more about wine than we do? *Au contraire, mon petit frère.* Not necessarily. It's just that they've been drinking it all their lives. In wine-drinking cultures, children used to be given a few drops of

WINE CRITIC ROBERT PARKER'S NUMERICAL RATING SYSTEM HAS HAD AN ENORMOUS INFLUENCE ON WINEDRINKING CONSUMERS

PARKER RATED THIS ONE A "92" AND THIS ONE AN "87." ARE THE ANDERSONS WORTH A "92"?

wine in their water to accustom them to the taste. People grow up with wine at the dinner table; it's part of the family meal. Since children aren't prohibited from touching the stuff, it doesn't become "forbidden fruit" like beer and wine do in our culture. As a result, kids *don't* bend over backward to get their hands on it when the adults aren't around, and then proceed to get drunk. In these cultures, wine is a *food* rather than a drug, and it is served and consumed with respect, but without much hoopla, at the table.

In fact, the idea many of us hold that Europeans in general actually know a lot about wine is a myth. Most of them don't even know any more than you do, for instance, about how wine is made. And the majority probably aren't familiar with more than one or two types of wine—they tend to know and drink what's local. Go to dinner five nights in a row with your average Frenchman, and you may be surprised to see that he's not ordering all over the wine list; he's sticking to the one or two wines he knows and likes.

Fear of wine is really a very basic fear of the unknown. Since most of us are not introduced to wine until we're adults and therefore much more fearful and set in our ways than children are, we're afraid of it.

This fear of the unknown is also rooted in history. Winemaking began in the United States in the early 1800s; it had even begun in what used to be Mexico and is now Texas and New Mexico as far back as the early 1600s. But production was relatively small until the California wine industry took off in the second half of the nineteenth century.

If things had gone along in this fashion, perhaps wine would now be as natural to Americans as it is to the French, and we'd never have developed oenophobia. Instead, what happened, in 1920, was Prohibition.

National Prohibition, a constitutional amendment that made the production, sale, or transportation of "intoxicating liquors" illegal in the United States from 1920 until it was repealed at the end of 1933, put a puritanical pall on the country and a damper on the wine business. Certain wineries were allowed to continue making wine for religious purposes, but by and large, vines died, wineries went under, people forgot how to make wine, and more significantly, how to enjoy it. Although some people made it at home, it was most likely plonk. (In case you don't know, "plonk" is the technical term for lousy wine.) Americans who drank wine with dinner for the most part had to drop the habit.

America suffered a great setback in both its winemaking capabilities and in wine appreciation. So if you suffer today from fear of wine, don't blame yourself, blame history.

Incidentally, Prohibition was also responsible for what has been until fairly recently in the century an embarrassing lack of culinary skills and food knowledge. Restaurants have always depended greatly on their income from wine and liquor; when they could no longer serve alcohol, the financial strain caused a tremendous number to fold in the 1920s. Speakeasies, not restaurants, were where all the action was, and like winemaking and wine appreciation, cooking and food knowledge fell by the wayside as well. After repeal, the Depression had already set in, so it took many years for restaurants to come back, and decades before people thought seriously about food and wine again. Not until the 1970s did haute cuisine really kick in again, and at the same time the California wine industry, which started to get back on its feet in the mid-1960s, began producing really good wines to go with the suddenly emerging really good food.

In other words, we lost a huge chunk of time in U.S. winemaking history, just as we did in food history. On the other hand, we've made up a lot of ground very quickly. Consider the fact that winemakers all over the world are borrowing styles and techniques from California and you'll realize that we've really come an impressive distance. We're already making world-class wines.

Besides our own wines, we're fortunate to have an amazing array of wines from all around the world available to us—which is not the case in most other countries. When you consider the pleasure that a glass of wine can bring to dinner (or even lunch!), it's a damn shame if we don't take advantage.

You may be saying to yourself at this point: Why bother?

First, wine makes food taste better. I don't know exactly why this is so, but I could make a few conjectures. Maybe the alcohol on the palate opens up the taste buds. Perhaps the flavors of wine just naturally complement cooking, much more so than, say, Orange Crush. Or maybe the conviviality associated with sharing wine with friends and family puts one in a more generous frame of mind.

Second, people around the world (or at least all up and down your block) are learning more and more about wine to enhance their enjoyment. If you ignore it, you'll be left in the cold. Imagine being the only one on your block who still thinks spaghetti is the only shape that pasta comes in!

Finally, and most importantly, for just about anyone who brings it into their regular course of living, wine improves the quality of life. Think of it this way: If you find that you really like it, *it'll be one more thing in your life that actually brings you pleasure!*

Once you start to enjoy wine and make it part of your life, you'll start to notice that life looks a little rosier. The sky will look a little bluer; you'll rest a little easier knowing some damn wine snob isn't going to make you look the fool at a dinner party; and your dinner table at home will become a place of chance, excitement, and sparkle, even if you're eating the same old meat loaf you've always eaten, which will suddenly begin to taste like filet mignon. When dining out, you'll no longer feel that awful dull gnawing feeling when presented with a wine list; on the contrary, you'll eagerly grab for it, and maybe even read it before you look at the menu! People will start insisting that *you* order the wine, even if deep inside you still feel you don't know all that much about it. But they asked you and hey—looks like they're paying, so you can even order something really expensive if you want!

And remember: Reading is one thing, but tasting is another. Taste as many different wines as you can, the more varied in terms of style and region, the better; and taste often. Your own taste will start becoming clear to you more quickly than you think.

In fact, why wait? Why not jump in right away? Start by running out to the nearest wineshop and picking something that appeals to you. Don't worry about why. Maybe you like the label, maybe you like the price, maybe the woman at the shop recommended it—no matter. Take it home. Open it. Pour a glass half full. Swirl it around. Smell it. Savor the smell. Don't worry about what you're smelling; just enjoy. Taste it. Swish it around

ARMING YOURSELF WITH A FEW WINE BOOKS AND REMEMBERING A FEW KEY FACTS CAN MAKE YOU APPEAR TO BE A WINE EXPERT

"A CABERNET IS A CABERNET WHEREVER IT GOES, BUT A PINOT NOIR TAKES THE CHARACTER OF WHEREVER IT GROWS."

your mouth. Swallow it. Did you like it? Does it have any lingering aftertaste? Was it pleasant? Horrible?

Whatever it was, *scary it was not.* Right?

Well, the beauty of it is that buying and tasting wine will never
be more scary than that. Wine is just wine. It's a liquid; nothing
more. All *you* have to decide is did you like it or not? Would you
buy it again, or never?

It's only what *you* like that counts. Good-bye forever to wine
anxiety.

Part I

OVERCOMING OENOPHOBIA

Chapter One

HOW GRAPES BECOME WINE

Fear not: I won't bore you with a lot of technical information about winemaking. You won't be tested on the definition of malolactic fermentation or carbonic maceration—or anything else for that matter. This will just be an incredibly brief—even terse and witty—summary of how grapes turn into wine, just enough information to let you get on with enjoying wine as fully as possible.

It all starts in the vineyard, where a wide variety of grapes are grown to produce wine. During the growing season, which lasts from spring through harvest in the fall, the grower (or *vintner*) pays close attention to the progress of the vines. He or she hopes that the weather won't often reach extremes, that the summer will last long so that the grapes can become very ripe, and that it won't suddenly start raining right before the harvest. It is weather that can make wines grown in one year taste better than others. So when people talk about good vintages (or years) these are the major factors they are considering.

As the grapes grow, they get riper and riper. Chemically, that

means that the amount of sugar in the grapes is increasing, which is why ripe fruit tastes sweeter than unripe fruit. As the time for harvest nears, the winemaker and the oenologist (the scientist specializing in winemaking who runs the winemaker's lab) will now become very interested in the grapes. If you go to wine country, you can see them out in the vineyards examining grapes with an instrument called a refractometer which tells them the exact sugar level on any given day. Probably they'll also use the old-fashioned method: tasting a grape to see if it's ripe. In general, they want to get that sugar level as high as possible at the time of harvest. If rain is forecast, the harvest becomes a race against time, since a lot of water can actually dilute the taste (and the chemical composition) of the grapes. If they become watery, so will the wine.

Once the grower or the winemaker gives the go-ahead, workers start picking the grapes. When the grapes in question will be used to make a high-quality wine, the picking becomes a fairly difficult job. The idea is to pick the grapes in bunches, leaving behind any that have turned to raisins, and making sure not to get any leaves in the large collection bins.

Now the bunches of grapes go to the winery. Depending on whether the wine will be red or white, two different things will happen.

White-Wine Making

White wine, believe it or not, can be made from grapes that are either white (actually, sort of yellow or green) or red (which could even be very dark, almost black). That's because color in wine comes from pigment in the skin, and if the winemaker removes the skin before the wine is made, the wine will remain white. After the grapes are picked, they're crushed and destemmed in a large machine. Then the juice, which at this point is called *free-run juice*, is drained off and collected, and the stems and skins pressed, so that additional juices can drain off as well. The stems and skins are left behind.

Next the juice, along with some yeast, goes into either a stainless-steel vat or a smaller oak barrel to be fermented. Fermentation simply means that the yeast "eats" the sugars, producing alcohol and carbon dioxide as by-products. The carbon dioxide bubbles up and disappears as the wine is fermenting, but the alcohol stays in.

The juice, which we now call "must," continues to ferment for anywhere from a few days to a couple weeks, until all the sugar has fermented into alcohol.

The yeast cells die, becoming what is known as "lees." You may have seen wines that say things like "aged on its lees" on their labels. ("On its lees" translates to *sur lie* in French—you might see that, too.) What it means is that the winemaker left the dead yeast cells in the wine as it aged instead of letting them settle to the bottom of the vat or barrel and draining off the clear juice, which is called "racking." Sometimes they'll even stir up the lees to increase their contact with the wine—and even brag about it on the label ("Stirred on its lees").

Malolactic Fermentation

Every wine is fermented at least once. Sometimes the wine goes through a second fermentation, either naturally, or helped along by the winemaker. In this fermentation, malic acid, naturally present in the grapes, turns into lactic acid, which tastes less harsh than malic acid. In white wines, malolactic fermentation is encouraged mainly in Chardonnays. Besides softening the acids, it can also add a "buttery" flavor and aroma to the wine.

Either way, the wine now has to age. Most white wine is aged in stainless-steel vats, which lets the flavors of the grape shine through loud and clear. Sometimes, though, white wine—especially wine made from the Chardonnay grape—is aged in oak (or other wood) barrels. The wine picks up a lot of flavor and aroma from the oak, especially those of vanilla and toast; when people talk about a wine being "oaky," they're usually talking about toasty vanilla aromas and flavors.

After barrel or vat aging, the wine is racked (if it hasn't been already) and stabilized. Then it will be *fined*, a process in which a substance is added to attract any extra particles floating around. Next the wine is drained off of the residue, filtered to make it clear and pretty, and bottled. At that point the wine is either released into the marketplace or held at the winery to age longer in the bottle.

TIP FROM CABERNET FRANK

Vinification is just a ten-dollar word for "winemaking."

Red-Wine Making

Winemakers go through the same basic process to make red wine, with only minor differences.

First, they want to get a lot of color into the wine. That means when the grapes are crushed, the

MAKING WINE

BREAKING THE SKINS

FERMENTING

HARVESTING THE GRAPES

BOTTLING

AGING

SELLING

Dave's Wine

Julia's Lemonade 5¢

Cabernet Sauvignon 50¢ glass $3 bottle

stems are removed, but the skins are left in. The skins contain most of the color pigment, but that's not all: They also have a lot of what are called *tannins*. In case you're wondering what tannin is like, you're probably already familiar with it: It's the substance in strong black tea that leaves your mouth feeling sort of dry. (It's also found in the seeds of the grapes and in the oak in which wine is sometimes aged.) As long as they're not overly harsh, tannins can be very important in red wine, since they give a backbone to the wine, and also preserve it for aging.

Unlike white wine, red wine is fermented *before* the skins are removed so they can stay in contact with the juice longer. In the production of very simple and inexpensive wines the skins may

Blending

Whether a wine contains 100 percent of one kind of grape or a combination of different grapes, it will usually need to be blended.

For wines such as California Meritage or red Bordeaux that contain several different grape varieties, each of the vats or barrels in the winery will contain the wine from only one particular grape. At some point before it's bottled, the winemaker and oenologist will taste samples from all the different vessels. Even if two different barrels are both filled with Cabernet Sauvignon, the grapes that went into them may have come from different vineyards, or even different spots in the same vineyard, and that will make them taste slightly different. Blending involves taking wine from different vessels, and putting them together in the best combination.

For certain wines, blending also means following a sort of recipe. For example, a Bordeaux might be a blend of 70 percent Cabernet Sauvignon, 20 percent Merlot, and 10 percent Cabernet Franc. Or the winemaker might want to include specific amounts of wine that has been made using different techniques. For instance, she may be making a wine entirely out of Chardonnay grapes, and she may want half of the grapes to have been barrel-fermented and half of them fermented in stainless steel.

be discarded after the fermentation (easily done, since they float up to the top of the vat). But for finer wines, the winemaker will want to keep them in there for a week or so longer: this is called *maceration*. The skins have to be punched down into the wine, or the wine pumped up over the skins, to encourage this process.

That done, the wine is racked, allowed to go through malolactic fermentation if desired (with fine red wines it often is), then put into either wood barrels or stainless-steel vats for aging. Oak aging is much more common for red wines than it is for white wines. When it has aged enough, the wine is fined, filtered, stabilized, clarified, and then bottled.

And that's it! That's all you have to know about winemaking.

Oh—there's one last thing you'll want to know. How on earth do they make rosé? Ladies and gentlemen, drumroll, please . . . Rosé, which is simply pink wine, is made one of two ways. In the first method, red grapes are crushed, and the skins left in contact with the juice for just a short time. Winemaking then proceeds nor-

Winemakers Make Such a Big Deal About Oak?

Oak barrels, which are pretty expensive, have much more flavor to give to the wine when they're new—no more than two years old. For that reason, winemakers have to keep buying new ones. Since they're spending a lot of money on them, the wineries like to tout this aspect of the process. Winemakers also make a big deal about where the oak was grown—whether the trees were American or French. The most prestigious oak is generally accepted to be French; however, some winemakers, such as many Spanish ones, prefer American oak.

Should they be bragging about it? Maybe, maybe not. Oak can add complexity to a wine, but when overdone, it can also mask the natural flavors and aromas of the grape variety.

Q: What does a winemaker do if he can't afford oak barrels, but wants to add some of that toasty, vanilla-y oak flavor?

A: Put the wine in stainless-steel vats, and dump in a bunch of oak chips, or even "oak essence." (Yes, it's true!)

mally, as if it were a white wine. In the second method, the wine-maker takes a bunch of white wine and mixes a little red wine into it. Really! In fact, that's how rosé champagnes are made.

IF YOU FORGET EVERYTHING ELSE YOU'VE READ IN CHAPTER ONE, JUST REMEMBER THIS:

1. The riper the grapes are at harvest, the more sugar will be available for fermentation into alcohol.
2. The color in red wine comes from the juice's prolonged contact with the grape skins.
3. Fermentation is the process of yeast "eating" the sugars

Wild Yeasts

Since yeast occurs naturally on the skins of the grapes, even if winemakers didn't add yeast to the juice, it would eventually ferment anyway. Winemakers need to control things a little more, though, so they "inoculate" the juice with a measured amount of yeast. Usually, this is a commercial yeast they have purchased, which has been carefully developed in a laboratory (especially in the U.S., Australia, and other "New World" wine-producing countries). However, there's a movement afoot in favor of using "wild" or "natural" yeasts. Winemakers who do so (and this includes many French winemakers) say that commercial yeasts make all wines taste pretty much the same, yet with "wild" yeasts, more individual, interesting flavors are allowed to come through. Detractors say their use is unpredictable, even a little dangerous, and accuse those who use them of doing so just as a marketing ploy. The only thing that's absolutely clear is that great wines have been made both ways.

in the juice, resulting in alcohol and carbon dioxide.

4. Lees are the dead yeast cells. Leaving them in during aging adds complexity to a wine.
5. Oak aging adds vanilla and toast aromas.
6. Tannins in red wine come from grape skins and seeds, as well as from oak barrels.

The average American drinks only 1.72 gallons of wine each year. Compare this with 40 gallons of soft drinks or 25 gallons of coffee—not to mention the 17 gallons of wine the average Frenchman drinks each year.

Chapter Two

HOW TO APPROACH A GLASS OF WINE

In this chapter you'll learn all you need to know about approaching a glass of wine. After you read through this, you'll be able to sit next to the most seasoned wine snob at a formal tasting and not make an ass of yourself.

Tasting vs. Drinking Wine

There's a world of difference between tasting wine and simply drinking it. You already know how to drink it—all you have to do is pour a glass and enjoy. Wine professionals and enthusiasts engage in a different type of activity, referred to as tasting.

Although this book really aims to tell how you can learn to enjoy *drinking* wine, you'll find that if you know the basics of *tasting,* you'll enjoy drinking wine in a way that you probably haven't before. If you know a little about how to taste, you'll also find that if you decide you like a wine, you'll have an idea about *why* you like it, and if you pronounce a wine "delicious" in front of a roomful of wine snobs, you'll be as correct as anyone else.

Learning More About Tasting

If you find you really like the serious *tasting* part of wine tasting (as opposed to drinking), you'll want to read more about it. Here's where to look:

- **The excellent first section of Michael Schuster's *The Simon & Schuster Beginner's Guide to Understanding Wine*, called "Wine Tasting Techniques." This is probably the most comprehensive.**
- **The "Judging Wine" chapter of Hugh Johnson's *How to Enjoy Wine*.**
- **The "On Tasting Wine" chapter of Kevin Zraly's *Windows on the World Complete Wine Course*.**

Finally, knowing the basics of tasting will allow you to find flaws in wine. That way, if you order a wine in a restaurant and you decide there's something wrong with it, you'll be able to say exactly *what's* wrong with it with confidence. If the person who has served it is inexperienced or ignorant and doesn't believe you, you can slap a label on the problem and insist that the house take it back.

Stemware

It's not necessary to have lots of different glasses in order to enjoy wine, nor need you even invest in one set of expensive glasses. All you really need in the way of stemware is one set of good all-purpose wineglasses for most table wines.

Perhaps you've seen books that describe in great detail the only type of glass that's proper for a white Burgundy, another that's appropriate for a red Burgundy, and yet a third for a red Bordeaux. If you pick up a copy of the popular *Wine Spectator* magazine, you can probably flip through the pages and find an advertisement for Riedel stemware. Riedel is an Austrian company that specializes in making the ultimate glass for each type

of wine. Each glass is designed to direct the bouquet found in each of the various types of wine right to your nose, and to send the wine into your mouth in order that it hits your tongue in all the right spots. What will people pay for this accessory? Up to seventy-nine dollars *for one glass*! Of course if you had all the money in the world, it would be wonderful to own such fabulous glasses. But if you spent that much on the glasses, think of the wine you couldn't afford to buy.

So put all that aside, and let's think about your set of inexpensive, all-purpose wineglasses. The glass you look for should be completely clear glass or plain (not elaborately cut) crystal. Any color, even in the stem, will interfere with your looking at the color of the wine in the bowl. Very thin glass or crystal, which is more elegant and expensive, makes tasting even more enjoyable, but it's certainly not a requirement.

The stem should be long enough so that your hand doesn't warm the contents of the bowl.

The bowl (the part where the wine goes) should be relatively large: twelve ounces is about right. (This means that you can pour twelve ounces in and the liquid will be almost to the top.) This way, if you pour four ounces of wine into it—the perfect serving in a glass of this size—you'll have plenty of room in which to swirl the wine around. You'll see that even though four ounces is a third of the actual capacity, the glass will appear to be just under half-full when it contains four ounces of wine.

The bowl should also taper slightly at the top. If the sides of the bowl don't taper, some of the bouquet will be lost. Slight tapering ensures that the wonderful smells you're looking for will be directed straight to your nose. (It also ensures that when you swirl the wine around, it doesn't wind up on the tablecloth or your shirt.)

Some people like the wide balloon-type bowl. A glass like this is typically used for mature red Burgundies. It's fine for any type of wine, although since traditionally white wines are served in smaller glasses, you might be happier with something else as an all-purpose glass.

Riedel, the stemware company mentioned above, actually makes an all-purpose glass, which it calls the "Gourmet Glass," designed for everyday use and tastings. Besides being affordable compared with all their other glasses, they're only six and a quarter inches high, which some wine lovers will like since they'll fit in the dishwasher. However, to my taste, the stem is awkwardly short.

Otherwise, you should be able to pick up an attractive, serviceable twelve-ounce wineglass for between five and eight dollars apiece at housewares stores such as Pottery Barn, Williams-Sonoma, and Crate & Barrel, or at many department stores.

On the other hand, you may be the type of person who really wants to have different glasses for different types of wine. This might be because you like to throw dinner parties, or perhaps you're a potential wine geek who would like to invest in a lot of apparatus, or you just want to enjoy each glass as fully and elaborately as possible.

If so, more power to you. Take a gander at the illustration on page 25, which shows the appropriate glasses for the various types of wine. Certainly champagne and sparkling wines are one exception to the all-purpose glass rule; they're really best enjoyed in a flute or tulip-type glass, which is not only festive, but also helps keep the bubbles in. Anyone interested in fortified wines such as port and sherry should probably invest in the right glasses for maximum enjoyment.

Temperature

Don't be put off by proclamations like "Red wine should be served between 58°F and 68°F." No one expects you to go around sticking thermometers in bottles! All you need to know here is that for serving, white wine is served cool, but not cold. Fifteen or twenty minutes out of the fridge should be fine. Red wine is served not quite at comfortable room temperature, just a few degrees cooler.

For *tasting*, though, you don't want your white wine as cool as you would if you were serving it with dinner. In this case,

THE RIGHT KIND OF CHAMPAGNE GLASS IS ESSENTIAL, THOUGH THERE ARE MANY MYTHS SURROUNDING ITS SHAPE

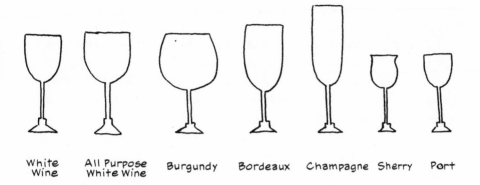

White   All Purpose   Burgundy   Bordeaux   Champagne   Sherry   Port
Wine   White Wine

both red and white wines should be a few degrees cooler than room temperature. (Sparkling wines should be tasted a little cooler than that.) Tasting a white wine that warm may seem a little odd at first, but you'll quickly get used to it. The reason we taste even whites at that temperature is that a wine needs to be that warm to have its aromas and flavors, as well as any flaws, really come out. It's a general rule that the colder something is, the less we can really taste it. For instance, if you make your own ice cream, you should make it a little sweeter than you really want it, because some of the perception of sweetness will be lost when it's frozen. A mediocre wine, chilled way down, will seem better than it is.

> **TIP FROM CABERNET FRANK**
> There are three basic types of wine: table wine, sparkling wine, and fortified wine.

If you feel a wine is too warm to taste properly, give it a little swirl in an ice bucket (or even a stockpot if you don't have an ice bucket) filled with ice and water. Ice alone doesn't do the job that well, and it takes much longer than you think to chill wine down in the refrigerator. The freezer is a little dangerous because if you're like me, you'll forget about it and the wine will freeze. (But then again, maybe you're not like me.)

Styles of Wine

Before you start to taste, the only other thing you need to know is that there are many different styles of wine. A wine may be sweet, bone-dry, or anything in between; still, sparkling, or faintly fizzy; and light-bodied to full-bodied. Think about where a wine falls along each of these scales as you taste.

Sweet vs. Dry

Grapes can be made into wines of varying degrees of sweetness, depending on the grape variety and on the region in which it's grown. Remember that the riper the grape, the more sugar will be available in the wine—either to ferment into alcohol or to remain in the wine as sugar. Winemakers can thus control the sweetness—even producing a range of sweetnesses within one grape variety.

It's usually white wines and rosés that are made sweet (though there are a few exceptions). When a winemaker wants to make a wine sweet, he can do this in a number of ways.

One is to let the grapes get riper than normal. That way there's lots of available sugar in the *must* (which is the grape juice before it's fermented into wine). Once the fermentation starts, the winemaker can either stop the fermentation, leaving some unfermented sugar left over, or let the wine ferment all the way, and then add a very sweet grape juice at the end. Either way, the wine will be sweeter than one made the normal way. In California, sweet wines made this way are usually called *late-harvest.*

Another way is to let the grapes freeze on the vine. That way, when they're made into wine, only very sweet concentrated juice goes into the wine—the watery part of the grape, in the form of ice crystals, is left out. This makes a very intense, sweet dessert wine called *eiswein,* since it was invented in Germany, or ice wine.

If you let grapes dry out and turn into raisins, that also makes them sweeter and more concentrated, and wonderful dessert wines are made this way. Vin Santo in Italy and Samos Nectar from Greece are two examples.

Perhaps the most celebrated method for making sweet wine is the one used in Sauternes, in the Bordeaux region of France. In certain areas of the world, foggy mornings are followed by warm afternoons, just before harvest. There, a mold known as *botrytis cinerea* attacks the grapes—with any luck. The grapes start to rot and shrivel up. This kind of rot is known in French as *pourriture noble*, or "noble rot." As they shrivel, the sugars concentrate, and when picked, they're turned into a beautiful sweet wine with an attractively unusual smell. Botrytis-affected grapes are also grown in South Australia, Germany, and even California. But you can think of Sauternes as botrytis Headquarters.

Still vs. Sparkling

Another aspect of the style of a wine is whether it's still or sparkling. What determines this? How much carbon dioxide is dissolved in the liquid. When the must ferments and the sugars turn to alcohol, a by-product of the process is carbon dioxide, the same stuff that gives sodas their fizz. For most wines, the carbon dioxide just bubbles off, never to be seen again.

But certain wines keep their bubbles. The most famous of these is champagne. But it's not easy: the monks who invented it went through hell trying to keep the bubbles in the bottle. After lots of experimentation, they invented the *méthode champenoise*, (the "champagne method"). With this method, they take a base wine that has already fermented once, put it in a bottle, add sugar and yeast, and plug it up. Then they let it age in the bottle, coaxing the deposits from the yeast into the neck of the bottle as it ages. Finally, they let the frozen plug of yeast fly out, and stop up the bottle again with a big, fat cork held into place with a wire cage. All this obviously involves a lot of work, which is expensive, so not all sparkling wines are made using this method. On those that are, the label will be marked either *méthode champenoise* or "fermented in this bottle."

You may find other wines that aren't *quite* sparkling, but still seem vaguely fizzy. You may even see just a few tiny little bubbles sitting on the inside of the glass. This is because all the carbon dioxide didn't dissipate. When you see that, it's usually done on purpose; in certain wines it adds a refreshing spritziness.

Looking, Smelling, and Sloshing

Tasting wine can be broken down into three phases: looking, smelling, and sloshing it around in your mouth. This last phase, sloshing, is what you probably think of as tasting. But in wine-

The Right Tool for Swirling

For maximum swirling possibilities, a glass of wine should never be poured more than half-full. Uninitiated friends may think you're just stingy and don't want to pour them a whole glass, but show 'em how to swirl 'n' sniff, and they'll get it.

One unpleasant side effect of the no-more-than-half-full rule is that if you order wine by the glass in a restaurant, the glass is usually pretty small and they'll pour it all the way to the brim. The management just wants to give you your money's worth, but it's robbing you of your swirling pleasure. If that happens, ask for a larger glass, which they probably won't have. I've gone to the ridiculous length of asking for an extra glass and pouring half the wine into it, which can not only alienate the staff, but the wine can end up in your lap! I don't care much if the wine is ordinary, but for restaurants that have a number of interesting selections by the glass, it's not a bad idea to mention to the manager that bigger glasses would be nice. Servers can then pour the same amount, and you can enjoy the wine—which the management has gone to some trouble to stock and store properly—to its fullest.

Color and Blind Tasting

A blind tasting is one in which the people doing the tasting don't know the identity of the wines they're about to taste. Why do they do this? It might be because they're critics who want to make an unbiased assessment of a particular wine. But it's also a popular game among wine enthusiasts and wine geeks.

In the case of blind tasting, the appearance of a wine becomes really important—it's a starting point for a lot of educated guesswork. It can give the taster big clues about what grape variety or varieties were used, whether the wine is mature, whether there are likely to be any flaws, the techniques used to make the wine (for example, was it filtered or not?), and how concentrated or flavorful the wine might be.

dom, all three phases are important, and the part where you put the stuff in your mouth is in reality not even the most important.

You might actually want to pour a glass and follow along with this little section to get the most out of it. All you need is a glass, some wine, and a white background—either a white tablecloth or a large piece of white paper to look at the wine against so the color's not distorted.

There are lots of things you can tell about a wine just by looking at it. Pour two or three ounces into your glass. Now observe it.

If it's white, it's not really white, right? Is it very pale? The color of straw? Is it pretty intensely colored, almost yellow? Is it golden? Greenish?

If it's red, is it really dark, almost purple? Is it the color of beets? Is it brick red? Is it pretty pale, almost pink?

Although looking at a wine is more important for the pros (see sidebar) the color of a wine alone will give you some clues to how it might taste.

To see the color of a wine, look straight down into it, either using the white tablecloth for background, or holding your piece of white paper under it.

For white wines, a very pale, almost colorless wine will probably be very light and fresh tasting. Whites with more color will tend to have more assertive flavors.

The same is basically true for reds. Anything very dark purple will probably have lots of pronounced flavor. Lighter-colored reds will often taste lighter; however, since red wines lighten somewhat as they age in the bottle, a lighter-colored wine may have more subtle and complex flavors.

Looking at the "rim" will tell you more about bottle age. To execute this move, simply tip the glass to one side, and look at the edge of the wine where it touches the glass. This is called the rim. For red wines, do you see an orangy or rusty brick-red tinge? This means the wine is probably somewhat aged. Is it more purply blue? You've got a young one. If it's brown, it's probably very mature.

White wines tend to get darker as they age. If it's starting to turn brownish, the wine may no longer be good. But if it's pretty golden yellow, you may have something that's simply mature. Since white wines, with some exceptions, are not made for long aging the way reds are, this might be a good thing or a bad thing. It could be good if it's a wine that has good aging potential; for instance a white Burgundy, which might be aged five to eight years (or even longer), or a Sauternes, some of which show their best at forty or fifty years old. But for many whites, long aging will send a wine over the hill.

The pros also look at a wine to assess its clarity and brilliance, since anything dull or hazy may be flawed. But since winemaking techniques have improved so much in the last decades, chances are that virtually all the wines you'll see will be clear and brilliant, so that you don't really need to worry about that.

> **TIP FROM CABERNET FRANK**
> If some wise guy asks why you're swirling your wine, just smirk and say, "I'm liberating molecules, bub."

How to Swirl Wine Without Getting It All Over Your Shirt

Choose a glass with a large bowl that narrows a little at the top. Pour in a little wine—about a third of the glass will do nicely. Choose a shirt to which you're not overly attached, in case early attempts don't meet with the success you've hoped for.

Place the glass of wine firmly on a table, and place your hand atop the glass's foot. Or if it's more comfortable, you may grasp the very bottom of the stem between your thumb and forefinger. Now gently move your hand (and thus the glass) in a small circle. See how the wine swirls around, but doesn't slosh?

After a short while this motion will begin to feel like second nature. You'll find yourself unconsciously swirling everything from coffee to lemonade. (It's very embarrassing to be caught at this.)

A little more practice, and you'll be playing with the big boys. Soon you'll be able to stand up with a glass of wine, holding it by the foot, and swirl it in the air without the steadying influence of a table, just like the wine geeks. It's a great skill to have if you visit a winery tasting room.

The French believe that swirling counterclockwise is very bad luck. Perhaps this is due to some ancient church-related idea that anything that goes to the left is sinister. However, if you're right-handed, swirling counterclockwise may be a much more natural movement, since the motion is inward, toward your body. Lefties will probably find clockwise more comfortable. Try it!

WINE TALK

Now swirl it around in the glass.

Why do we swirl wine around in the glass? Several reasons. The first is to release the aromas of the wine. Swirling actually frees up molecules of the wine so they can travel right up to your nose and you can smell it better. (Can you tell that here we're already venturing into the second phase, smelling? Think of swirling as a segue.)

The second is to look at the body of the wine. Is it sort of thick, almost viscous? If so, it is probably fairly high in alcohol, and perhaps sweet.

The third: It's fun! After you taste this way for a while, you won't be able to help it.

Now smell. Wine experts fall into two camps on the best way to do this. Try both, and most likely you'll find that one works better for you.

The first camp takes a very quick, light whiff, just for an initial impression. Sit back and jot a note about this first impression. Then go back and take a big, deep smell, sit back, and concentrate on what you smell.

The second camp believes that since first impressions are the most reliable, you should make your very first whiff a big and heartfelt one.

Either way, sit back and think about what you smell. Take a little time, because this phase, the smelling, is by far the most important. What we normally think of as our sense of taste is really to a large degree our sense of smell. There are actual scientific reasons for this that I won't really go into, other than to say that tasting is experienced in the brain in the olfactory center, which is mostly connected to sensors that are mostly in our noses.

When people first try to figure out what they smell in a wine, they sometimes become discouraged because they just don't know *what* they smell. They keep smelling it over and over again to try to figure it out, but then their senses get worn-out, and they get frustrated and give up.

It helps, however, if you know what kinds of smells to look for. Aromas to look for:

- fruit (often the easiest to find)
- herbs and spices
- flowers
- smells associated with desserts
- earthy, woody scents
- unpleasant smells

Q: When people claim to smell dozens of different aromas in a wine—violets, raspberries, vanilla, and so on, are they really smelling these things, or are they imagining them?

A: They can really smell them. It doesn't mean there are actual raspberries in the wine, but there *are* hundreds of "flavor compounds" in any given wine. The compounds share the same chemical structure as the flavor compound in the things they smell like.

Sometimes I find one kind of aroma right off the bat, say a couple of fruit smells. It's then helpful to sort of run through the other types of smells in the Rolodex of smells in your mind. Can you find anything floral? Sometimes there might be an aroma of violets, for instance, that's easy to miss if you weren't thinking about flowers.

Professor A. C. Noble, who teaches a "sensory evaluation" course in the Department of Viticulture and Enology at the University of California at Davis, has done a lot of thinking about all the aromas potentially found in wine. She believes that being able to find exactly the right word to describe an aroma you pick up greatly enhances your ability to enjoy any particular wine, as well as remember the way it smelled and tasted. To that end, she created the Wine Aroma Wheel, which is a very handy tool for sorting out aromas. (See the box on page 35.)

If you want to really remember particular wines you taste, keep a little tasting notebook, jotting down your impressions of the aromas (and texture, body, finish, and length, which we'll learn about shortly) along with the information on the label, and whether you liked it or not. If you do this, you'll have a permanent record of everything you've tasted. This can be particularly useful if you see something on sale and you want to remember whether you liked it enough to buy it.

Once you know what to look for, finding aromas in wine becomes wonderfully fun. And it may make you feel better to know that wine professionals aren't necessarily born with marvelous senses of smell; it's something they work on, something they exercise. How do they do this? By tasting often and keeping notes on what they taste.

A few also keep their noses sharp with the aid of a tool called *Le Nez du Vin*, which means "the nose of wine." This French-made boxed-set contains dozens of concentrated smells; professionals use them to remind themselves of exactly what each specific aroma smells like. If you can't get your hands on one of these puppies (which are pretty hard to find, even in France, and cost several hundred dollars), you might try my own invention, "The Smelling Game" (see page 36–37).

The Wine Aroma Wheel

Professor A. C. Noble's Wine Aroma Wheel begins with the most general kind of aromas (divided into "floral," "fruity," "chemical," "microbiological") in the center of the wheel, and becomes more specific as it radiates outward for a total of three tiers. Thus in the wedge labeled "fruity" in the center, the middle tier divides into six categories, "citrus," "berry," "(tree) fruit," "(tropical) fruit," etc. Each of these categories divides into subcategories; for instance "berry" divides into "blackberry," "raspberry," "strawberry," and "blackcurrant (cassis)." On the back are listed characteristic aromas to look for in different types of wine.

Large, sturdy, plastic-coated, full-color copies of the Wine Aroma Wheel may be obtained for approximately five dollars (plus tax, where applicable) from Department of Viticulture and Enology, University of California at Davis, CA 95616 (916) 752-0380. Proceeds will benefit the department's ongoing research program.

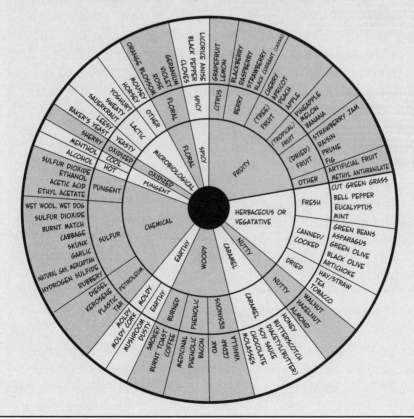

The Smelling Game

The sense of smell is the most underrated of all our senses. Human beings are inherently very good at it, and incredibly affected by it. Consider the phenomenon of pheromones, which give off a scent so subtle it's virtually undetectable. Yet scientists credit them with playing a huge role in sexual attraction. If an undetectable smell can have that kind of effect, imagine the range of smells we're capable of enjoying in our wine.

For some reason, we undervalue our sense of smell, and therefore we don't exercise it. Many of the aromas commonly found in wine are also found right in your kitchen. The Smelling Game will help you get accustomed not only to these smells, but to using your nose in general; thus sharpening your tasting skills.

To play, all you do is blindfold a friend, then raid the kitchen for ingredients with distinctive smells. Look in the refrigerator or pantry, the fruit bowl or the spice rack. Choose something you think will be incredibly easy first, such as a banana. You might want to break off a little piece and smash it, so the aroma is released. Now hold it under your friend's nose.

Often what happens is the person smelling says, "Oh, I *know* that smell!" But then they can't put their finger on it. You'll have to tell them.

The game is way more fun than it sounds.

Phase three of tasting is loudest: sloshing.

If the way we experience taste has more to do with our sense of smell than anything that happens on our tongues, that's because what happens on our tongues is actually pretty limited. Taste buds on different parts of the tongue register different tastes. Sweetness is tasted at the front, sourness (acidity) on the

SOME INGREDIENTS TO TRY:
a strawberry (cut in half)
blackberries or raspberries (crushed a little)
a slice of apple
a slice of ripe pear
a slice of pineapple
orange juice (harder than it sounds)
lemon peel
lime peel
Dijon mustard
fresh basil
fresh thyme
a smashed garlic clove
a piece of fresh ginger
cinnamon
butter (this one's tough)
a stinky cheese
coffee beans (or ground coffee)
vanilla extract
chocolate (break it up a little)
rose-flower water
orange-flower water
vinegar
anchovies
shredded coconut
toothpaste (not from the kitchen, so it really
    stumps 'em!)

sides, saltiness on top, and bitterness at the back. But that's all we can taste: sweet, sour, salt, and bitter.

Our sense of smell adds complexity and nuance to what we normally think of as our sense of taste. In addition to the aroma receptors that are in the nose, there are also aroma receptors at the back of the tongue, near the throat. So even when something

WORDS FREQUENTLY USED IN WINE TASTING

is in your mouth, you're smelling it at the same time (even if you hold your nose!).

Now take a sip of wine and give it a good slosh around your mouth, making sure it touches all the different parts of the tongue. You won't taste salt, but you may taste some sugar, if it's a relatively sweet wine, or sour, or bitter. Now, with the wine still in your mouth, try drawing some air into your mouth through your teeth. Notice any deepening of the flavors? That's because you're aerating it further, making it more volatile. Keep the wine in your mouth, sloshing it around for as long as you keep tasting things, and then either swallow it or spit it out.

Now just sit back a moment and keep paying attention to what you're tasting. Is there an aftertaste? If so, is it a pleasant one? Notice how long the aftertaste lasts: this is what the big boys refer to as "length." More length is good.

Okay, so we've tasted the wine. What, you're probably wondering, were we supposed to look for?

One of the most important things in judging any wine is deciding whether it's "balanced." To be balanced, several elements in the wine should exist in pleasing proportions so that no one of these elements draws too much attention to itself.

For white wines, we're looking for a balance of acid, sugar, and alcohol. Think of fresh lemonade: you want it not too sweet and not too sour. If it's too sour, you feel it on the sides of your tongue, right where the "sour" taste buds are, and your mouth puckers up unpleasantly. But add sugar, and suddenly it's delicious. Notice how you didn't have to remove any of the acidic lemon— you just had to add something to balance it. If you add too much sugar, however, it becomes too sweet; it seems gooey and cloying. Now you can hardly taste the acid of the lemon. Add a little more lemon, and perhaps some water, and now it's balanced again.

It's the same idea with white wine. Even if you can't taste the sugar in a white wine, it's there (even if in very small amounts). In that case you want enough acid to keep the wine bright, but not so much that it overwhelms. If the wine is perceptibly sweet, it needs more acid to balance it. Now and then you might taste a wine in which the sugar overwhelms the acid, and that can taste cloying (like our overly sweet lemonade) and dull.

Also consider whether the alcohol is balanced against the acid and sugar. Too much alcohol leaves a sort of hot, burning sensation on the palate. If none of those three elements overwhelms you, the wine is balanced.

For red wines, there's another element thrown in: tannin. Tannin, you'll remember from Chapter One, is the substance that comes from the skins and seeds of red grapes, used in making red wine. To refresh

> **Q: What's that terrible sucking sound that wine geeks make when they take a sip?**
> **A: They're drawing air over the sip of wine in their mouth to help bring out the flavors.**

TIP FROM CABERNET FRANK
The two surest clues that what you're tasting is a particularly good wine: an intensely pleasant nose and a very long finish.

your memory about what it tastes like, it's the substance in strong black tea that leaves your mouth feeling sort of dry.

With red wines, look for a balance of sugar, acid, alcohol, and tannins. The sugar in red wines is usually perceptible as a fruit taste; this may be backed up with some zippy acid in the background, especially in red wines made to drink young, such as Nouveau Beaujolais. In big young red wines, such as a Cabernet Sauvignon, Barolo, or Bordeaux younger than four or five years old, you may be overwhelmed with the tannins. That much tannin may seem like a flaw, but the reason is that these wines are made to age, and the tannins help preserve them as they develop in the bottle. The tannins themselves will soften somewhat with age, but if they're very rough, they'll always be rough.

Sometimes it's easy to confuse acids with tannins. If you're not sure which you're tasting, pay attention to what happens in your mouth after you swallow the wine or spit it out. Does your mouth feel very dry? That means there were a lot of tannins. Is your mouth watering? That means there were lots of acids.

Just as the sense of smell is important to wine tasting, so is the sense of touch. Things that taste "spicy-hot" to us, such as jalapeño chiles, are not actually tasted; rather they're *felt*. Irritation inside our mouth caused by the peppers gives the impression of "hotness." Touch is actually the sense we use to perceive the

---

Q: When people refer to a *palate,* what do they actually mean?
A: Your palate, physically speaking, is simply your mouth. But when someone refers to a person who has a *great palate,* this means he or she has an excellent sense of smell and a well-developed ability to discern subtle nuances of aroma and flavor.

presence of tannins as well—we *feel* them as astringent.

We also use touch to enjoy the *texture* of the wine, the way it feels in our mouth. Okay, take another sip and slosh it around. Does it feel thick or thin? Like velvet or satin or wool or water? Are there other words you might use to describe it? Is the feeling pleasant or unpleasant? That's the texture.

The idea of *body* is also important to wine enthusiasts. Is a wine light-bodied, medium-bodied, or full-bodied? A higher percentage of alcohol makes a wine appear thicker, or more viscous, more full-bodied. Wines with a lower percentage of alcohol are thinner, light-bodied. Before you even feel body in your mouth, you can see it, back in phase one. Swirl your wine around in the glass again. How does it look against the side of the glass—thick or thin? Are there "legs" dripping down the sides? Legs are a sign of viscosity, indicating relatively high alcohol or sugar.

Voilà! You've done it! You know how to taste—there's nothing scary, and no mystery. Go through the whole process once more—look, swirl, smell, and slosh, notice the body and flavors; swallow or spit, taste the aftertaste, notice the length. Now ask yourself the most important question of all: Do you like this wine?

Guess what—you're now ready to taste with the best of 'em. You have the tools to decide what you like or don't like and why.

Do you have to do this every time you're presented with a glass of wine at dinner? Of course not! But whenever you try a wine you haven't sampled before, you might just want to take a moment,

> **TIP FROM CABERNET FRANK**
>
> **When tasting red wines, especially big, young wines with lots of tannin, eat a little mild-flavored cheese on a cracker. The cheese does the same thing to the tannins in the wine as milk does when you pour it into tea: the tannins will "eat" the protein in the cheese. Bound together, they become smoother and more palatable. This is also why people tend to serve meat with big red wines.**

> **Q: What's the difference between *aroma* and *bouquet*?**
> **A: Aroma usually refers to the smells that come from the grape variety, while bouquet refers to the smells that come from a combination of the grape, the fermentation process, any wood aging, and bottle aging. However, any odor detected in a wine may be called an aroma.**
> **Q: What are the aromas that come from the wine having had contact with oak?**
> **A: Vanilla, toast, cloves, carnations, and coconuts.**

silently go through the steps, and form an opinion. Then forget everything you've been concentrating on, sit back, and simply enjoy drinking the wine as part of your dining experience.

IF YOU FORGET EVERYTHING ELSE YOU'VE READ IN CHAPTER TWO, JUST REMEMBER THIS:

1. Tasting is different from drinking.
2. The only glass you really need is a clear, twelve-ounce wine goblet.
3. Taste reds a few degrees cooler than comfortable room temperature.
4. Taste whites a little warmer than you think.
5. For dry wines, the riper the grapes when they're picked, the higher they'll be in alcohol.
6. *Body* and *texture* refer to the alcohol content and mouth-feel of a wine. (*Light-bodied* means low in alcohol; *full-bodied* means high in alcohol.)
7. Approach tasting in three phases: looking, smelling, and sloshing in your mouth.
8. Much of what we look for in a wine is in the *nose*.
9. Balance is the harmonious relationship between acids, tannins, sugars, and alcohol.
10. Try to associate aromas and flavors in wines to other familiar ones.

Chapter Three

MESSAGE IN A BOTTLE

How to get the wine out of the bottle and into a glass? This annoying problem has plagued wine lovers, winemakers, and waiters for centuries. Permit me to bore you with a little wine-bottle history.

In ancient Greece (as well as Rome and Egypt), wine was stored in large jars called amphoras. Corks were sometimes used to close them, and the Romans gave their amphoras airtight seals using pitch, as far back as the second century B.C.

Everything was going along just fine, until suddenly the Moors conquered what is now Spain and Portugal (where most of the cork trees grew), no one could get corks, and everybody had to scramble to find a way to keep the air out of their vessels. Oh, they tried all kinds of things—wax and pitch, wooden plugs tightened up with pieces of cloth, you name it.

Fast-forward to the seventeenth century: glass bottles now came into widespread use. People tried using glass stoppers (like the ones we use today for decanters), but that was a tad expensive. Then they remembered what they did once upon a time, and went back to using cork.

However, the cork could only be pushed down partway into the bottle, since no one had bothered to invent the corkscrew

yet. Imagine everyone's frustration when the corks got pushed down too far! Though it is possible to remove a cork from a bottle without any implement whatsoever by hitting the bottom of the bottle against a tree (this is something that fledgling wine geeks used to do in college to impress dates on picnics), it's really a pain in the neck, and besides—how often do you have a tree next to you when you want to open a bottle of wine?

Opening the Bottle: Ritual Aspects

First, cut the foil, using either a small, sharp knife or a nifty little tool cleverly called a *foilcutter*. To do this, just slice it off right where it meets the top of the bottle, exposing just the top of the cork. If it's easier, you can certainly cut the whole foil off.

Next, wipe the rim of the bottle with a cloth. This is particularly important if the wine bottle is old and crusty, since you don't want all that crusty stuff to fall into your wine as it's poured. However, it's probably a good idea all the time, since little chemical problems can collect there. If there was a little leakage

TIP FROM CABERNET FRANK

As Marie Antoinette might have said, if you don't have a corkscrew, drink champagne!

through the cork, for example, there could be a trace of spoiled wine on the rim, which might not ruin the whole bottle, but could make the first impression unpleasant, and perhaps even fool you into thinking it's bad.

Next, remove the cork, by whatever means pleases you best.

Corkscrews: Choosing Your Weapon

THE "ARMPIT" OPENER

That's what I call it, anyway. When the two "arms" are raised, you can see little gears underneath that look suspiciously like armpit hairs. And it gets even worse from there. This type of corkscrew, which is the one we see around most often, happens to be one of the worst. It's no wonder so many people are petrified to open the wine, considering how difficult it is to use. See the "screw" part? It's the type called an *augur*, a straight piece of metal with threads, rather than something that looks like a curly pigtail. These things destroy corks. Plus the augur is often too short to go all the way down into the cork. They're a royal pain in the ass, and I wouldn't recommend them to my worst enemy. Okay, maybe to my worst enemy.

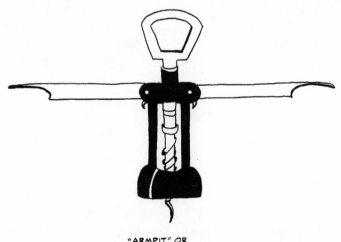

"ARMPIT" OR
"WINGED" CORKSCREW

Let's cut to the chase, then, shall we? The best corkscrew you can buy is called a *Screwpull*.

SCREWPULL

It's not cheap—but buy one, and you'll agree it's the best eighteen bucks you've ever spent. The Screwpull is completely foolproof and incredibly easy to use—easier even than a can opener. All you have to do is place the apparatus over the bottle, guide the screw a little way into the cork, and start turning the top of it gently in a clockwise direction. The screw moves down into the cork and pulls it up in one continuous motion.

THE WAITER'S FRIEND

The next serious contender in the world of corkscrews is the one called the *waiter's friend*. The problem: Only waiters seem to be able to negotiate them successfully, and not even all of them have mastered the technique. To use it, screw the waiter's friend into the cork manually, place the notched part over the lip of the bottle, and use leverage to pull out the cork. It sounds tricky, and

it is—it requires a lot of practice to be able to send the screw straight down the cork with no guidance, and some force is still needed. What always winds up happening with me is I get the screw down into the cork, but I somehow can't get the leverage, and I wind up having to place the bottle on the floor between my feet and pull it straight up with tremendous force. It works, but I look like a complete idiot. However, those who can use the waiter's friend with ease like it because it's very quick if you've got the knack. I don't recommend it unless you're a waiter and have to open a lot of bottles quickly.

THE TWO-PRONGED OPENER

With this one, you slide the longer end down in between the cork and the bottle, push it in a little ways, then place the shorter end on the opposite side. Wiggle the opener down back and forth, little by little, until it is all the way in. Now, using a twisting motion, pull it straight up. Because it doesn't penetrate the cork, the two-pronged opener works well for old wines or other wines that might have a crumbly cork. However, it's difficult to use with very tight corks.

Getting the Wine into the Glass

Here's where all the big arguments begin: the breathing and decanting debate. Since red wines may be young and tannic ("closed up"), or old, with lots of sediment in the bottle, while white wines aren't pestered by these issues, both "breathing" and "decanting" are strategies that apply only to reds.

> **TIP FROM CABERNET FRANK**
> Imagine: corks were used to seal bottles of wine some 1,700 years before anyone bothered to invent the corkscrew!

The Cork Problem

Unlike the wine inside the bottle, which evolved greatly in the couple of millennia we've been drinking it, the cork, so necessary for keeping the wine in the container and the air out of it, has barely progressed at all.

You may be surprised to learn that corks drive winemakers crazy. Due to the growing popularity of wine throughout the world, and the relative paucity of cork trees throughout the world (they grow almost exclusively in Portugal and Spain), winemakers are having a harder and harder time getting quality corks for their wines. As if that weren't enough, the bleaching process used to disinfect corks can cause the formation of a chemical called trichlorophenol (TCA), which results in such an unpleasant smell that the wine is said to be "corked" or "corky," ruining the bottle. Up to 5 percent of all wine is "corked," and according to *Wine Spectator* magazine, corked wines cost winemakers and consumers between two billion and three billion dollars a year.

To that end, some winemakers are experimenting with synthetic corks. Since they know that wine lovers may miss the traditional aspect of real corks, some try to make them look real. Others use brightly colored synthetic corks.

But synthetic corks won't solve one aspect of the problem that also conspires to drive winemakers nuts: the fact that consumers have such a rough time removing corks from bottles that it discourages them from buying wine. There is a solution at hand, but it goes so counter to the image and mystique of wine that winemakers are reluctant to use it: the screwtop.

Foiled Again!

Traditionally, the foil that covers and protects the cork is made of lead, but due to concern over lead poisoning, American winemakers now use alternatives such as aluminum or plastic. The French, of course, think this is ridiculous. Since our enjoyment of wine is so much an aesthetic and sensual experience, perhaps we lose something when we have to hack a thick piece of plastic off the bottle.

Certain California winemakers have been experimenting with alternative closures to try to solve the problem, and the most interesting result must be that devised by Napa producer Robert Mondavi. Several Mondavi wines now come in a bottle without foil or plastic, so there's nothing to remove except the cork itself. Beeswax lies over the cork, a small disk of paper directly above that, and the redesigned bottle has a small lip on the edge of it. It looks a little odd, but it's kind of neatly satisfying simply to place the corkscrew into the cork, right through the paper and beeswax, and pull out the cork.

Breathing

Breathing refers to exposing the wine to air before drinking it. Traditionally, this takes the form of opening the bottle a half hour, an hour, or even longer, before pouring it. The idea is that exposing the wine to oxygen helps it "open up," allowing all the flavors to come through. At restaurants, where normally one can't open a wine much in advance, the waiter or wine steward (also known as a *sommelier*) will often suggest pouring the wine into the glasses and letting it sit.

In case of confusion about the term "opened up," it can actually refer to two things. Besides the above, it also applies to a red wine designed for long aging, in which the tannins have softened sufficiently. In either case, think of wine that has "opened up" as a wine that is finally approachable.

The problem with the whole idea of letting wine "breathe" in the bottle is that studies have shown that the area exposed to air, just a tiny disk below the opening of the bottle, is far too small to let much oxygen in at all. Gerald Asher, the wine columnist for *Gourmet* magazine, calls the efficacy of that kind of breathing "useless wine lore," and most wine writers, including the authors of the definitive *Oxford Companion to Wine*, agree with him. (Try telling that to tens of thousands of residents of the Bordeaux region of France, who have done it all their lives!)

However, letting a youngish red wine "breathe" in the glass probably does make sense. Both the aeration the wine gets from being poured and the increased area above the surface of the wine in the glass will expose it to much more oxygen.

Decanting

There is another way to aerate the wine: by decanting it into another container sometime before serving it. Although decanting is traditionally performed for older wines that might have a lot of sediment collected in the bottle, many people find that it's a useful way to aerate a red wine, especially a young one. Gerald Asher writes that at some point in his life, he noticed that "Any remnant of red wine left over from dinner always seemed to taste better with lunch the next day. That's how I came to accept the basic logic of decanting—that red wine needs to be aerated to be enjoyed at its best." Certain restaurants in California's wine country, such as Mustard's Grill in the Napa Valley, routinely decant red wines for their customers under this theory.

This is where the arguments begin. The *Oxford Companion to Wine* cites Professor Emile Peynaud, a granddaddy of oenology in Bordeaux, as one of many experts who consider decanting in order to aerate wine "oenologically indefensible." (Ouch!) These guys say that exposing a wine to oxygen ahead of time causes it to lose many of its aromas.

Okay, so what about decanting for the traditional reason of separating the clean wine from its sediments?

This is something you probably won't have to do often, if ever, unless you're very fortunate and you get your hands on a monster of a wine, since a wine has to be pretty old and serious to have any deposits. If you do have something with some age (at least ten years in the bottle) such as a classed-growth Bordeaux, you might want to decant it; if you're serving a vintage port, you'll have to.

Decanting is an almost medieval-looking operation that scares a lot of people, including inexperienced waiters. But it's really quite easy. All you have to do is make sure the bottle has been standing upright for at least twenty-four hours so any sediment settles into the bottom. Then have a decanter (or even a glass pitcher) ready—very clean, with no soap residue left in it. Light a candle. Say a prayer. (Just kidding.) Now hold the top third of the wine bottle right in front of the candle as you pour so that the candle's light illuminates the "shoulder" of the bottle. Pour the wine slowly and gently into the decanter, looking at the shoulder the whole time to make sure the wine in it is clear. When the bottle is almost empty, you may start to see a little residue appear in the shoulder. That's when you stop, and leave the rest in the bottle. If you don't see any, keep on pouring—there wasn't any sediment.

When to Decant

This depends on whom you believe about the whole "breathing" issue. If you're decanting a young red wine in order to aerate it, you might want to do it anywhere from a half hour or so before serving (for perhaps a relatively young Pinot Noir from the Pacific Northwest or California) up to as long as three or four

> **Most people who live in the Bordeaux region of France like to pour young wines into the glass with great gusto to get lots of air into it and release the aromas into the glass. They crack up when they see oenophobic Americans carefully pouring a delicate trickle into the glass.**

Wine-Bottle Shapes

The shape of a wine bottle can tell you something about whether the wine inside might one day need to be decanted in order to remove sediment. Wine that comes in bottles with *shoulders,* such as red Bordeaux and California Cabernet Sauvignon, may throw a deposit upon aging, and the bottle's shoulder is designed to catch the sediment as it's decanted. Bottles containing red Burgundies or American Pinot Noirs don't need a shoulder like that, since they rarely throw deposits.

Burgundy   Bordeaux

Opening Champagne and Other Sparkling Wine

Opening a bottle of champagne or sparkling wine (a bottle of "bubbles," as they say in the California wine trade . . .) obviously requires an entirely different technique than still wines. This is because the carbon dioxide bubbles in the wine cause tremendous pressure to build up in the bottle, and if you're not careful, the cork can fly out dangerously. (You could put an eye out that way!)

Opening a bottle of champagne frightens lots of people, too, but it's really quite easy.

First, remove the foil.

Next, being careful not to point the cork toward anyone, twist the loop on the wire cage until it is disengaged. Carefully remove the cage.

Grasp the cork with one hand, keeping the hand over the cork to prevent it from flying out while you use the other hand to twist the *bottle* gently but firmly until it's opened. There won't be a loud pop, but hey—there's not supposed to be! You should hear just a gentle little "*phssht*" sound.

Pour about an inch of wine into each glass, and then go back and fill them up. This technique prevents them from bubbling over.

Cheers!

hours (for a three- or four-year-old Bordeaux, Hermitage, California Cabernet, or Barolo). A knowledgeable wine merchant can advise you on specific wines.

If you're decanting something older for possible sediment, you might want to play it safe and decant just before serving.

> Q: What does it mean when someone says a wine is
> *closed up*?
> A: When a red wine made to age for a long time, such
> as a classed-growth Bordeaux, is tasted when it is still
> fairly young, it is often said to be closed up. This
> means that the tannins are still so overwhelming that
> the flavors of the wine can't come through yet. That's
> because as it ages in the bottle, the molecules of
> tannin start collecting, getting larger and larger. This
> leaves an impression of more tannin. After some
> years, the clumps of tannin molecules get so large that
> they start falling apart. At that point, the wine seems
> to get "softer," and the wine is said to have *opened up*.

Saving Leftover Wine

You know how to open it. You know how to pour it. You know
how to drink it. But what if you don't finish the bottle?

For white wines, it's most convenient simply to recork them

What's in a Label?

Many American winemakers seem to have irrepressible urges to brag on their labels about how they made the wine. Whether or not the technique they're mentioning is anything to brag about, this can be intimidating. The following is a brief review of the techniques you may see flaunted on labels.

- *Oak-aged:* Aging a wine in oak barrels adds lots of flavors and aromas. Since new oak is expensive, winemakers like to brag about using it when they've forked over that much dough. Of course oak aging can be a great thing, adding richness and complexity, and it's important in many of the world's great wines. But overoaking can also harm a wine, masking its natural aromas.

- *Barrel-fermented:* This means some or all of the wine was fermented in oak barrels rather than the regular stainless steel. Too much oak aging makes a wine just smell like vanilla and toast. But fermenting wine in oak, as opposed to aging it in oak later, can add complexity while keeping down the vanilla smell.

- *Malolactic fermentation:* This is the second fermentation some wine undergoes, in which the harsh malic acids are converted to softer lactic acids. Winemakers can control when and if this happens. While it does reduce the acid in overly tart red wines and add buttery flavors that can be attractive, it's not necessarily anything to brag about.

- *Aged sur lie:* This refers to aging the wine with the dead yeast cells that result after the wine is finished fermenting. Although doing so can certainly add complexity and allure to a wine, many winemakers overly romanticize the practice.

and put them in the refrigerator. They'll probably be fine for a few days, after which they'll start to deteriorate.

For sparkling wines, place a spoon or other flatware in the bottle, leave it open, and put it in the fridge. With any luck, it'll still be bubbly tomorrow.

For reds, the easiest thing to do is to pick up a little vacuum pump (packaged under several different brand names, such as "VacuVin"). These inexpensive gadgets are easy to use—just place the rubbery cork that comes with it in the bottle, place the small plastic pump on top, and pump the air out of the bottle. A valve in the stopper prevents air from getting back in. Wines may be kept up to a few days, unrefrigerated, if pumped this way a couple of times a day. (Note: A prominent wine writer recently wrote about testing this device, and claims they're useless. However, I haven't thrown mine away. . . .)

Alternatively, you can recork a bottle of red and keep it in the refrigerator for up to a few days as well. It's best if you can pour the wine into a smaller bottle, so there's less air sitting on top of it. Just remember to remove it several hours before you want to drink it, since it'll take that long to come up to an acceptable drinking temperature.

Of course any kind of leftover wine may be used for cooking instead of drinking. Or you can make your own excellent vinegar from it.

IF YOU FORGET EVERYTHING ELSE YOU'VE READ IN CHAPTER THREE, JUST REMEMBER THIS:

1. The best corkscrew is a Screwpull.
2. A chemical called TCA is what causes a wine to be "corked," giving it an off smell.
3. Allow young red wines to "breathe" for a half hour or so in the glass, or else decant them roughly to aerate them before serving.
4. When opening a sparkling wine, you don't want a loud *pop*. Point away from people, hold the cork firmly, and twist the bottle to open.

Chapter Four

THE GRAPES AND WHAT THEY TURN INTO

Imagine this scenario: Out to dinner with friends, upon arriving at the restaurant, you find there's a wait. No problem; you saunter up to the bar to wait for your table and decide to have a glass of wine instead of a cocktail. Familiar enough scenario, right? The bartender says, "What can I get you this evening?" "Glass of Chardonnay," you say, without missing a beat, and your friends all happily chime in, "Same for me."

What's wrong with this picture? Nothing, you say? Well, don't get defensive; you've only done what millions of other people do. You went right to Chardonnay without even considering any other white-wine varieties. To you, white wine, which is the apéritif wine color of choice among American diners, *means* "Chardonnay."

What's wrong with *that*? Well, nothing, except for the fact that there are white wines made out of lots of other wonderful grape varieties besides Chardonnay which you may like even better at certain times. And if you keep ordering Chardonnay, and keep paying whatever price for it that the producers are demanding, producers will continue replanting their vineyards that used to grow other varieties with only Chardonnay, and restaurants will start offering fewer and fewer other white wines besides Chardonnay, and your local wineshop will stop stocking other white wines besides Chardonnay, and one day, when you get tired of Chardonnay, you won't have any other white wine to drink.

Okay, you're probably saying, you've made your point. But I *like* Chardonnay. Why *shouldn't* I drink it all the time?

Two reasons.

One, it's not the best wine for every job. Take your little before-dinner drink, for instance. You were probably drinking a Chardonnay from California—usually a big, rich, buttery, oaky wine that's very high in alcohol. As such, it's a wine that's much better suited to food. Wines that are crisper and more refreshing, such as Sauvignon Blancs or Rieslings, usually make better apéritifs, and they're not as alcoholic (don't forget, you haven't even eaten yet—what if it's an hour before your table is ready?) or as tiring to the palate.

The second reason is that you're limiting yourself to one varietal. What if it turns out later you find you like Sauvignon Blanc way better than Chardonnay—won't you feel silly? Drinking only Chardonnay is like wearing only blue shirts: blue shirts may be wonderful, but they're far from the only game in town.

How did Chardonnay get to be the white wine of choice among Americans? One reason is that it's easy to pronounce— fear of wine doesn't kick in the moment you have to utter the word. An interesting footnote is that in the 1970s, California winemaker Robert Mondavi wanted to bring wines made from Sauvignon Blanc—a fabulous grape that hadn't gotten enough play in the U.S.—to the attention of the American public. But Mondavi's no dummy—he knew that we might have trouble pronouncing "sauvignon." Did he let that stop him? No sirrr-eee—he renamed the varietal "Fumé Blanc." (It's easy to say "foo-*may*.") More on that later.

With red wines, Americans are almost as unadventurous. Cabernet (again, easy to pronounce: ca-ber-*nay*) means red wine to far too many people. Don't get me wrong—I love Cabernet; it might even be my favorite grape variety, if I had to choose (which I don't). But it's tough to match with food, especially given today's lighter diets, and lots of times I'd prefer a wine made from Pinot Noir or Syrah or Zinfandel or another red variety.

Okay, okay—what is a grape variety, anyway? And how is it different from what people call a "varietal"?

Grape Varieties

Just as there are different types of table grapes, such as Thompson Seedless, Concord, and Red Globe, there are also different types of grapes used to make wine. Even if we're accustomed to only drinking Chardonnay or Cabernet, and maybe one or two others, winemakers throughout the world use *hundreds* of different types of grapes (known as grape varieties) to make different kinds of wine. Certain wines are made from only one grape variety, and others are made from a combination of grapes. Whether it's one or more depends on a number of things: tradition, taste, the vagaries of the market, or even the law of the land of whatever wine region we're talking about.

Besides Chardonnay, a few wine-grape varieties you may have heard of are Riesling, Sauvignon Blanc, Cabernet Sauvignon, Merlot, Pinot Noir.

Varietals vs. Regionally Named Wines

To complicate things even further, in some wine regions of the world, wines are named after the principal grape they're made from. If so, they're referred to as *varietals*. In other regions, wines are named after the regions themselves.

Take again, for example, the Chardonnay grape. In California, a wine made from 100 percent Chardonnay grapes is called— you guessed it—Chardonnay. In France, however, a wine made from 100 percent Chardonnay is generally known as white Burgundy. (Other types of wine are made from Chardonnay in France, but Burgundy is the region most famous for this type of wine, and therefore Chardonnay is practically synonymous with white Burgundy in France.)

Easy, *n'est-ce pas*? If it were that simple, we could all go home now, and you could return this book and get your money back. No such luck!

In the regions wine professionals call the New World, including not only the Americas, Australia, and New Zealand, but also South Africa—in other words, any major wine region outside of Europe—varietals reign supreme. In other words, the wines are named for their principal grape rather than for their region. But as the wine world becomes more and more a global community, bastions of winemaking tradition, such as France and Italy, are beginning to market some varietally labeled wines. This, they feel, makes the wines more attractive and less intimidating to Americans—who are huge importers of wines from all over the world.

In California, the labeling of wines as varietals began in the

SOME GRAPE VARIETIES STAND OUT MORE THAN OTHERS

late 1950s and into the 1960s. At that time wines (most of which were cheap jug wines) were named after regions they had nothing to do with. Lots of red wine in California was called "Burgundy," despite the fact that in the Burgundy region of France, red wines called Burgundy contain 100 percent Pinot Noir grapes, while in California these wines usually contained no Pinot Noir whatsoever—they were made from inferior, more easily grown grapes. And chew on this: Sparkling wine made in California used to be called "champagne." But champagne isn't a *style* of wine; it's actually a region in northeast France where the famous bubbly comes from. Sparkling wine made in other parts of France cannot be called champagne. Nor would anyone want to call it champagne—that would be just like winemakers in New York State calling their wine "California wine." It would just never occur to them. You can imagine how mad this made the French—selling wine made in California as "champagne"!

In France, although the wines are almost always named after places (Bordeaux, Châteauneuf-du-Pape, Côte de Beaunes, Champagne, etc.), there are some exceptions. Most notably, the French region of Alsace—whose wines, such as Riesling, Sylvaner, and Gewürztraminer—have always been named after their grape variety. Similarly in Italy, although most wines are named for their zone, occasionally you'll see one that's named for a grape. Barolo, for instance, is made from Nebbiolo grapes, but it's named for the town in Piedmont around which the grapes are grown. However, Pinot Grigio is named after a grape (the one we refer to as Pinot Gris). Go figure.

Terroiristes vs. Techno-Dudes

This basic difference in the way New World and European wines are named reflects a profound difference in philosophy, which is in turn reflected in the wine. In France, winemakers believe that all the magic's in the soil. It's a notion of the land, the earth, as being all-important, but not just in a chemical way; it has to do with the soul of the land as well. *Terroir* is what they call it. They believe that the site of each specific vineyard determines how a wine will ultimately taste. The vintners must grow the best grapes possible in that site (and the fewer grapes, the better— smaller vineyard yields make more complex wine), and the wine- maker's job is to make the wine with as little interference as possible in order to let the *terroir,* the expression of the earth, emerge. Given this reverence for the land (which, by the way, is very French), it should come as no surprise that the French would name their wines after geographical locations.

"What a crock," New World winemakers have been saying. "Gimme a break." In the United States and Australia particularly, where the winemaking business has been influenced by science and universities (such as University of California at Davis), the philosophy has been that it's all in the grape itself and the techni- cal winemaking know-how. Tremendous attention has been paid by these techno-dude winemakers in the New World to clonal selection of grapes, pH levels, refractometers to check sugar lev- els, and the like. In these regions, the winemaker seeks self-ex- pression through the winemaking process rather than as an expression of *terroir.*

That's been the story in California for the last twenty-five years or so, but here's a funny footnote: It has lately become very fashionable in California for winemakers to talk about *terroir.* More and more wineries there are paying attention to exactly which vineyard the grapes in a given wine are from, and more and more they've started putting that information on the label. But still, it smacks more of science than any kind of mystical bond with the earth; vintners take soil samples and check them for mineral content, and chalk up any interesting flavors that come out as belonging literally to whatever minerals are con- tained therein.

Style

What complicates matters is also, paradoxically, one of the things that makes wine so endlessly fascinating. It's what winemakers *do* with the particular grapes in each region that makes the wines coming out of those regions very different. That's what wine aficionados call *style*. The style of California Chardonnays differs tremendously from the style of French white Burgundies. One is big, fruity, oaky, and alcoholic; the other is bone-dry, elegant, earthy, and even austere.

A Rundown on the Grapes

Enough said. On to the grapes. If something strikes your fancy and you want more info, flip ahead to Part II, and look under the region which interests you. Varieties are listed in the following order: whites you really ought to know about, reds you really should know, less well-known "extra-credit" whites, and "extra-credit" reds.

Must-Know White-Grape Varieties

CHARDONNAY

It's become a cliché that Chardonnay is synonymous in America with white wine. That's because Americans drink wines made from it like it's going out of style. And they needn't fear that it is because it's the most widely planted grape in California.

In the U.S. (including California, Washington, Oregon, and New York State), wines made from the Chardonnay grape are labeled "Chardonnay," as they are in Australia and New Zealand. In France, the Chardonnay grape is used to make white Burgundies (such as the very famous Montrachet and Meursault), Chablis, and it's one of the grapes used to make champagne.

The Chardonnay grape is one of what winemakers refer to as the *noble* grape varieties, meaning, roughly, that it's a great grape that produces world-class wines. It's a fairly neutral grape that can either let the *terroir* come through, or pick up flavors from the winemaking process. Often winemakers age, and sometimes ferment, the Chardonnay in barrels made from oak, and the wine picks up a lot of flavors from the oak itself—more than you'd think. Oak can give Chardonnay a characteristic vanilla aroma,

or one of cloves or nuts. The *malolactic fermentation*, in which the
winemaker lets the wine ferment twice, will give Chardonnay a
buttery aroma and a richness.

There's a world of difference between Chardonnays from different regions, however, both because of the styles of winemaking and the way the grapes grow in different climates.

Burgundy, Chardonnay's traditional home, has a relatively cool
climate. This region produces wines from Chardonnay that are
exceedingly elegant, lean and rich at the same time, with not
much apparent fruit flavor since the fruit doesn't ripen that
much. Instead, the earthy, minerally, sometimes nutty, site-specific
flavors of the Burgundian *terroir* emerge. (If France is the *terroir*
capital of the world, then Burgundy is the *terroir* capital of
France.)

The Chardonnay-growing regions of California and Australia
are much warmer than Burgundy, and the grapes get riper. For

Chardonnay Bashing

**You may be surprised to know that lately it's become
very fashionable to make fun of California Chardonnay—
and often for good reason. Although it's very easy to
grow, very easy to vinify (make into wine), and fetches
incredibly high prices on the marketplace, winemakers
bitch and moan that consumers won't try anything else,
and critics complain that the fruit is too obvious and the
oak overwhelms and masks what in France is a subtle and
complex grape. Mary Ewing Mulligan, a wine educator in
New York and a Master of Wine, says, "Think about
canned pineapple juice sort of revved up with high
alcohol and bittered up with oak—then you have a
good idea of the typical California Chardonnay
today."**

this reason, Chardonnays from these regions often have pronounced fruit aromas—apple, citrus, pear, and pineapple are
most common. California Chardonnays often suffer from too
much oak—if you sample one with an overwhelming vanilla
aroma that hits you over the head, that's what caused it. Poorly
made Chardonnays can smell like grapefruit Life Savers or
candied pineapple, and they're often sweeter than their French
confrères.

Chardonnays may be consumed when young and fresh, from
one to five years after bottling, or the better ones may be aged—
up to twenty years or so for the best white Burgundies.

SAUVIGNON BLANC

Wines from this grape are also very popular in the U.S., where
they are called either Sauvignon Blanc or Fumé Blanc (they're
exactly the same), and Australia and New Zealand, where they're
called Sauvignon Blanc. Chile has begun to produce some as
well; it's the number-one white wine produced for export there.

In France, Pouilly-Fumé, Sancerre, and other dry white wines
from the Loire Valley are made from the Sauvignon Blanc grape.
It is also an ingredient in dry white wines from Bordeaux such as
Entre-Deux-Mers and white Graves, as well as in sweet white
wines from the southwest of France such as Sauternes, Barsac,
Loupiac, and Monbazillac.

Sauvignon Blancs are crisp, refreshing, aromatic wines, known
for their distinctive nose, which is often described as freshly cut
grass, bell peppers, asparagus, or even, believe it or not, cat pee!
When a Sauvignon Blanc has a cat-pee nose, it's considered a
positive thing, since it's a good example of its variety. If the
grapes were picked when they were underripe, these aromas can
become quite pronounced. You may also find some pear, apple,
peach, apricot, fig, melon, citrus, floral, and spicy aromas. In most
regions where they're produced, Sauvignon Blancs are fermented
and aged in stainless-steel tanks because the cleanliness of the
stainless steel allows the character of the grape to come through
loud and clear. New Zealand put itself on the wine map for its
excellent Sauvignon Blancs made this way.

Poor examples of Sauvignon Blancs can taste unpleasantly green: leafy, "weedy," or overly herbaceous.

In some regions, winemakers will use oak (either fermenting the wine in the barrel or aging it for a time in the barrel) to give the Sauvignon Blanc an added richness. This may add aromas of vanilla, spice, and butter (just as the oak does in Chardonnays). Some California winemakers are doing this; it is common practice in Bordeaux.

Sauvignon Blancs, especially the unoaked ones, make wonderful apéritifs, since they're light, aromatic, and refreshing; their crispness (which you may notice as a bright acidity) lets them go well with a wide variety of light foods, including simply grilled chicken and fish. Plus, they're well priced—bargains, in fact, compared with comparable Chardonnays. Ten dollars or so buys you some mighty fine ones. Sauvignon Blancs should be drunk while young and fresh—within two or three years of the vintage date.

RIESLING

Though it's one of the finest white-wine grapes in the world, American producers don't make much Riesling. It's not because they don't want to, but because they can't sell it—since all the public seems to want is Chardonnay. However, Rieslings make such wonderfully aromatic, low-alcohol wines, that I'm predicting a future Riesling trend, in part because Rieslings go so well with the Pacific Rim cuisines that continue to grow in popularity, as well as many other kinds of food. Dry and off-dry Rieslings also happen to go well with spicy foods; they're also charming on their own as apéritifs (as are the lightly sweet ones); and the sweetest ones make delicious dessert wines.

In fact, sommeliers and chefs love Rieslings. Daniel Johnnes, the sommelier at New York City's renowned Montrachet restaurant, sings Riesling's praises. On his wine list, Johnnes features Rieslings from Germany, Alsace, and Austria, but his patrons tend to shy away from them unless the staff recommends them. Which they do, enthusiastically. "We recommend them," Johnnes explains, "because they have real personality and character as well as real value, and they're food-friendly. It's especially interesting to recommend a Riesling to people who want to learn something or try something different, especially if they want to show their knowledge to their guests. Riesling provides an opportunity to show something that's really impressive. With a Chardonnay or a great white Burgundy, people have expectations, and they can be let down. With Riesling, they might not have any expectations, and they're thrilled." Sounds as if the guy likes the stuff . . .

Since the Riesling grape thrives in very cool regions, the best Rieslings come from Germany and Alsace (Austria, too, but they're tough to find in the U.S.); they also do well in South Australia, New Zealand, the cooler regions of the U.S., and Canada. Rieslings seem to confuse people, perhaps because they are called by so many different names in different regions.

In the U.S., varietals made from true Riesling are known as Johannisberg Riesling or white Riesling. Much of California is too warm to produce dry Riesling; so instead it's allowed to overripen, and made into a sweet "late-harvest" Johannisberg Riesling. Oregon has a great climate for Riesling, but winemakers there have been forced by the craze for Chardonnay to cut back on its production, a trend I hope will reverse itself.

Riesling is much more popular in Australia and New Zealand than it is in the U.S., and winemakers there do a wonderful job with dry Rieslings, which they call "Rhine Riesling."

> **TIP FROM CABERNET FRANK**
> If you think, "Yuck—a sweet wine" when you hear the word "Riesling," think again. Rieslings from Alsace are typically dry and very lovely. German Rieslings are often sweet, but that doesn't stop them from being gorgeous wines. Try one— you won't be disappointed.

Riesling reigns supreme in its German home and in the Alsace region of France, where it is known simply as "Riesling." Germany is known for varying degrees of sweetness in its Rieslings, while Alsatian Rieslings tend to be dry (though not always). Austria and northern Italy also produce Rieslings in small quantities, as does Chile, though not of the same quality.

Aromas to look for: petroleum, citrus, apricot, peach, pineapple, floral scents, honey in the sweeter ones.

VIOGNIER

Even though Americans will have a rough time pronouncing this grape (vee-*yohn*-yay), it's the trendy white varietal du jour in California. One of the reasons for its present popularity: It harkens from France's Rhône Valley, traditional home of several currently trendy grape varieties (see Syrah and Grenache). Viognier grapes produce a highly perfumed, rich, dry white wine, with heady aromas of pear, melon, orange blossoms, and lime blossoms, even jasmine. It's a *pretty* wine.

However, not all winemakers like it. "I'm somewhat underwhelmed by Viognier," says Randall Grahm, the winemaker at Bonny Doon Vineyard in California's Central Coast region. "I think it's something of a fad." This despite Grahm's reputation as one of a number of Californian champions of Rhône varietals. (Grahm believes that California's climate resembles the Mediterranean, and that Mediterranean varieties should be grown there— see Chapter Six.) Viogniers are quite pricey—the good ones from California cost twenty-five or thirty dollars retail. Grahm does concede, however, that "It's nice for a special occasion."

Why do you need to know about it? You'll probably be seeing a lot of it in the future, and wine snobs may use it to try to bully you. Plus, you may find it delicious.

In France, it is known as Condrieu or Château-Grillet, both from the northern Rhône; and lately more wines coming from the Languedoc region are varietally labeled as "Viognier."

Extra-Credit White Varieties

PINOT GRIS

This grape makes a rich, low-acid wine that goes well with food since it's not overly aromatic. Most famous are those from Alsace, where wines made from this grape are called "Tokay d'Alsace." In Italy, you might know it as "Pinot Grigio," but Italian ones aren't as rich or concentrated, and some are even sparkling. Germany,

Austria, Switzerland, and Hungary produce wines from Pinot Gris. Pinot Gris has done well in Oregon; and it's even being planted in California.

PINOT BLANC

In Alsace, Germany, Austria, Italy, and Hungary, this grape produces a full-bodied white. In Alsace, Italy, and Hungary, wines made from Pinot Blanc are dry; in Germany and Austria, they can be either dry or sweet. Some Pinot Blanc is made in California, but there's a big argument about whether it's all really Pinot Blanc or whether some of it is an inferior grape called Melon. It's also grown in France's Burgundy region.

SÉMILLON

This grape is usually blended with other grapes, though Australia (where it used to be called "Hunter Valley Riesling," even though it has nothing to do with Riesling), South Africa, and Chile produce unblended Sémillon; in the U.S., a small amount is produced in California and Washington.

Sémillon is rich and full, dark yellow–colored, with low acid, yet it ages very well.

Sémillon's lusciousness, as well as its susceptibility to botrytis, contributes to the unmatchable sweet white wines of Sauternes and Barsac. Blended with Sauvignon Blanc (in combinations usually around 80 percent Sémillon to just under 20 percent Sauvignon Blanc, with a little bit of a third variety, Muscadelle, thrown in for good measure), this grape is the main ingredient of dry white wines from Graves in France. Both these and Sauternes benefit greatly from aging—even up to thirty or more years for the most famous Sauternes, Château d'Yquem.

Aromas to look for: honey, nuts, pears, apples (especially in Barsac), lanolin (especially in Australia).

GEWÜRZTRAMINER

This grape, pronounced geh-*vertz*-tra-mih-ner, makes an approachable full-bodied wine with an appealingly spicy, fruity nose, from dry to very sweet. For some reason, it's out of fashion at the moment—perhaps because it's more fun to smell than it is to drink. It can hit you over the head with its full flavor. Look for peach, apricot, litchi, citrus, honey, rose, and spice (*gewürz* means "spicy" in German) aromas.

MARSANNE AND ROUSANNE

In France, these two varieties from the Rhône Valley are almost always blended together. In the northern Rhône, they make up white Crozes-Hermitages and white Hermitages; in the southern Rhône, white Châteauneuf-du-Pape. They make full-bodied wines, without much acidity. Aromas to look for: apples, pears, nuts, spice, almonds, and glue(!). From Australia, you may find Marsanne on its own; in Switzerland, it's called Ermitage Blanc. Rousanne is the fancier grape of the two—it's more elegant and aromatic, but tougher to grow. In California, blends of the two are becoming popular; Bonny Doon makes one called "Le Sophiste." Several California wineries bottle varietal Marsanne as well.

CHENIN BLANC

Wines made from Chenin Blanc may be found in the Loire Valley (where it's called Pineau de la Loire), New Zealand, South Africa (where it's called "Steen"), and the U.S. Chenin Blancs can be quite good, but they're often dreadful. They can be bone-dry all the way up through very sweet. In the Loire, they're still to slightly fizzy to full-on sparkling; in California, South Africa, and New Zealand, they're made still.

California produces a lot of awful ones, and for that reason Chenin Blanc has a lousy reputation there. However, Chappellet Vineyards makes a very appealing one, but because of Chenin Blanc's reputation, they named it "Old Vine Cuvée," instead of giving it the regular varietal name. Unfortunately, several other California producers of admirable Chenin Blanc have stopped making it for lack of consumer interest.

Aromas to look for: apple, flowers, citrus blossoms, melon, spice, honey (okay, darling?).

MUSCAT

What we normally call "Muscat" is actually Muscat Blanc à Petits Grains. There are three other distinct varieties that have the word "Muscat" in them, but they're not as good, and you probably won't bump into wines made out of them.

Muscat is one of the oldest grape varieties, known for its perfumed aroma, which more than any other variety smells like—grapes! But it's even prettier than that—often it's grapes perfumed with flowers, orange blossoms, and spice. Once you smell any wine made from this grape, you won't forget its distinctive aroma.

Muscat produces both dry wines and sweet wines, wines relatively low in alcohol and high in alcohol, table wines and fortified wines, and both sparkling and still.

There are lots of different wines made from Muscat the world over, but four stand out:

- Moscato d'Asti, a delicately sweet, slightly fizzy dessert wine from the Piedmont region of Italy. Think of it as a refined, elegant cousin of the well-known but undistinguished, often sticky-sweet Asti Spumante.
- Muscat de Beaumes-de-Venise, a vin doux naturel. (Vin doux naturel is the French term for a wine to which the winemaker added a spirit to stop the fermentation and keep the wine sweet.) This golden dessert wine is rich and luscious.
- Muscat d'Alsace: a dry, light wine from the Alsace region of France. If you've ever tasted either Moscato d'Asti or Muscat de Beaumes-de-Venise, the nose on this will be immediately familiar to you—it may even trick you into thinking it's going to be sweet—but it's not: it's bone-dry!
- Muscat of Samos, the second-most-famous Greek wine. Like Muscat de Beaumes-de-Venise, Muscat of Samos can be made as a vin doux naturel or a vin de liqueur. It can also be made from dried grapes. All three are sweet dessert wines.

The Muscat-eer Club

Muscat, Muscadet, Muscadelle, Muscardin: These may sound like the conjugation of an obscure verb in an unknown language, but they're not; they're four distinctly different grape varieties. The only one you really need to know is Muscat, short for Muscat Blanc à Petits Grains, also known as Muscat Blanc, Moscatel de Grano Menudo, Muscat of Frontignan, Moscatel de Frontignan, Muscat d'Alsace, White Muscat, Moscato d'Asti, Moscato Bianco, Muscat Canelli, Muskateller, and Muskadel.

Other wines made from Muscat grapes include:

Dessert wines from California, including Bonny Doon's Vin de Glacière, which identifies the grape on the label as "Muscat Canelli" (which is just another name for Muscat Blanc à Petits Grains), Quady's Orange Muscat, or Preston's Muscat Brûlé, two fortified wines.

Dry wines from Austria are called Muskateller.

Must-Know Red-Grape Varieties

CABERNET SAUVIGNON

I'll admit it: Cabernet Sauvignon (also known, simply, as "Cabernet," or fondly, as "Cab") is one of the best grapes in the world. It makes wines that are full and concentrated, and the presence of lots of tannins in its thick skin gives the wine structure and allows it to age for a very long time.

Cabernet, in turn, makes some of the world's greatest red wines: the wines of the Bordeaux region of France. Some Bordeaux winemakers combine Cabernet with another grape or two; usually Merlot, and often Cabernet Franc.

In California, Australia, Chile, and Argentina, this grape makes the varietal Cabernet Sauvignon.

Look for blackberry, blackcurrant, bell-pepper, and black-pepper aromas in Cabernet Sauvignon; you might also find mint or tobacco, chocolate, vanilla, or butter, or, in Australian and a few California Cabernets, eucalyptus.

MERLOT

Often Cabernet Sauvignon's partner in crime, Merlot rounds out the classic Bordeaux blend, imitated more and more in California, where it is often called "Meritage."

But it can also make wonderful wines on its own. Although once upon a time it was planted in the Bordeaux region as sort of an insurance policy because it did better in poor weather than Cabernet, today there are certain Bordeaux that are made from 100 percent (or close to 100 percent) Merlot, mostly in the Saint-Emilion and Pomerol districts. In California, Washington State, Australia, Chile, and Argentina, among other regions, you'll find varietals called Merlot. They're softer, rounder (the wine pros

TIP FROM
CABERNET
FRANK
In California,
the wine-
drinking public
continues to be
gaga over
Cabernet
Sauvignon.
Winemakers, on
the other hand, get
tired of the whole
subject—when
dining among
themselves, the call
is often for
"ABC," "Anything
but Cab."

say "fleshier"), and more approachable than Cabernets. The downside is, depending on the region, they often have less structure, and are less complex.

Americans have been going crazy over Merlots for the last few years, probably because the tannins are less harsh than they are in Cabernets, so they seem "friendlier." Look for berry, black cherry, olive, black pepper, vanilla, and mint and other herbal aromas.

PINOT NOIR

The most famous wines made from the noble Pinot Noir grape are red Burgundies, such as Pommard, Volnay, Côte de Beaune, Nuits-Saint-Georges, and so on. Winemakers in this region find the Pinot Noir grape neutral enough to let the *terroir* find its expression, and that's why these wines can be so fabulous.

Pinot Noirs from the United States, namely California and Oregon, are much fruitier, though they can be bone-dry. Though usually not as *raffiné* and subtle as their French cousins, they can be delightful wines (and many are even better than delightful), which happen to go wonderfully with a wide range of food. In fact, sommelier Daniel Johnnes says that along with Riesling, Pinot Noir is "the most food-friendly wine."

The Pinot Noir grape variety also makes an appearance as a possible ingredient in sparkling white wines! Together with Chardonnay, Pinot Noir makes up the base wine for champagne; and on its own, you'll sometimes see a sparkling wine called "Blanc de Noir"—this sparkling wine, often from California, can be slightly tinged with pink.

Pinot Noir grapes are fairly thin-skinned, so the wines aren't as tannic or darkly colored as Cabernet, and they're usually made

to drink younger, about two to six years after bottling, though *grand cru* Burgundies can age much longer.

Look for cherry, strawberry, raspberry, spices, butter, and vanilla on the nose.

SYRAH

If you don't know this grape, you're in for a treat. The Syrah grape makes wines that are big, dark, and concentrated, with lots of

Meritage

Meritage is not a varietal; it is a Bordeaux-style combination of Cabernet Sauvignon, Merlot, and perhaps Cabernet Franc and/or Malbec, made in California. The name "Meritage" is a result of a contest held in California in the 1980s to come up with a name for the blend. This one probably won because it sounds suitably French, without actually being French, and also suggests the idea of marriage, as in a marriage between several grape varieties.

roasty flavor. Don't confuse it with Petite Sirah, a relatively obscure variety (see Extra-Credit Reds, on page 78). It's a totally different grape.

The most famous incarnations of wines from the Syrah grape are from France's northern Rhône Valley, where the best-known examples are called "Hermitage" and "Côte-Rôtie." Australians love this grape, too—they call it "Shiraz," which actually may be the original name for this grape if it came from Persia, as some people think; South Africans call it Shiraz as well. Syrah is starting to be grown in California.

Aromas to look for: roasted beets, leather, blackberries, blackcurrants, smoke.

GRENACHE

The second-most widely planted red grape variety in the world, Grenache is the numero uno grape for red wines in the southern end of the Rhône Valley, where it's the main ingredient in Châteauneuf-du-Pape, Côtes du Rhône, and other wines. It also turns into rosé—Tavel being one of the most famous. Lately Grenache is becoming popular in California in the form of several southern Rhône-style blends (Joseph Phelps's Vin du Mistral Le Mistral and Grenache Rosé, for two; Bonny Doon's Le Cigare Volant, for another). It does well in California, because it loves the warm climate, and even survives drought.

In Spain, Grenache is known as Garnacha; it's used, blended with Tempranillo, in Riojas, as well as many other wines. It's called Cannonau in Sardinia.

ZINFANDEL

Why do you have to know this? Because you're American, and this is an American grape! Or so most American winemakers think, anyway; many Italians think it's actually the same thing as Primitivo, an Italian grape. Wine made from Zinfandel is dark purple, with lots of fruit "up front," as they say (meaning it's the first thing you notice). Though most people prefer to drink it young while it still shows its wonderful fruit characteristics, it can also age well.

Look for strawberry, blackberry, raspberry, plum, black pepper, raisins, and spices in the aroma.

Zinfandel, dark though it is, is also made into the very popular blush (very pale pink) wine called white Zinfandel (other grapes may be added into the blend as well). Here the skins are only left in contact with the juice for a very short time, giving it that pink tinge. This wine was created by accident by Bob Trinchero of Napa Valley's Sutter Home in 1972; he released it anyway and the public went crazy. White Zinfandel is fairly sweet, often slightly fizzy.

SANGIOVESE

Sangiovese is important because it makes Chianti, which, as time marches on, will become more and more popular and important, as well as the very yummy Brunello di Montalcino and Vino Nobile di Montepulciano. The grape makes wines with appealing red fruit and floral aromas and bright acidity.

California winemakers are starting to use it, too, so wine-lovers-on-the-go should know it!

NEBBIOLO

This is the last must-know. Nebbiolo makes some of the best Italian wines: Barolo and Barbaresco. These deep, dark, intense, complex wines are Italy's serious, brooding types, and can age for

BLUSH WINES ARE CONSIDERED "FRIVOLOUS" BY SERIOUS WINE DRINKERS

Blush Wine Drinkers   Red Wine Drinkers

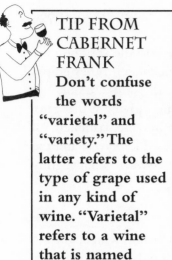

TIP FROM CABERNET FRANK Don't confuse the words "varietal" and "variety." The latter refers to the type of grape used in any kind of wine. "Varietal" refers to a wine that is named after the grape it's made from.

a very long time. Look for fig, roasted-plum, nutty, and earthy aromas.

Extra-Credit Reds

Some of these are used mostly in blends with other wines; others may be less present in the market as the grape varieties listed above.

CABERNET FRANC

This is one of the varieties blended with Cabernet Sauvignon and Merlot to make the classic blend in Bordeaux; it's being used in California as well for Meritage. Since it is less intense in color and lighter in tannin than its friend Cabernet Sauvignon, winemakers in the Loire Valley use it for several light-style reds such as Chinon, Saumur-Champigny, Bourgueil, and Anjou-Villages. Long Island and Washington State are also starting to make Cabernet Franc varietals.

MALBEC

Once upon a time this was part of the Bordeaux blend, and though it's used in California Meritage, in Bordeaux it's not used much anymore. However, it's really big in Chile and Argentina, where it appears as a varietal.

MOURVÈDRE

Winemakers in the southern Rhône blend this, along with Grenache, and sometimes Syrah, Cinsault, and other varieties, to make Châteauneuf-du-Pape. California's Bonny Doon Vineyards has a 100 percent Mourvèdre proprietary red called "Old Telegram."

TEMPRANILLO

In Spain, this intense, dark grape gets blended with Garnacha (Grenache) to make Rioja; it's the major variety in Tinto Fino from Ribera del Duero; and used also in Penedès. In Portugal, it's part of the blend used for ports, among other things.

PINOTAGE

This grape variety, unique to South Africa, was born from a cross between Pinot Noir and Cinsault. The result is a dark purple, concentrated red wine reminiscent of Syrah, that can be chewily delicious.

GAMAY

This grape variety makes a light red wine, with freshness, fruitiness, crisp acidity, and not much depth. You know it as Nouveau Beaujolais. It also makes other kinds of Beaujolais, for instance Beaujolais-Villages. A small amount is grown in California, for Nouveau Beaujolais–type wines.

PETITE SIRAH

This California grape variety, unrelated to Syrah, was long thought to be an obscure French variety called Dourif. However, genetic research at UC Davis is showing that Petite Sirah is its own unique grape. The wines it produces are inky dark, fairly intense, with big fruit. When they're well made from grapes from old vines, they can be wonderful; otherwise they might take the enamel off your teeth.

Now—don't worry if you don't remember all that, because a handy-dandy chart follows, showing each of the major grape varieties and the wines it produces in the different regions of the world. You'll find more information about each in Part II, which covers all the regions.

TIP FROM CABERNET FRANK

Wine professionals often refer to grapes as *berries,* a term that can be very confusing to those not in the know.

Grape Varieties and the Wines They Make

VARIETY	A.K.A.	BLENDED WITH	WINES
Varieties Used for White Wine			
Chardonnay			Chardonnay, white Burgundy, Chablis, Blanc de Blancs champagne
Chardonnay		Pinot Noir, Pinot Meunier	Champagne
Chardonnay		Sémillon	Sémillon–Chardonnay (Australia)
Sauvignon Blanc	Fumé Blanc		Sauvignon Blanc, Fumé Blanc, Sancerre, Pouilly Fumé
Sauvignon Blanc		Sémillon	white Graves, Sauternes, Barsac, Loupiac
Riesling			Riesling, white Riesling, Johannisberg Riesling, Rhine Riesling
Viognier			Viognier, Condrieu, Château-Grillet
Pinot Gris	Pinot Grigio		Pinot Gris, Pinot Grigio, Tokay d'Alsace, Rülander (Germany), Grauer Burgunder (Germany)
Pinot Blanc			Pinot Blanc, Weissburgunder (Germany)
Sémillon			Sémillon, "Hunter Valley Riesling" (Australia)
Sémillon		Sauvignon Blanc	Sauternes, white Meritage (California)
Gewürztraminer			Gewürztraminer
Marsanne			Marsanne, Ermitage Blanc (Switzerland)
Marsanne		Rousanne	white Hermitage, white Crozes-Hermitage, white Châteauneuf-du-Pape

Chenin Blanc	Pineau de la Loire, Steen	Chenin Blanc, Stein (S. Africa), Anjou blanc, Saumur, Savennières, Vouvray (Loire Valley)
Muscat Blanc à Petits Grains	Muscat, Moscato Bianco, Muscat of Frontignan, Muscat Blanc, Muscat Canelli	Muscat de Beaumes-de-Venise, Muscat d'Alsace, Muscat of Samos, Moscato d'Asti, Muskateller (Austria)
Trebbiano	Malvasia Bianco	Vin Santo, Galestro, Vernaccia di San Gimignano, Frascati

Varieties Used for Red Wine

Cabernet Sauvignon		Cabernet Sauvignon, red Bordeaux
Merlot	Cabernet Franc	Pomerol, Saint-Emilion
Merlot		Merlot, Pomerol, Saint-Emilion
Cabernet Sauvignon	Merlot	red Bordeaux
Cabernet Sauvignon	Merlot, Cabernet Franc	red Meritage (California), red Bordeaux
Cabernet Sauvignon	Sangiovese (optional)	"Supertuscans"
Pinot Noir		Pinot Noir, red Burgundy, Spätburgunder (Germany)

VARIETY	A.K.A.	BLENDED WITH	WINES
Syrah	Shiraz (Australia & S. Africa)		Hermitage, Crozes-Hermitage, Côte-Rôtie, Syrah, Shiraz
Grenache	Garnacha (Spain), Cannonau (Sardinia)		Châteauneuf-du-Pape, Côtes du Rhône, Tavel (rosé), Grenache Rosé, various cute-sounding Rhône-esque proprietary names (California)
Grenache		Tempranillo	Rioja
Zinfandel			Zinfandel, white Zinfandel
Sangiovese	Prugnolo Gentile		Chianti, Brunello di Montalcino, Vino Nobile di Montepulciano, Sangiovese
Sangiovese		Cabernet Sauvignon	"Supertuscans"
Nebbiolo			Barolo, Barbaresco
Cabernet Franc			Chinon, Saumur-Champigny, Bourguiel, Anjou-Villages, Cabernet Franc
Tempranillo		+ miscellaneous others	Rioja, Tinto Fino, Penedès
Gamay			Nouveau Beaujolais, Beaujolais-Villages, Beaujolais Cru
Barbera			Barbera d'Alba, Barbera d'Asti
Corrino		Rondinella, Molinara	Valpolicella, Amarone, Bardolino

IF YOU FORGET EVERYTHING ELSE YOU'VE READ IN CHAPTER FOUR, JUST REMEMBER THIS:

1. Different wines are made from different types of grapes.
2. When a wine is named after the grape it's made from, it's called a *varietal*.
3. Chardonnay and Cabernet aren't the only game in town.
4. Most wines in France and Italy are named after the region in which they were made.
5. Pinot Noir makes red Burgundy.
6. Chardonnay makes white Burgundy.
7. Cabernet Sauvignon, Merlot, and Cabernet Franc make red Bordeaux.

Part II

THE REGIONS

THE GLOBALIZATION OF WINE

Now let's go on a world tour. It's a great time to take the trip, since the last twenty years or so have seen incredible strides in winemaking all over the globe. In the United States, we're fortunate enough to have on the shelves of our wine merchants' shops wines from dozens of countries, and the future holds even more diversity in store.

Not only can we choose from the wines of more and more regions, but winemakers are crossing their regional boundaries like crazy, to share winemaking knowledge, or to take advantage of the climate and soil of distant lands, bringing their expertise to newly emerging regions. Look at the French: winemakers from Bordeaux and Champagne have transplanted themselves to California's Napa Valley (as have Italians and Spaniards); Burgundians have descended upon Oregon, Pinot Noir grapes in hand; winemakers from the southwestern French region of Madiran are even starting up in China!

MANY FRENCH WINEMAKERS HAVE COME TO CALIFORNIA TO MAKE WINE

Italian winemaker Angelo Gaja is taking Grignolino (an obscure grape variety in California, but appreciated in Italy's Asti province) from California to Italy. And the varietal-labeling influence of California wines has spread (for better or worse) to pockets of Italy, and even to France.

In Part II, you may notice a somewhat unbalanced amount of attention paid to the U.S. and France, compared with the rest of the world. Is this twisted, narrow, and unfair? You bet! Consider the fact that before the breakup of the Soviet Union, that nation produced more wine than any other. But do we ever see Russian wines on our supermarket shelves? No! So why should you bother about them? The United States and France are given unequal weight because French and American wines comprise most of what you'll run into, both in wineshops and on restaurant wine lists.

But that's not the whole picture, of course.

Depending on where you live, you'll probably find many other wines from the "Old World," especially those from Italy, Spain, and Germany. If you haven't tried them, they offer a wealth of new tastes to explore.

And as other "New World" wines, such as those from Australia, New Zealand, South America, and even South Africa, show up on more and more shelves, you'll want to discover them.

This book doesn't attempt to cover all the wines in the world, an overwhelming prospect. We'll just concentrate on the ones you're most likely to bump into, plus a few others that might be worth seeking out. If you're looking for something encyclopedic covering a specific region, Chapter Thirteen will guide you toward more specialized books and courses.

Chapter Five

THE UNITED STATES OF WINE

Congratulations! You've picked the best possible time in history to take up an interest in American wines. Why? Because we're on the move, baby! At this moment in history, with California winemakers perfecting what they've learned in the last twenty years, improving the quality of their grapes, and experimenting with new varietals; with Washington and New York states really coming into their own, and Oregonian winemakers jumping into the fray with plenty of guts, smarts, and good taste, the excitement is here and will only continue to build.

Which is not to say these are the only states producing wines: they're just the most established wine regions in the country. But there are wineries all over—from New Jersey, Connecticut, and Maine to Virginia, North Carolina, Georgia, Missouri, Illinois, Ohio, even down into Texas, which, incidentally, had quite a little wine industry of its own in the nineteenth century. In fact forty-four different states produce wine.

Why don't we hear more about wines from all these places?

Well, to be frank, they're just not as good as the wines in the more established regions. But give them time; some of them may just get there.

We all know about the reputation and quality of California wines, which have in the last twenty-five years or so made the United States one of the leading wine regions of the world. Since California wines are probably the most widely available across the country, we'll look at them a little more closely than any of the other regions covered in this book.

California may not be the *oldest* winemaking region in the United States, but it's the best established. Although a few wineries there have been making serious wine for most of the century, such old wineries are rare. Beaulieu Vineyards, for instance, continued uninterrupted through the Depression, producing sacramental wines.

In the 1930s, according to Louis Foppiano, Jr., whose family's Foppiano Vineyards in Sonoma County has been around since 1896, very little wine in California was bottled by the wineries: they sold it in huge barrels at the winery's "retail sales" room (the early incarnation of the modern-day tasting room) and customers had to bring their own jugs to fill up from the barrels. The wineries also sold the wine to grocery stores in smaller barrels; the grocer bottled it for sale in jugs. At that time each of the wineries made just one or two wines: red wine and white wine. These were cheap blends of whatever grapes the winemaker happened to have lying around. "You'd just set up three different barrels with a tasting glass under each one," Foppiano explains. Each barrel would contain the same wine. "One would say 'five cents a gallon,' one would say 'ten cents a gallon,' and one would say 'fifteen cents a gallon.' And people would take the little glass out, they'd taste all three, and invariably they'd say the fifteen-cent tank was better."

We've come a long way since then—or have we? Have you ever noticed how if a wine is expensive, people automatically think it's good?

By the end of World War II, people became accustomed to

JUG WINES (WINES SOLD IN VERY
LARGE BOTTLES) ORIGINATED
IN CALIFORNIA

buying wine in bottles, and in the 1950s, jug wines (inexpensive wines sold in large bottles) were a common sight on supermarket shelves throughout the land. Now you could see lots of variety: in the reds, Burgundy, Claret, Barbarone, and Zinfandel; in the whites, Sauterne (sic), Rhine, Chablis. The funny part is they were all still the same old blends: the "Burgundy" and the "Barbarone" were just a combination of whatever red-wine grapes the winery happened to have on hand (there was a lot of Zinfandel in those days), and the different whites were all blends as well, with absolutely no regard for the grape varieties included. Wineries called them by different names in an effort to try to market them to different ethnic groups—German immigrants would go for "Rhine" rather than "Chablis," even though there was no difference. Italian immigrants preferred "Barbarone," while French immigrants (and people who craved things that seemed French) went for "Burgundy." And of course "Sauterne" had nothing in common with luscious French botrytis-affected Sémillon/Sauvignon Blanc, properly spelled with a final "s."

AMERICAN WINE-LABEL TECHNICALITIES

Today in the United States, wine falls under the purview of the federal Bureau of Alcohol, Tobacco, and Firearms (BATF), which regulates its labeling. Many people think a more appropriate regulatory agency would be the Food and Drug Administration (FDA), since wine is a food, with nutrients, vitamins, etc., and a potentially beneficial health value.

In any case, the system is a total mess, and untangling it probably won't help you choose a good bottle of wine.

However, you should know that when a wine is varietally labeled ("Chardonnay" or "Cabernet"), the law states that the wine must contain at least 75 percent of that grape variety. Sometimes you'll see a label that boasts "100% Chardonnay," or something like that; they just want you to know that it's more "pure." However, closer to 100 percent isn't necessarily better. While some winemakers blend in cheaper grapes, with higher-quality wines it's more likely that they'll be blending in other varieties that really *help* the wine. For instance, even though a wine is labeled "Merlot," the winemaker may decide to blend in 10 percent of Cabernet Sauvignon to give it more "structure," often a sound decision.

With American wines, you'll often have a choice between "Reserve" or a regular labeling, or you may see the same wine from different vineyards. Unlike regions such as Italy or Spain, in the U.S., "Reserve" doesn't mean anything specific; sometimes the grapes come from a vineyard that the winemaker particularly likes, or the wine is made a little differently; for instance, it might be fermented in the barrel, or spend a little more time aging in the barrel. But that doesn't necessarily mean you'll like it better (you may in fact prefer less oak). If a winemaker sees fit to mention a vineyard on the label, it may be that it's one he or she is proud of—a clue that there could be something interesting inside the bottle.

The question of appellations is much more tangled—even Kafkaesque. When you look at a bottle of California wine, it will have an appellation—that is, an indication of where the grapes were grown, just as a French wine will. Unlike French wines,

American wines won't say the word *appellation* anywhere on the bottles. What you'll see is an American Viticultural Area (AVA), which is a place name—and that *is* the appellation, although the label won't even say "AVA" on it. It might say the name of a state, such as "California," or a region, such as "Central Coast" or "Napa Valley," or a county, such as "Sonoma County," or a more specific AVA, such as "Rutherford," or "Edna Valley." What that means is that at least 85 percent of the grapes used must come from the specific AVA mentioned. If the AVA is "California," then at least 85 percent of the grapes must come from California—anywhere in the state. If the AVA is "Russian River Valley," then 85 percent of the grapes must come from that very small AVA within Sonoma County. The remaining 15 percent might come from elsewhere in Sonoma County, or even anywhere else in the state.

The problem with AVAs is that they don't really tell you much. Plus the system has loopholes. Take the appellation "Napa Valley" for example. For a wine to boast "Napa Valley" on its la-

Visiting Wineries

If you live near (or can make a trip to) California, Oregon, Washington, or New York State, visiting wineries is a wonderful way both to learn about wine and to taste wines you haven't tried before. The most user-friendly region for touring, of course, is the Napa Valley, where most of the wineries are open to the public and have tasting rooms. Smaller wineries may be available for tours and tastings by appointment, but don't take up a small staff's time unless you intend to buy a case or so. The nearby Sonoma Valley, though it isn't set up as well for tourists, is gorgeous, too, a little more rustic.

The best way to plan a tour is to pick up a book that describes each winery and lists the hours. The Gault Millau *Guide to the Best Wineries of North America* is one such book.

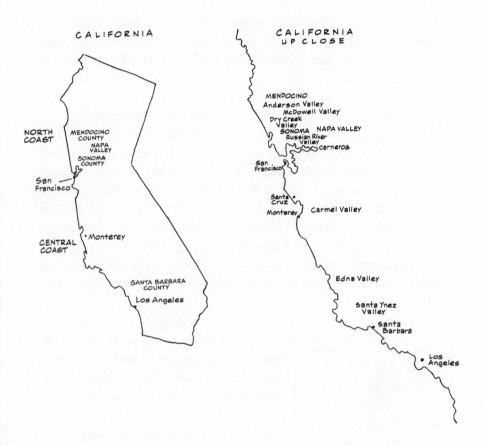

bel, 75 percent of the grapes must come from Napa Valley, unless the winery existed before a certain date, in which case they can pretty much do what they want.

Note: The winery itself isn't necessarily located within the AVA on the label, since many wineries own or buy grapes from vineyards in neighboring areas.

So why bother thinking about AVAs? Because as winemakers move toward the idea of *terroir*, we'll begin to notice more the differences between grapes grown in various specific areas.

California

California wines underwent a major renaissance in the sixties and seventies, during which time the number of wineries in the state exploded. At the same time quality took a major leap forward, as winemakers began concentrating their efforts on high-quality varietally labeled wines for the first time.

A now famous tasting in Paris in 1976 really turned things upside down. Unbeknownst to the winemakers whose wines had been entered, an entirely French panel of judges rated several California wines above some of Burgundy's and Bordeaux's finest offerings in a blind tasting; the winners were a 1973 Château Montelena Chardonnay and a 1973 Stag's Leap Wine Cellars Cabernet, which the judges were convinced were top French wines. A 1970 Château Haut-Brion and a 1970 Château Mouton Rothschild (two of the most prestigious wines in the world) rated just below the Stag's Leap Cab. The rest, as they say, is history.

The most significant part of that history is that California wines could now take their rightful place in the pantheon of the best wines of the world; and now finally, Americans could find something on their supermarket shelves other than those dopey jug wines of yesteryear. They could now choose varietals—varietals of high quality—and start to have opinions about them and decide that they liked certain wines better than others.

> **TIP FROM CABERNET FRANK**
>
> **A sorry side effect of California's wine boom was that the wine geek began to flourish, as did his kissin' cousin, the wine snob.**

Although Napa Valley has long been California's wine glamour spot, Sonoma County has been quietly making wonderful wines for just as long. Mendocino County, the Central Coast (around Santa Cruz and Monterey), and, farther south, Santa Barbara County have also come into their own.

CALIFORNIA WINES VS. FRENCH WINES

Looking at the big picture, California wines for the last twenty-five years have followed the lead of the French. The grape varieties that have been widely planted—Chardonnay, Cabernet, Merlot, and Pinot Noir—are imports from Burgundy and Bordeaux, and that's one important reason winemakers attempt to make wines in roughly the same styles.

But though they're French in basic style and in grape, the California attitude toward winemaking that developed in the 1970s was diametrically opposed to that in France. The difference can be summed up in five words: University of California at Davis. The prestigious Department of Viticulture and Enology at UC Davis pumps out winemaking graduates and spits them into the wineries of California, where they become oenologists (officially the people who head up the wineries' laboratory operations), winemakers (the top of the oenological heap in terms of decision making about the wines), and grape growers. All of it is approached very scientifically, with lots of attention paid to fancy high-tech equipment, highfalutin technical issues such as clonal

selection of grapevine rootstocks, and degrees Brix of the grapes at harvest. Europeans often criticize this approach as too sterile and soulless, though lots of UC Davis technology has been imported all over Europe.

Meanwhile, California winemakers historically haven't paid as much attention to the quality of the grapes themselves, acting under the mistaken impression that quality lay entirely in what the winemaker did with those grapes. Not surprisingly, winemakers became celebrities, much as chefs were gaining star status for the first time in California (a situation that continues to flourish). The idea of winemaker-as-celebrity is completely contrary to the French conception of what it means to make wine.

As far as the grape growers were concerned, the prevailing idea in California was that *more* was better (especially since they're paid by the ton for their produce). That idea is totally contrary to the Old World idea of quality winemaking, now widely accepted all over the world, that less is more. In other words, lower yields from the vineyards—fewer grapes—make better wines.

In recent years, winemakers and growers have understood their missed opportunity, and these days growers are working more closely with the winemakers to grow the highest-quality grapes.

Although California renditions of French wines (Chardonnay as an imitation of white Burgundy, Pinot Noir as an imitation of red Burgundy, Cabernet as an imitation of red Bordeaux, etc.) are similar in some ways to their French counterparts, the result is ultimately very different. In general, California varietals are fruitier, oakier, and less subtle than their French counterparts, and they don't require (and in many cases can't withstand) as much aging. Critics accuse them of being overblown and too much alike.

CALIFORNIA AVAS

At the same time specific AVAs within California are gaining recognition. You may have heard of Carneros, Howell Mountain, Stags Leap, Alexander Valley, or Russian River: these districts are all specific AVAs within their regions. For the first time people are talking about the specific character of each of these appellations, and the way the land is expressed in the wines; and as a result, winemakers are keeping grapes from the different growing regions separate.

Why do you need to know this arcane information? The more you taste California wines, the more you'll start seeing these appellations prominently displayed on labels and on wine lists. As you taste, you might start noticing that you particularly like the wines from certain AVAs: Pinot Noirs from Carneros, for instance, or Chardonnays from Russian River.

At this point, although an abbreviated list follows, you don't need to memorize all the California AVAs and the characteristics of the wines they produce. If you're moved to really get into it, James Halliday's *Wine Atlas of California* is an excellent and well-explained (not to mention beautiful) reference.

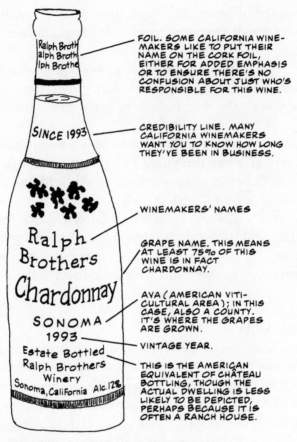

FOIL. SOME CALIFORNIA WINE-MAKERS LIKE TO PUT THEIR NAME ON THE CORK FOIL, EITHER FOR ADDED EMPHASIS OR TO ENSURE THERE'S NO CONFUSION ABOUT JUST WHO'S RESPONSIBLE FOR THIS WINE.

CREDIBILITY LINE. MANY CALIFORNIA WINEMAKERS WANT YOU TO KNOW HOW LONG THEY'VE BEEN IN BUSINESS.

WINEMAKERS' NAMES

GRAPE NAME. THIS MEANS AT LEAST 75% OF THIS WINE IS IN FACT CHARDONNAY.

AVA (AMERICAN VITI-CULTURAL AREA); IN THIS CASE, ALSO A COUNTY. IT'S WHERE THE GRAPES ARE GROWN.

VINTAGE YEAR.

THIS IS THE AMERICAN EQUIVALENT OF CHÂTEAU BOTTLING, THOUGH THE ACTUAL DWELLING IS LESS LIKELY TO BE DEPICTED, PERHAPS BECAUSE IT IS OFTEN A RANCH HOUSE.

CALIFORNIA WINE: A QUICK VISUAL

California Wine Trends

THE BURGUNDIAN BANDWAGON

It's become very chic for California winemakers who are making Chardonnay and Pinot Noir to describe their techniques and the resulting wines as "very Burgundian." This is code for "We know that California wines can hit you over the head with their fruit and oak and high alcohol. We want to do something a little more subtle—restrained and sophisticated."

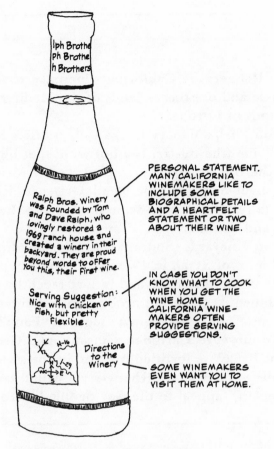

Ralph Bros. Winery was founded by Tom and Dave Ralph, who lovingly restored a 1969 ranch house and created a winery in their backyard. They are proud beyond words to offer you this, their first wine.

PERSONAL STATEMENT. MANY CALIFORNIA WINEMAKERS LIKE TO INCLUDE SOME BIOGRAPHICAL DETAILS AND A HEARTFELT STATEMENT OR TWO ABOUT THEIR WINE.

Serving Suggestion: Nice with chicken or fish, but pretty flexible.

IN CASE YOU DON'T KNOW WHAT TO COOK WHEN YOU GET THE WINE HOME, CALIFORNIA WINEMAKERS OFTEN PROVIDE SERVING SUGGESTIONS.

Directions to the Winery

SOME WINEMAKERS EVEN WANT YOU TO VISIT THEM AT HOME.

CALIFORNIA WINE: BACK LABEL

THE RHÔNE RANGERS AND ITALOPHILES

There's also a movement in California, led by a loosely affiliated group of winemakers who call themselves the "Rhône Rangers," who believe that although they are widely planted, Cabernet Sauvignon, Chardonnay, Pinot Noir, and Merlot (known as *continental varieties*) are not ideally suited to the California climate (or climates, since the weather around the state varies widely). Rather, they argue that California's climates much more closely resemble those of the Mediterranean, and therefore winemakers should be looking toward the grape

A Few Rhône Rangers

Rhône Rangers are California winemakers who imitate
the style and use the varietals of the Mediterranean
regions of Europe.

Joseph Phelps Winery (Napa Valley) offers its "Vin du
Mistral" line (the mistral is a hot wind that blows through
the southern Rhône Valley), including "Le Mistral," a
Châteauneuf-du-Pape type blend; Grenache Rosé du
Mistral (a refreshing pink wine made from the Grenache
grape), and Viognier.

Preston Vineyards (Sonoma), which serendipitously
planted a lot of Syrah in 1978, confusing it with Petite
Syrah, is in the forefront, and in fact recently
discontinued its Cabernet production. Besides Syrah,
Preston also offers Marsanne; Viognier; "Faux" (a blend of
Syrah, Mourvèdre, Carignan, Cinsault, and Grenache);
"Muscat Brûlé" (a fortified Muscat, in the style of Muscat
de Beaumes-de-Venise). Rhône-style wines, says owner
Lou Preston, "appeal to the way people like to drink

varieties of the Rhône Valley (Syrah, Grenache, Marsanne, Rousanne,
etc.), and of Italy (Sangiovese, Nebbiolo, etc.).

To that end, several wineries have introduced Rhône-style and
Italian-style varietals and blends.

VINTAGES

Vintages are not as important with California wines as they are
with French wines since the weather is less wildly variable. But
there has been a spate of excellent years in California lately for
both red and white wine, particularly 1990 through 1993, which
simply means that the wines from those years are likely to be
good, even among lesser producers. A number of disappointing
vintages in France (particularly Bordeaux) from 1991 to 1993
will put California wines of these years in the limelight.

wines most of the time. They're ripe but fruity and soft." Preston also offers some Italian styles, such as "Moscato Curioso" (similar to Italy's Moscato d'Asti, low in alcohol, and a little spritzy, available only at the winery); Barbera and Sangiovese are in the works.

Quivira (Sonoma County) produces Dry Creek Cuvée, a Châteauneuf-du-Pape-type blend of Grenache, Mourvèdre, and Syrah.

Qupé (Santa Barbara County) produces varietals Syrah and Marsanne.

Bonny Doon Vineyards (in Monterey County) has a wide range of Rhône-style selections: Le Cigare Volant, a Châteauneuf-style blend (Grenache, Mourvèdre, Syrah, and Cinsault), Old Telegram (100 percent Mourvèdre—the name is a translation/pun of the famous Vieux Télégraphe, of which Mourvèdre is an ingredient), Le Sophiste, a Marsanne and Rousanne blend, a varietal Syrah, and a number of Italian-style wines under the Ca' del Solo label.

NAPA VALLEY

Napa is really the heart of California wine country; its prestige is well-known all over the world. The main varietals here are Cabernet Sauvignon, Chardonnay, Sauvignon Blanc, Zinfandel, and Pinot Noir, though there is by far more Cabernet and Chardonnay than anything else.

The landscape in Napa changed radically in the 1970s, when hundreds of wineries opened in the valley. Unfortunately, due to a recent outbreak of phylloxera, an insect that destroys vineyards, the scene will probably be changing again soon. (A major phylloxera infestation destroyed most of the vineyards of Europe in the 1860s.) Sadly, the phylloxera louse has already wiped out entire California vineyards, and no doubt much more damage will be done; some existing wineries will close,

Q: If California wines are labeled as varietals, how come some of them have names like "Vin du Mistral" or "Ca' del Solo, Il Pescatore"?
A: These *proprietary names* **usually refer to blends of two or more grapes rather than a single varietal. The winery decided just to think up their own cute name for the blend, since there's no other handy alternative. Think of it: they couldn't call a Marsanne/Rousanne blend a "white Hermitage" since "Hermitage" refers to a region in France. That would be like calling Chardonnay "white Burgundy" when it's not in fact from Burgundy.**

others will replant and become stronger for it, and new ones will emerge.

For now, here's what some of Napa's different AVAs have to offer. And no, you don't have to memorize it.

Rutherford: Home of Beaulieu Vineyards (B.V.), Franciscan Vineyards, Grgich Hills, Flora Springs, Niebaum-Coppola Estate, and some of the best Cabernet Sauvignons, which are known for a flavor referred to as "Rutherford Dust." Also red Meritage blends (Cabernet, Merlot, and Cabernet Franc), and Chardonnay.

Oakville: Two of Napa Valley's most famous vineyards may be found here: Martha's Vineyard, whose grapes are sold to Heitz for its Martha's Vineyard Cabernet, and Backus Vineyard, whose grapes are sold to Joseph Phelps for its Backus Vineyard Cabernet. Home to wineries such as Robert Mondavi, Opus One, Caymus, Far Niente, Mumm Napa, and Cakebread, among others—Oakville is a veritable wine walk of fame! The Cabernet grown here is known for a distinctive mint-and-eucalyptus aroma. Sauvignon Blanc does well, too.

Howell Mountain: Up in the hills to the east of the valley, this is the home of *serioso* Cabernet. Dunn Vineyards leads the way. La Jota Vineyard also finds a home here. Oddly, Château Woltner, owned by two of the former owners of Château Haut-Brion, one of the top châteaux in the Graves district of Bordeaux, has opted to make only Chardonnay, which traditionally comes not from Bordeaux, but Burgundy.

Carneros (also known as *Los Carneros*): Part of this AVA at the southern end of the valley lies in Napa Valley and the other part in Sonoma County. This region, cooler than most of Napa since it's close to San Pablo Bay and foggy at night, is ideal for the Burgundian varieties Chardonnay and Pinot Noir, and these are almost exclusively what's grown here. Since these are the two varieties used in sparkling wine, lots of the grapes used for California sparkling wine come from here. Acacia Winery, Domaine Carneros, Bouchaine, and Saintsbury are a few of the wineries in Carneros, and lots of wineries buy grapes from this AVA too.

Stags Leap District: This district, which runs along the Silverado Trail on the east side of the Valley, grows almost exclusively Cabernet and Merlot, which are known for their ripe berry flavors.

Stag's Leap Wine Cellars and Stags' Leap Winery, both of which were founded in 1972, had, once upon a time, a huge battle over the use of the name, at the time when this district was becoming a sub-AVA. Notice the result: No apostrophe on the Stags Leap AVA itself, an apostrophe before the final *s* on Warren Winiarski's winery, and one after the *s* at Carl Doumani's place. Clos du Val, Robert Sinskey, and Chimney Rock may also be found here.

Mount Veeder: A ridge that runs along the border of Napa and Sonoma, known for its intense Cabernet, Chardonnay, and some Zinfandel. Wineries include the Hess Collection, Mayacamas, Jade Mountain, Mount Veeder Winery, and Château Potelle.

Areas that aren't AVAs, but worth knowing:

Spring Mountain: Just next to Mount Veeder, and home of Cain Cellars, Spring Mountain, Robert Keenan, and others. Cabernets here are softer than Mount Veeder.

Diamond Mountain: Here you'll find Diamond Creek, a small winery producing very expensive Cabernets with names that scream *terroir* (Cabernet Sauvignon, Volcanic Hill; Cabernet Sauvignon, Red Rock Terrace; Cabernet Sauvignon, Gravelly Meadow).

Calistoga: At the north end of the valley, and home of the famous mud baths, as well as Château Montelena, Peter Michael Winery, Cuvaison, Sterling, Schramsberg, and others. Calistoga is known for its big, rich Cabernets and flavorful, chewy Zinfandels.

Atlas Peak: Known primarily for Atlas Peak Vineyards (owned by famed Italian winemaker Piero Antinori), which account for about half of the Sangiovese grown in California.

SONOMA
With a history as rich and long as Napa's, Sonoma seems to tread quietly beside its more glamorous neighbor. But that doesn't

mean its wines aren't as good! The town is lovely, and all in all, the feeling isn't as touristy as Napa Valley.

Carneros (Also see Napa, since part of the AVA falls in Napa Valley): Buena Vista, Gloria Ferrer, and Sonoma Creek fall in the Sonoma portion of Carneros.

Alexander Valley: Many different varieties are represented. Jordan, Geyser Peak, and Simi are all located here.

Russian River Valley: Since it's kind of damp and cool, Chardonnay and Pinot Noir do particularly well in the Russian River Valley. Sonoma-Cutrer, Rodney Strong, Williams & Selyem, Dehlinger, and Iron Horse call it home; Kistler, among others, uses grapes from this region.

Dry Creek Valley: Sauvignon Blanc loves this AVA, as do Zinfandel and Cabernet; Rhône varieties are also on the rise. Ferrari-Carano, Preston Vineyards, Dry Creek Vineyard, and Quivira are all in Dry Creek Valley.

MENDOCINO COUNTY

Anderson Valley: Chardonnay and Pinot Noir are two of the many varieties that do well here, and wonderful sparkling wines have emerged (Scharffenberger and Roederer Estate). Zinfandel, Gewürtztraminer, and Riesling also do well. Navarro Vineyards, Lazy Creek Vineyard, Husch Vineyards, Handley Cellars; Kendall-Jackson Vineyards also has a vineyard here.

McDowell Valley: This tiny AVA only boasts one winery—McDowell Valley Vineyards, which is concentrating on Rhône varietals under its Vieux Cépages label (Syrah, Viognier, and Grenache).

OTHER NORTH COAST AREAS

Santa Cruz Mountains: Still considered North Coast, even though it goes right down into the center of the state. The Santa Cruz Mountains region boasts a wine history more glorious than one might think, dating back to the late nineteenth century. It reestablished itself after the repeal of Prohibition relatively early: Martin Ray was founded in the early 1940s (it's since been reincarnated as Mount Eden); Ridge and David Bruce were founded in 1959 and 1961, respectively. Because of the soil and climate, grapevines really have to struggle here and low yields result— which might sound terrible, but it's a recipe for great wines! Bonny Doon Vineyard is also here.

CENTRAL COAST

The Central Coast, which runs from just north of Monterey to a little south of Pismo Beach, is an exciting wine region that you don't hear that much about, except for the region's wonderful wines themselves. Some of the best Chardonnay grapes are grown in this area; wineries in many other regions buy grapes from various Central Coast AVAs for their Chardonnays.

Monterey: The Salinas Valley is home to the Monterey AVA, which includes a number of smaller AVAs in a confusing puzzle. In any case, it's mostly white-wine-land, with Chardonnays and Riesling leading the pack. Jekel Vineyard, Estancia, and the Monterey Vineyard are all here.

Mount Harlan: An AVA unto itself, located between Salinas and Holister, with only one winery (Calera) in it, Mount Harlan produces Pinot Noir, Viognier, and Chardonnay.

Chalone: On a mountain ridge inland and a little south of the city of Monterey (east of Highway 101), Chalone Vineyard is the only winery in this AVA, producing Burgundian-style Chardonnay and Pinot Noir as well as Pinot Blanc and Chenin Blanc.

Edna Valley: Just south of San Luis Obispo, Edna Valley is Chardonnay land because of its cool ocean climate. Edna Valley Vineyards is the most famous winery here.

SANTA BARBARA COUNTY

To my mind, this is the most exciting emerging region for Burgundian-style varieties; and there's interesting Rhône varietal action happening, too.

Santa Maria Valley: Some great Chardonnay and Pinot Noir, as well as a little Sauvignon Blanc, Pinot Blanc, Riesling, Viognier, Marsanne, Cabernet, Merlot, and Syrah come from this AVA. Several vineyards (Bien Nacido, Tepesquet, Santa Maria, and Sierra Madre) produce grapes for wineries from all over the state.

Wineries to watch: Au Bon Climat, Byron, Qupé Cellars, and Foxen.

Santa Ynez Valley: Riesling, Chardonnay, Pinot Noir, Sauvignon Blanc, Sémillon, Cabernet, and a smattering of Rhône and Italian varieties are grown in this AVA just north of the city of Santa Barbara. Firestone Vineyard, Fess Parker Winery (owned by the guy who played Davy Crockett and Daniel Boone on TV), Sanford Winery, Santa Barbara Winery, and Zaca Mesa Winery are among those located in the AVA.

The Rundown on California Varietals and Blends

Are you totally lost? Was that way too much info? Well, relax, breathe through your nose (a good habit for wine lovers anyway). Now we'll get to the nitty-gritty: what to look for.

CHARDONNAY

While California winemakers bemoan the fact that Americans are stubbornly unwilling to try anything at all besides Chardonnay, they're still happy to ride the wave of its overwhelming popularity: Chardonnay sales are growing by about 20 percent each year. The most widely planted grape variety in California, 24,143 acres were planted to Chardonnay in 1984, and by 1993, acreage had more than doubled to 62,701.

For the most part, California Chardonnays are overoaked, overalcoholic, and overpriced. Your best bet in finding one that isn't (and there are some excellent ones) is to look in certain AVAs: Carneros, Sonoma's Russian River, Edna Valley, and other Central Coast AVAs, and Santa Barbara County's Santa Maria and Santa Ynez Valleys.

It helps a lot to stick with good producers. Here is a sampling of impressive Chardonnays from a range of wineries. But be cautioned: They can be expensive.

Byron Vineyard and Winery
Au Bon Climat

Peter Michael Winery
Château Woltner
Kistler
Matanzas Creek Winery
Grgich Hills
Chalone
Edna Valley Vineyard
Sonoma-Cutrer
Frog's Leap (Chardonnay Carneros)
Hess Collection
Far Niente Winery
Stags' Leap Winery
Bouchaine
David Bruce Winery
Long Vineyards
Ferrari-Carano Winery

SAUVIGNON BLANC

For my money, this is where the white-wine action is in California: for ten dollars and under, there are plenty of delicious wines to be had. Some are vinified in stainless steel, so the characteristic Sauvignon Blanc varietal qualities come through—similar in style to the wines of the Loire Valley. Others are either barrel-fermented or aged in oak, and they're a little fatter and richer, and sometimes they have some Sémillon added for depth (in which case they may be labeled as white Meritage). These wines, which are trendy at the moment, are more reminiscent of those from Bordeaux, though they're fruitier.

In any case, since they're not expensive, you can experiment! A few reliable producers:

Murphy-Goode Estate Winery
Cakebread Winery
Flora Springs Winery
Matanzas Creek Winery
Robert Mondavi Winery

SPARKLING WINES

Dozens of producers are making charming and relatively inexpensive sparkling wines in California using the *méthode champenoise*. But don't confuse it with Champagne: remember, that's a region in France, not a drink. Most of the California producers have cooperated with the French by not calling their sparkling wines "Champagne" on the bottle, though Schramsberg, the longest-established California sparkling-wine producer, persists, as does Gloria Ferrer.

In fact, many of the California producers of sparkling wine are actually owned by French champagne firms: for instance Mumm Napa (owned by Mumm); Domaine Carneros (owned by Taittinger); Domaine Chandon (owned by Moët-Hennessy, parent company of Moët et Chandon), etc. Two are owned by Spanish firms that produce Cava, Spain's celebrated sparkling wine: Gloria Ferrer Champagne Caves (owned by Freixenet), and Cordoniu Napa (owned by Cordoniu).

The quality of California sparkling wines, for the most part, is high (Gloria Ferrer's sparkling wines, in fact, are much better than owner Freixenet's Spanish *cavas*). And the wines represent a much better value than French champagnes.

Some excellent producers:

Mumm Napa
Domaine Chandon
Domaine Carneros
S. Anderson Vineyard
Scharffenberger Cellars
Schramsberg Vineyards
Roederer Estate
Piper Sonoma
Gloria Ferrer
Maison Deutz

OTHER CALIFORNIA WHITES

Chenin Blanc: Most are awful, with a few notable exceptions, including Chappellet (labeled as "Old Vine Cuvée," but it's Chenin Blanc).

Viognier: This traditional northern Rhône variety has only recently come to California; at the moment it's trendy and expensive. The best I've tasted were from Calera and Alban; Joseph Phelps also makes a good one, labeled "Vin du Mistral Viognier."

Riesling: There isn't too much interesting Riesling action going on in California, since it's mostly a little warm for it. In any case it's referred to in the U.S. as white Riesling or Johannisberg Riesling, and it's made in varying degrees of sweetness.

Miscellaneous Whites: A few producers are making interesting blends of Rhône varieties, including Bonny Doon's Le Sophiste (Marsanne and Rousanne). Preston makes a varietal Marsanne. Bonny Doon also offers an attractive Ca' del Solo Malvasia Bianca, which is an Italian variety. Both wineries offer Muscats (Preston's is fortified, while Bonny Doon's is an ice wine).

Blush and Rosé Wines: Several wineries are producing lively Grenache Rosés, such as Joseph Phelps (Vin du Mistral Grenache

Rosé), and Bonny Doon (Vin Gris de Cigare). White Zinfandel, which was invented by accident by Bob Trinchero at Sutter Home, is incredibly popular, but to my palate it's more like soda pop than wine.

PINOT NOIR

In California, Pinot Noir, like Chardonnay, is best suited to cooler regions such as Carneros, Russian River, and Santa Barbara County. A lot of California Pinot Noirs are too fruity and overblown, but more and more producers are going for subtlety, and when these wines are good, they're very nice indeed. A few of my favorites:

Chalone Vineyards
Au Bon Climat
Acacia
Gary Farrell
Calera Wine Company

Byron Vineyard and Winery
Dehlinger
Saintsbury
El Molino
Bouchaine Vineyards
Robert Mondavi
Etude
Williams-Selyem Winery

MERLOT

California Merlots can be a little mushy and characterless, although they're big sellers. However, one outstanding bottle is Beringer Howell Mountain Bancroft Ranch 1990—but it costs about thirty dollars. Ferrari-Carano and Matanzas Creek make nice Merlots; Arrowood also consistently garners good reviews.

CABERNET SAUVIGNON AND MERITAGE BLENDS

Cabernets are really the wines that put California on the world wine map; most of the best are from Napa Valley and Sonoma County. In the last ten years more and more wineries have been offering what they call "Meritage" blends, which are blends of the classic Bordeaux varieties, Cabernet, Merlot, and Cabernet Franc. Because a wine only has to contain 75 percent Cabernet Sauvignon to be labeled as such, many wines labeled as "Cabernet" are actually Bordeaux-style blends as well. With California Cabernets, there are interesting choices at every price level. At the top of the heap are the super-luxury wines, wines we usually only read about, which might cost between twenty-five and one hundred dollars. Obviously these wines are out of the reach of most of us mortals. Then we have the fairly expensive Cabernets; wines we might consider for special occasions for around fifteen to twenty-five dollars. Below that, but often very delicious, are premium wines, available for between eight and twelve dollars, but perhaps up to fourteen or so. Some of these might be "second labels" of wineries with great reputations. And below that, you'd have your under-eight-dollars Cabernets, which can be wines of good quality, but without the complexity and ageability of the others.

Consistently good Cabernet and Meritage producers:

Caymus Vineyards
Robert Mondavi Winery (try the Unfiltered Cabernet)
Château Montelena
Beaulieu Vineyards (B.V.)
Benziger
Dunn Vineyards
Duckhorn Vineyards
The Hess Collection
Franciscan
Heitz Cellars
Estancia (try the Meritage)
Rodney Strong Vineyards
Stag's Leap Wine Cellars

ZINFANDEL

Although people used to think it came from Italy, Zinfandel is now generally believed to be California's very own native grape. When these unintimidating, friendly wines are good (a lot of them are, and I'm not talking about white Zinfandel here), they offer up generous peppery fruit (look for berries), and they're pretty inexpensive. Cabernet lovers who have been afraid to branch out should try them! Some reliable producers:

Grgich Hills Cellars
Château Potelle
Foppiano Vineyards
Ridge Vineyards
Storybook Mountain
Quivira
Château Souverain
Cakebread Cellars (only available for sale at winery)
Preston Vineyards
Deloach Estate
Benziger

Ultra-Fancy-Schmancy Cabernets and Meritage Blends

Heitz Cellars Martha's Vineyard (about $55)

Dunn Vineyards Howell Mountain (about $40, if you can find it)

Joseph Phelps Backus Vineyard (about $35)

Joseph Phelps Eisele Vineyard (about $45)

Joseph Phelps Insignia (about $40)

Cain Five Napa Valley (about $35)

Caymus Vineyards Napa Valley Special Selection (about $75)

Flora Springs Napa Valley Reserve (about $33)

Flora Springs Trilogy (about $25)

Robert Mondavi Napa Valley Reserve (about $48)

Opus One (about $65)

Peter Michael Winery Les Pavots (about $25)

Beaulieu (B.V.) Georges de la Tour Private Reserve (about $40)

Dominus Estate (about $40)

Grace Family Vineyards (about $75)

Diamond Creek Vineyards (Gravelly Meadow, Volcanic Hill, and Red Rock Terrace) (about $50)

The Hess Collection Napa Valley Reserve (about $38)

OTHER RED VARIETALS AND BLENDS

Joseph Phelps Vineyards and Bonny Doon Vineyard make attractive Rhône-style blends.

Foppiano and Stags' Leap Winery offer excellent Petite Sirahs.

As for wines made from the Italian grape varieties, all of this is still pretty new in California. But we probably have lots of good wines to look forward to made from Sangiovese (the grape that Chianti and Brunello are made from) and Nebbiolo (the

Great Cabernet Bargains

Estancia Cabernet Sauvignon (about $10)
Hess Select Cabernet Sauvignon (about $9)
Château Souverain Cabernet Sauvignon Alexander Valley (about $11)
Geyser Peak Cabernet Sauvignon Sonoma County (about $10)
Rodney Strong Cabernet Sauvignon Sonoma County (about $11)
St. Francis Cabernet Sauvignon Sonoma County (about $10)
Beaulieu Vineyard (B.V.) Cabernet Sauvignon Napa Valley Beautour (about $9)

Barolo/Barbaresco grape). Bonny Doon is already producing pretty good ones; Preston makes a nice Barbera. Other producers to watch: Il Podere (Santa Barbara County), and Napa's Atlas Peak, Robert Pepi, and Sutter Home Winery.

Washington

Why don't we hear more about Washington State wines? Not only are there some wonderful examples to be found here, they're also reasonably priced. How's that for good news? The very top of the line is no more than twenty-five or thirty dollars, but the vast majority is attainable for more like ten or so dollars. In fact, there are lots of high-quality bargains.

In Washington, Merlot is king. Lots of critics contend that the best Merlots in the U.S. come from Washington, and I'd have to agree. Cabernet is very big, too, which might come as a surprise to anyone who thinks of Washington as having a cold and rainy

WASHINGTON STATE WINEMAKERS
LIKE TO POINT OUT THAT THEIR STATE
IS ON THE SAME LATITUDE AS
BORDEAUX

MARGARET
AND I WERE BORN
IN TACOMA, BUT
BORDEAUX IS OUR
SPIRITUAL
BIRTHPLACE.

clime. The main wine-growing regions, the Yakima and Columbia River valleys, are pretty far inland from the coast (and from
Seattle), and during the growing season, they get long, hot days
and cool nights—just like in Bordeaux. In fact, we may think of
the state as being pretty far north, but actually it's in the same latitude as Bordeaux.

Washington also produces Chardonnay, Riesling, Sauvignon
Blanc, Chenin Blanc, Gewürtztraminer, and Sémillon.

Reliable producers:

Columbia Crest
Columbia
Château Ste. Michelle
Andrew Will
Quilceda Creek
Leonetti

Oregon

Want to be on the cutting edge of American wine? Think Oregon—an emerging region if ever there was one.

If Washington is Merlot-land, Oregon is Pinot-ville. In terms of white wine, Riesling used to be the most widely grown grape variety, and there are still plenty of them, including late-harvest dessert models. But Chardonnay recently surpassed Riesling, due in large part to the fact that we Americans behave as if Chardonnay were the only white wine on earth. Oregon also produces Pinot Gris and Gewürztraminers worth looking into.

Although its wine industry is not new, Oregon has had some trouble really getting started. However, in the last few years the state has made huge leaps, which some people associate with the arrival of Robert Drouhin, the owner of Joseph Drouhin, the Burgundy importer. His new Domaine Drouhin, under the direction of winemaker Véronique Drouhin (Robert's daughter), has been releasing delicious Pinot Noirs. These days Oregon is seen as America's little slice of Burgundy.

The main wine region in Oregon is the Willamette Valley,

IT RAINS SO MUCH IN OREGON THAT WINEMAKERS
THERE HAVE HAD TO EMPLOY CREATIVE GRAPE-
GROWING TACTICS

which runs along the Willamette River, not too far from the coast, between Portland and Eugene.

Although the prices for the best Oregonian wines are a little higher than those from Washington, there are still lots of bargains to be unearthed.

Producers to seek out:

Domaine Drouhin
Ponzi
Adelsheim
Knutsen Erath
Argyle
Sokol Blosser
Willamette Valley
Bethel Heights

New York State

People who don't know that New York State has the oldest established wine industry in the country sometimes crack up when they hear about New York wines. Maybe they're picturing a guy squishing grapes in the shadow of the Empire State Building or something.

In any case, there's lots of action: New York is second in wine production only to California, and the number of wineries in the state more than quadrupled between 1983 and 1993. At press time, there are somewhere around one hundred.

Although there are six AVAs in the state, most wine-making takes place in three of them: Finger Lakes (way upstate, near Buffalo), the Hudson River region, and the North Fork of Long Island. In New York, small wineries are referred to as *farm wineries*, and it is here where the most promising wines are made.

The reason you may not have heard too much about New York as a region is that it was long thought unsuitable for growing grapes of the *vinifera* species—basically, these are all the varieties we've been talking about throughout the book, such as

NEW YORK STATE WINES STILL FACE SOME SKEPTICISM

HOW CAN THE SAME STATE THAT GROWS A GRAPE NAMED "ELVIRA" BE TAKEN SERIOUSLY AS A WINE REGION?

Tasting-Room Etiquette

1. Find out ahead of time whether the winery is open to the public without an appointment, either by looking in a guidebook or calling. If an appointment is necessary, be sure to be there on time or call and cancel.
2. Don't ask the winery staff at a by-appointment-only winery to take their time to show you around unless you intend to buy at least a case.
3. Don't be surprised when you only get about an inch of wine in your glass: it's for tasting, not drinking!
4. This is one of the only times in life that spitting makes you appear more poised (be sure to do it in a spittoon).
5. Don't show up five minutes before closing and expect to taste everything.
6. If you suspect a wine is corked, you may discreetly tell the person pouring. That way they can smell it, and if so, discard the bottle and start a new one.
7. If you dislike a wine, but there's nothing *wrong* with it, keep it to yourself.
8. Don't loudly announce all the particular wonderful aromas and flavors you're finding—the power of suggestion is very strong, and you'll interfere with others trying to taste.
9. Don't ask the staff to open up bottles other than those being poured.
10. If you're drinking, rather than spitting, don't drive.

Cabernet Sauvignon, Chardonnay, etc. So even though, for instance, the North Fork of Long Island has been producing wine since the seventeenth century, the native grapes were what are called *labrusca* or *labruscana* and the wine made from these usually isn't good enough to make high-quality table wines. A few of these varieties are Concord, Catawba, Delaware, Niagara, and Elvira, many of which are used to make wine coolers and that sort of thing.

Today there are plenty of hybrids—crosses between *labruscana* and *vinifera* varieties, and there's more and more *vinifera* finally being grown, including Chardonnay, Riesling, Gewürztraminer, Sauvignon Blanc, Cabernet Sauvignon, Merlot, Pinot Noir, and Cabernet Franc.

> **TIP FROM CABERNET FRANK**
> **Do as the California winemakers do: When you feel like a glass of sparkling wine, champagne or otherwise, say, "Let's have something with bubbles."**

IF YOU FORGET EVERYTHING ELSE YOU'VE READ IN CHAPTER FIVE, JUST REMEMBER THIS:

1. California renditions of Burgundy and Bordeaux tend to be fruitier and less subtle.
2. There's a trend in California and Oregon toward Pinot Noir and Chardonnay that are more "Burgundian" in style—more subtle and complex.
3. Certain AVAs in California are gaining recognition, such as Carneros, Howell Mountain, Russian River, and Alexander Valley.
4. California sparkling wines, made by the *méthode champenoise,* are charming wines at attractive prices.
5. Viognier is the trendy varietal du jour.
6. In Washington State, Merlot is king.
7. Oregon is the new Pinot Noir hot spot.

Chapter Six

FRANCE

Ah, la France! Why is it the French seem to hold such a tenuous monopoly on all things *raffiné*—perfume, couture, cuisine? Easy: because they're French!

Besides being the most famous wine region in the world, France is also the best merchandiser of wine. As such, France

IT'S A FUNNY THING. FOR SOMEONE WHO'S NEVER VISITED THE COUNTRY, DOESN'T SPEAK THE LANGUAGE AND HATES THEIR POLITICS, FRANK WILL *ONLY* DRINK FRENCH WINES.

FRANCE

Seine

Paris

CHAMPAGNE
• Rheims
• Epernay   ALSACE

LOIRE VALLEY

• Chablis

BURGUNDY

Nantes
Loire River

Cognac

Rhône River

RHÔNE VALLEY

BORDEAUX

Languedoc   Côtes de Provence

Armagnac   Minervois

has conditioned the wine-buying public to the cachet of its wines. Much of this is well deserved—great wines like Château Pétrus or Romanée-Conti don't exactly happen in New York State. Yet some of it wreaks havoc with our native insecurities, and the adjective "imported" always sounds more alluring than what we have here, much in the same way that salad dressing at somebody else's house always tastes better than our own.

Just because a wine is French doesn't mean it has to be expensive. I've seen more than one French visitor to the U.S. rant and rave upon visiting wineshops here and noticing that many French bottles are less expensive than they are in France! In fact, despite their reputation, French wines, at this moment in history, represent some of the best values around. Sure, many of them are outrageously expensive, but at the lower end of the scale, wonderful wines are to be had for seven to ten dollars. As a matter of fact, if you're looking to spend ten dollars on a bottle of red wine to bring to someone's house for dinner, you'll probably have a wider selection of fine wines from France in that price range than just about anywhere else.

Wine is made all over France, but there are six major growing regions. (Take a look at our highly inaccurate map to get an idea of their relative locations in France.) They are:

Bordeaux
The Rhône Valley
Alsace
Champagne
The Loire Valley
Burgundy

French wines are named after the region whence they come—this reflects the French fondness for place names, of which there are zillions—rather than the grape variety used. Many Americans become overwhelmed when confronted with them, but fear not—we'll sort out the whole mess within just a few pages.

With French wines, the vintage is important, much more so than, say, with California wines, where the relatively even, temperate climate has less bearing on quality from year to year. There were an extraordinary number of good years in France in recent history, especially in the late 1980s to 1990, which still should be available in stores. Newer releases, from 1991 to 1993, are generally not as good, with the exception of Burgundies.

You might want to pick up a little plastic chart listing the relative quality of the vintages of French wines (available in better wineshops), and keep it in your wallet. Contrary to what you might think, whipping out this puppy in a wineshop or fancy restaurant doesn't make you look like a geek; rather it imparts an air of knowledge and sophistication.

THE *APPELLATION CONTRÔLÉE* (AC) SYSTEM
Invented in the 1930s, this system organizes most of the wines of France geographically. What you'll see on a label is "Appellation

_____ Contrôlée." The blank will be filled in with either a region (such as Côtes du Rhône or Bourgogne—i.e., Burgundy), or a district, which is a smaller part of a region (such as Côtes de Nuits, which is a district of Burgundy), or a commune (such as Nuits-Saint-Georges, which is a village in the district of Côtes de Nuits in the region of Burgundy). Or it might even be the name of a specific vineyard, such as Les Cailles, which is a specific vineyard in the commune of Nuits-Saint-Georges in the district of Côtes de Nuits in the region of Burgundy. Get it? That one might say "Appellation Les Cailles Contrôlée." In general, all over France, the more specific the *appellation contrôlée*—that is, the smaller the piece of land described—the better the wine will be.

Once you get to the most specific appellations, which are the vineyards themselves, another hierarchy kicks in: you see, the French, in their incredibly organized yet completely crazy-making fashion, have even found a way to rate the vineyards themselves. When you see something on a bottle like "Grand Cru Classé" or "Premier Cru Classé" or simply "Grand Cru" or "Premier Cru," that's what's going on. Is this hierarchy, then, the same in all regions? No, that would be too easy! Don't forget, *we're dealing with the French*! But don't worry, it'll come clear as you read about each region.

Bordeaux   Burgundy

The wine world divides neatly into those who think the best
red wines in France come from Bordeaux and those who think
they come from Burgundy. It is said in wine circles that those
favoring Bordeaux are the intellectuals, while those who love
Burgundy are the sensualists. Yet somehow that's never sounded
quite right to me. Burgundian winemakers and vintners tend to
approach what they do with sort of a mystic reverence. To fully
appreciate Burgundies, you have to put yourself into a spiritual
state in order to find the *terroir*. Bordeaux seems more sensual
to me in an earthy kind of way. The wines are deep, generous,
and complex, to my mind less demanding intellectually (unless
you consider memorizing châteaux and notable vintages "intel-
lectual") —sublime, yet approachable.

Which is all well and good until you consider the Rhône Valley!

The first step in seeming like you know something about
French wine is to decide which camp you'll join—and you can
do this randomly if you wish. Don't worry too much about
making the wrong choice; you can easily convert later.

In any case, since the Bordeaux region is closest to the Atlantic, and therefore to us, we'll start there.

Bordeaux

For an introduction, you might want to pick up a bottle of red
wine labeled "Appellation Bordeaux Contrôlée." That means all
the grapes used come from the region of Bordeaux. You can
pick up one of these for a song (six or seven dollars), and you'll
see what the reds are like in general. It'll probably be pretty
young (usually what you'll find at that level are wines about
three or four years old), and that's fine for a simple wine. Look
for the aromas you'd expect in anything made with Cabernet:
berries, herbs, blackcurrants, etc. The wine will be deeply purple, packed with flavor, with firm tannins. Have a little piece of
cheese with it.

THE PLOT THICKENS

Bordeaux itself is divided into thirty-five wine districts, but five of them stand out above all others. It is only these five with which we'll concern ourselves, since they're the most important, and since wines from these districts are most likely to turn up on wine lists and in wineshops. They are Pomerol, Saint-Emilion, Médoc, Graves, and Sauternes. If you commit these to memory, you'll already know more about French wine than most of the people on your block.

The first three districts (Pomerol, Saint-Emilion, and Médoc) specialize in red wines, Graves in both red and white, Sauternes in white. Each district uses different blends of grapes: Cabernet Sauvignon, Merlot, Cabernet Franc, and Malbec for the reds, and Sauvignon Blanc and Sémillon for the whites. Each individual winemaker decides what percentage of each grape to use in making the wine.

As if we didn't have enough to worry about, one of the five main districts of Bordeaux, the Médoc, birthplace of many of the best wines in Bordeaux, happens to be divided into areas known as "communes." These are not places where French hippies run around engaging in free love and making big pots of overcooked lentils for dinner, but rather wine neighborhoods or communities. The top four communes of the Médoc are: Pauillac, Saint-Estèphe, Margaux, and Saint-Julien. If you're thoroughly

PAUILLAC
robust,
Full-bodied

SAINT ESTÈPHE
wiry, lean

MARGAUX
delicate, Feminine

SAINT JULIEN
consistent,
solid

CORK. THIS KEEPS THE WINE IN THE BOTTLE. DESPITE THE FACT THAT SCREW-ON TOPS MAKE IT EASIER TO CLOSE THE BOTTLE AFTER IT'S BEEN OPENED, A CORK KEEPS THE WINE LONGER.

FOIL. THIS PROTECTS THE CORK AND KEEPS IT IN PLACE. USE A KNIFE TO REMOVE BEFORE OPENING.

FILL LINE OR "ULLAGE." MAKE SURE THE WINE LEVEL IS AT LEAST THIS HIGH. DON'T BELIEVE ANY WINE SALESPERSON WHO TRIES TO TELL YOU THE WINE "SETTLED" DURING SHIPPING.

COLOR. CHECK TO DETERMINE WHETHER THE WINE IS RED OR WHITE. BORDEAUX MAKES BOTH. HOLD UP TO THE LIGHT IF NECESSARY.

ORIGIN. MAKE SURE THE WINE IS FROM BORDEAUX, FRANCE, RATHER THAN, SAY, BORDEAUX, INDIANA, OR BORDEAUX, ARGENTINA.

VINTAGE YEAR. CHECK YOUR VINTAGE CHART TO SEE IF THIS IS A GOOD YEAR.

ARCHITECTURE. EXAMINE THE PICTURE OF THE CHÂTEAU. DETERMINE WHETHER OR NOT YOU LIKE THE BUILDING.

RATING DESIGNATION. "SUPÉRIEUR" SOUNDS AWFULLY GOOD, BUT THERE IS AN ELABORATE RATING SYSTEM INVOLVED.

CERTIFICATE OF AUTHENTICITY. THE APPELLATION CONTRÔLÉE IS YOUR GUARANTEE THAT THE WINE CAME FROM WHERE IT SAYS IT DID. SORT OF THE VINOUS EQUIVALENT OF USDA APPROVAL.

CHÂTEAU BOTTLED. THIS MEANS THE WINE WAS BOTTLED AT THE CHÂTEAU ITSELF, RATHER THAN HAVING BEEN TRUCKED DOWN THE ROAD TO SOMEONE ELSE'S CHÂTEAU.

IMPORTER. THESE ARE THE GUYS WHO BROUGHT IT INTO THE COUNTRY. AND NATURALLY WANT A LITTLE CREDIT FOR IT.

ALCOHOL CONTENT. MORE ALCOHOLIC WINES HAVE A LONGER LIFE THAN THOSE WITH, SAY, 9%.

BORDEAUX: A QUICK VISUAL

confused, stare at the illustration for a few moments; you'll immediately feel much better.

The first thing you'll notice, if you examine a bunch of bottles of Bordeaux, is that most of them are called "Château" something-or-other. *Château,* as you'll remember from high-school French, means "castle"; in Bordeaux, this means the winery.

In terms of taste, red Bordeaux wines are big, deep, rich, and complex; whites from Graves are usually dry, rich, and a little

earthy; and Sauternes are thick, sweet, and lush, though not cloying.

Most red Bordeaux wines, though not all, need some additional time in the bottle after they're released. Many simple, inexpensive reds are ready to drink as soon as you see them in the stores. Otherwise, you probably don't want to drink anything much younger than about five years old; and for the fancier bottles, make it more like ten to twenty.

Systems of Classification for the Five Districts of Bordeaux Wines

MÉDOC

In 1855, a consortium of growers, shippers, and merchants in Bordeaux

> **TIP FROM CABERNET FRANK**
> Don't confuse the *premier cru* **Château Margaux with other wines from the Margaux commune of the Médoc district labeled simply "Appellation Margaux Contrôleé."**

"CRU BOURGEOIS?" DEAR ME, I'M AFRAID THE SIMPSONS MIGHT MISINTERPRET.

TIP FROM CABERNET FRANK

Don't turn up your nose at *cru bourgeois* **Médocs. Le Cirque, one of New York's toniest restaurants, pours Château Larose-Trintaudon— incidentally the largest of all the** *cru bourgeois* **producers—as its house wine.**

judged all the wines of Médoc, classifying them in order of their quality. Even though it rewards a few wines that are not what they used to be and underrates a few that have since become great, the classification still stands almost exactly as it was. We're starting with the most complicated region first, so don't be put off by the involved explanation; it's all downhill from here for the rest of Bordeaux.

Premier cru: At the top of all the Médocs is *premier cru*, which is usually translated as "first growth." This translation sometimes leads to a lot of unnecessary confusion, since it makes it sound as though each vineyard might produce a number of consecutive growths, which is not the case at all. So when you hear *premier cru* or "first growth," think of this as "top-dollar wine" or "first-quality vineyard." But do get used to the French, since this is what you'll see on labels and on wine lists. The *premiers crus* represent the best of the Médocs; you will pay dearly for these, but of course they're all fabulous. There are only five at the top of this Bordeaux heap, and you may well have heard of one or two: Château Latour, Château Lafite-Rothschild, Château

> **TIP FROM CABERNET FRANK**
> **There were only two years in all the eighties in Bordeaux that weren't very good: 1984 and 1987.**

Mouton-Rothschild, Château Margaux, and Château Haut-Brion (which is actually from the Graves district, but so good they had to include it in this most prestigious of classifications).

Deuxième cru: These "second growths" are the second-level wines. Many are of superb quality; some, such as Château Léoville-Las-Cases, Château Pichon-Longueville, and Château Cos d'Estournel, even rivaling the first vineyard wines. *Troisième, quatrième,* and *cinquième crus* are the third, fourth, and fifth

OKAY, SO I DIDN'T CHOOSE A FIRST-GROWTH BORDEAUX. BUT THAT'S NOT BECAUSE IT'S YOUR MOTHER WHO'S COMING TO DINNER!

TIP FROM CABERNET FRANK
Château Ausone and Château Cheval-Blanc are known as the A-list of the eleven Saint-Emilion *premiers grands cru classées*.

growths. They, too, produce some excellent-quality wines, such as Château Palmer *(troisième cru)* and Château Lynch-Bages *(cinquième cru)*, especially in good years. Bottles from the second through fifth growths will sometimes simply read "Cru Classé" or "Grand Cru Classé," indicating they were rated somewhere in the 1855 classification, a great distinction in itself.

Cru bourgeois: This doesn't mean that if you drink this, you're a nouveau-riche jerk; it's just the next step below *grand cru classé* and there are some very respectable wines to be found, even at this level, such as Château Citran, Château Larose-Trintaudon, Château Sociando-Mallet, Château Haut-Marbuzet, and Château Meyney. If you find *cru bourgeois* wines in exceptional or very good years, they're bound to be pretty damn good.

VINTAGES
What are very good and excellent years in Bordeaux? If you don't feel like buying a vintage chart, all you have to remember is anything in the 1980s except 1984 and 1987. 1989 and 1990 are excellent, and 1988 is very good. Buy one of these, and you can't go wrong. Other vintages in the early 1990s weren't great (1991, 1992, and 1993), so do your best to get your hands on something from the

TIP FROM CABERNET FRANK
If you happen to find yourself sipping a wine from the Graves district with a Frenchman, look at the wine, frowning, and say, "*Putaing—ça c'est Graves.*" (Pronounced *peu-taing, sa say grahv.*) Not only will he know that you can correctly identify the wine, but he'll also understand a hilarious pun, for the phrase also means, "Damn, that's serious." Gets 'em every time!

TIP FROM CABERNET FRANK

Pssssstt. Yeah, you—the one with the corkscrew. C'mere. I've got the recipe for Château Pétrus: It's 95 percent Merlot and 5 percent Cabernet Franc. Let's go make a batch!

eighties, since pretty soon we won't be seeing them around much.

SAINT-EMILION

The ranking of the red Bordeaux wines of Saint-Emilion is easier to grasp than the complicated Médoc mess: all you really have to remember is *premier grand cru classé* ("first great vineyards"—the real boffo stuff), *grand cru classé* (which you can think of as other "great classified vineyards"), and *grand cru* in that order. Unlike in Médoc, just having one of these three titles doesn't mean that much.

But you should know that most Saint-Emilions are Merlot blended with a little Cabernet Franc (with the notable

Regions, zones, districts, communes, vineyards—these words sound so similar, it's easy to confuse them and sound like a dope. It's a little easier if you think of France's hierarchy this way:

Bordeaux, the Loire Valley, and Champagne are examples of *regions.*

Within each region are *districts,* such as Médoc, Graves, and Saint-Emilion in the Bordeaux region.

Certain districts, such as the Médoc in Bordeaux, or the Côtes d'Or in Burgundy, are also divided into *communes,* such as Pauillac, Saint-Julien, and Margaux, in the Médoc district.

Within each commune or district are *vineyards, châteaux,* or *properties,* such as Château Lynch-Bages, Château Latour, or Château Clerc-Milon in the Pauillac commune.

Easy Bordeaux Pronunciation Key

Bordeaux: bore-*dough*
Pomerol: poh-muh-*rol*
Saint-Emilion: san-teh-meel-*yoh*
Médoc: may-*dock*
Graves: *grahv*
Sauternes: soh-*tehrn*
Pauillac: po-*yack*
Saint-Estèphe: san-tess-*teff*
Margaux: mar-*goh*
Saint-Julien: sah-zhoo-*lyeh*
Château: sha-*toh*
Premier cru: pruh-myeh-*creu*
Deuxième cru: duhz-yem-*creu*
Grand cru classé: grhah-creu-clah-*say*
Lafite-Rothschild: lah-feet-rot-*sheeld*
Haut-Brion: oh-bree-*yoh*
Château d'Yquem: sha-*toh*-dee-*kehm*
Léoville-Las-Cases: lay-oh-*veel*-lahss-*cahss*
Pétrus: pay-*treuss*

exceptions of Château Figeac and Château Villemaurine, which also use Cabernet Sauvignon).

GRAVES
These include both red and white wines; all you have to remember is to look for *crus classés*.

The most famous of all the Graves is Château Haut-Brion, which you'll remember (if you were paying attention) is classed *premier grand cru* along with the four fanciest Médoc wines. Château Haut-Brion and many of the other fancy Graves châteaux are located in a separate new appellation called Pessac-Léognan.

The dry white wines from Graves, made from Sauvignon Blanc and Sémillon, can be outstanding as well. (In fact Château Haut-Brion makes one. Another famous one is Domaine de Chevalier.) The good ones are rich, supple, elegant, and unlike many other dry white wines, they benefit from long aging—ten years or so.

POMEROL

Pomerol is the smallest of the five districts, and it was never classified. However, one of the most famous wines in the world (and the most expensive)—Château Pétrus—comes from Pomerol. If anyone ever offers you a bottle of it—or even a sip—don't turn it down.

In fact, think of Pomerol as the Beverly Hills of Bordeaux. Besides Château Pétrus, whose 1990 retails for a whopping $450 a bottle, it's also home to Château Le Pin ($275 a bottle) and Château Lafleur ($200 a bottle). Yowch!

SAUTERNES AND BARSAC

People who don't know anything about wine think of Sauternes as an el-cheapo cooking wine. Not so! A *real* Sauternes, that is, one that actually comes from France, and therefore the Sauternes district of Bordeaux, is one of the finest, most interesting wines in the world.

Most people think of it as a dessert wine, since it's sweet and rich, but natives of Bordeaux love it with foie gras as a first course. Sauternes' distinctive character comes from *noble rot*, a mold that grows on the grape when conditions are right, which doesn't happen every year—that's why Sauternes can be very expensive. Sauternes and Barsac are both made from a blend of Sémillon and Sauvignon Blanc.

Sauternes and Barsac are classified into three categories:

Grand premier cru: One wine stands alone in this category, the big cheese of the Sauternes world, and that is Château d'Yquem. If you get to taste this once in your lifetime, you will be lucky indeed. This is a wine that needs twenty or thirty years in the bottle to reach its full potential.

Premier cru: Eleven Sauternes fall into this excellent category.

Some of them are even affordable for special occasions!

Deuxième cru: The twelve wines at this level are nothing to shake a stick at either.

The Rhône Valley

Wines from this region, starting near the town of Avignon in the south and extending up the Rhône River to a town called Vienne, just below Lyons, suddenly became very chic in the late 1980s, though they have a long and glorious history, with which I won't bore you. The only interesting tidbit really worth knowing at this point is that the intensely colored wine made from the grapes of this region used to be snuck around France and added to vintages from other regions, including Bordeaux and Burgundy (where the winemakers had trouble getting a deep enough color in their red wines).

Appellation Côtes du Rhône Contrôlée red wines, widely available in wineshops, are simple wines, fine for everyday fare, but not terribly interesting. They consist of mostly Grenache, with some other varieties, such as Carignan and Syrah, thrown in. Much of this is made as rosé, which is very popular in France. A tiny amount of it is white.

If you can, try to find the next level up, Appellation Côtes du Rhône Villages, since these wines offer more interest, especially if they have a village name attached to them, such as Gigondas or Vacqueyras. Tavel, another such wine, is a charmingly fruity and inexpensive dry rosé, which is pretty widely available in the U.S. (Drink it chilled.) On a wine list,

> **TIP FROM CABERNET FRANK**
>
> **Part of the Côte-Rôtie is divided into the Côte Brune and the Côte Blonde, which means "brunette slope" and "blonde slope." These refer not to the hair color of the babes who live there, but rather to the type of soil found on each.**

Easy Rhône Pronunciation Key

Côtes du Rhône: coat-deu-*rone*
Gigondas: zhee-gohn-*dahss*
Hermitage: air-mee-*tahzhe*
Crozes-Hermitage: *crohz*-air-mee-*tahzhe*
Cornas: cor-*nahss*
Côte-Rôtie: coat-roh-*tee*
Guigal: ghee-*gall*
Chapoutier: sha-poo-*tyay*
Négociant: nay-goh-see-*yahn*
Muscat de Beaumes-de-Venise: moo-*skah* duh bohm-
    duh-ven*eez*
Châteauneuf-du-Pape: sha-toh-nuhff-duh-*pahp*
Vieux Télégraphe: vyeuh tay-lay-*graff*
Beaucastel: boh-cass-*tell*

---

you might see these village wines listed simply by the village name and the producer.

THE NORTHERN RHÔNE

The more serious wines of the Rhône Valley divide into those from the northern Rhône and those from the southern Rhône. Let's start north and head south. If you're a fan of big red wines, and you haven't tried any of these, I envy you the pleasure!

Although the northern Rhône boasts an impressive history, its winemaking reputation had fallen somewhat by the wayside for some years, but in the last ten years or so, the quality has improved so much, helped by several excellent vintages, that these wines are once again exciting. However, many of them are expensive, relegating them for most of us earthlings to the realm of special occasion wines.

Hermitage is probably the most famous of the northern

HERMITAGE HAS
OFTEN BEEN
CALLED "THE
MANLIEST WINE
ON EARTH"

CHECK THE
LABEL FOR
CHEST
HAIRS

Hermitage

Rhône wines; in fact for most of winemaking history, going
way back to Roman times, Hermitage was considered the finest
wine in the world. George Saintsbury, a British journalist and
wine lover, wrote in his very famous and still-reprinted *Notes on
a Cellar-Book* (first published in 1920) about an 1846 Hermitage he had tasted, referring to it as "the *manliest* French wine
I ever drank." Somehow the adjective stuck, and now people use
it to describe all red Hermitage, which is an intense, deeply colored wine, made entirely from the Syrah grape, known, along
with other northern Rhône wines, for a distinctive "gunflint"
aroma. (That assumes a lot, doesn't it? When was the last time
you smelled a gunflint? For that matter, what *is* a gunflint?)

Hermitage is one of the greatest wines of the world, one that benefits from long aging. Its greatness, unfortunately for wine lovers, is reflected in the price.

White Hermitage, made from Marsanne and Rousanne grapes, is known for its generous fruit nose and nutty richness.

Crozes-Hermitage wines are also wonderful, and a bit less expensive than Hermitage. The reds, also made from Syrah, are not quite as "manly" as Hermitage, but almost. They're concentrated wines with hints of leather and tar alongside their generous fruit aromas. The *white Crozes-Hermitages,* like white Hermitages, are made from a blend (usually) of Marsanne and Rousanne.

Saint-Joseph, a delicious, unpretentious wine, is even more affordable, if you can find it. It's what the region's residents drink with lunch; drink it young.

Cornas has all of a sudden become fashionable. Why? Because it produces great red wines made from Syrah. On and off, the region has had trouble producing the best wines possible, but now the district is on the rise.

At the top of the Rhône Valley, *Côte-Rôtie,* which means "roasted slope," produces fabulous red wines known for their intense roasted-fruit and floral aromas. They're also made from Syrah, sometimes with a little Viognier thrown in for texture and

CHÂTEAUNEUF-DU-PAPE MAY BE COMPOSED OF UP TO 13 DIFFERENT GRAPE VARIETIES

CHÂTEAUNEUF du PAPE
HAS A FEW DISTINCTIVE
FEATURES

CROSSED KEYS. NOT A
TRIBUTE TO REGIONAL
LOCKSMITHS BUT AN
INDICATION OF
DOMAINE
BOTTLING

VERY LONG CHÂTEAU
OR DOMAINE NAMES.
SOMETIMES
CONTINUED ON THE
BACK.

CHÂTEAUNEUF
DU PAPE
VIEUX
TELEGRAPHE
ETC.

finesse. The vineyards here, probably the oldest in France, date back to around 70 A.D.! The most famous Côte-Rôties are from three vineyards: La Turque, La Landonne, and La Mouline, which are all owned by a producer called Guigal.

Wines called *Condrieu,* a district just next to Côte-Rôtie, are all dry white wines made from Viognier. They're very aromatic and rich, with lots of body, sometimes aged in oak, and sometimes not. Within the boundaries of Condrieu is a little island of an appellation, one so small that there's only one winery in it, *Château-Grillet.* This, too, produces Viognier. Since the appellation is so small and the wines therefore rare, Château-Grillet is pretty expensive. Probably wines from these districts will become very fashionable as Americans' interest in the Viognier grape continues to grow. (Or then again, maybe they won't. . . .)

One of the best things about the Rhône Valley is that there's not some horribly complicated *cru* hierarchy to learn. Plus, you can drink many of the red wines young or old. 1988, 1989, and 1990 were all very good years. Just look for the type of wine you want from a good producer or *négociant,* a merchant who blends and bottles wines. You can't lose!

Here are some reliable producers of northern Rhône wines:

E. Guigal (Côte-Rôtie, Condrieu, Hermitage, Côtes du Rhône)

M. Chapoutier (Hermitage, Crozes-Hermitage, Côte-Rôtie, Saint-Joseph)

Paul Jaboulet Aîné (Hermitage, Crozes-Hermitage, Cornas, Côte-Rôtie, Saint-Joseph)

Gérard Chave (Hermitage, Saint-Joseph)

A. Clape (Cornas, Côtes du Rhône)

Delas Frères (Hermitage, Crozes-Hermitage, Cornas, Condrieu, Côte-Rôtie)

THE SOUTHERN RHÔNE

Not a lot to remember here, just two wonderful wines to think about now and then, and try whenever you get the chance! One of them, a dessert wine called Beaumes-de-Venise (also known as *Muscat de Beaumes-de-Venise*) is covered in Chapter Nine, since it is a *vin doux naturel,* which is a type of fortified wine.

The other is *Châteauneuf-du-Pape.* This red wine is a blend made of mostly Grenache (no more than 80 percent) with any combination of another thirteen varieties, including Syrah, Mourvèdre, and Cinsault, blended in. They come in two styles: a fairly light one, meant to drink young, and a richer, more intense one, made to drink between five and twenty years old.

To buy these, look for a medieval-looking coat of arms pressed into the glass in the neck of the bottle: this tells you it's estate-bottled, which is the best way of making sure you're getting a good Châteauneuf. If you happen to find a white Châteauneuf-du-Pape, you're looking at something of a rarity: only about 3 percent of this wine is white.

THE GRAPE VARIETALS OF ALSACE ARE NOT AS READILY IDENTIFIABLE AS THOSE OF OTHER FRENCH WINES.

LOOK, FRIEDRICH, IF WE COULD LOSE A FEW SYLLABLES ON THIS GEWÜRZTRAMINER I THINK WE'D HAVE A WINNER.

Some reliable Châteauneuf-du-Pape producers:

Vieux Télégraphe
Beaucastel
Clos des Papes
Rayas

Alsace

Unlike all the other wines of France, the wines of Alsace are named by the grape variety, so learning them is a breeze. (Think this is getting easier and easier? Well, just wait until you get to Burgundy, heh, heh, heh.)

Although it does produce some Pinot Noir, think of Alsace as mostly white-wine land. Unlike the German wines from right next door with which they're often confused, the white wines of Alsace are traditionally dry (with the exception of some special late-harvest wines, which can be sweet). They're also beautifully aromatic, and—here's the best part—usually reasonably priced!

You only need to know three things, and you'll be in fat city: the varietals found in Alsace, the hierarchy of wines, and some reliable producers.

ALSATIAN VARIETALS

With one or two exceptions, all Alsatian varietals are composed of 100 percent of the grape in question. The biggies are Riesling, Gewürztraminer, Pinot Gris (also called Tokay Pinot Gris), and Muscat, although production of Muscat is on the decline. You'll find Sylvaner and Pinot Noir as well, though in this region, these two varieties aren't as prized.

THE HIERARCHY

Dry Alsatian wines are either *grand cru* or not. Period. That's all you have to worry about. The *grand cru* wines must be either Riesling, Gewürtztraminer, Pinot Gris, or Muscat, and come from one of approximately fifty *grand cru* vineyards. If it's a regular bottling, not *grand cru*, the bottle won't say anything about a *cru*, just Appellation Alsace Contrôlée.

Although the next two categories take up a lot more space,

> ### TIP FROM CABERNET FRANK
>
> **If you're in the mood for a sparkling French alternative to champagne, try Crémant d'Alsace. An inexpensive and often attractive sparkling wine, Crémant d'Alsace may be made from a blend, in varying combinations, of Pinot Blanc, Pinot Noir, Pinot Gris, Auxerrois, Riesling, and Chardonnay. Did you notice it's not varietally-named? There's an exception to every rule.**

Easy Alsace Pronunciation Key

Alsace: ahl-*zass*
Vendage Tardive: van-*dahzhe* tar-*deev*
Sélection des Grains Nobles: say-leck-*seeoh* day *ghrah nobl*
Zind-Humbrecht: *zind-oom*-breckt
Hugel: euh-*ghel*

they're rare compared with the *grand cru* and regular bottlings, so you won't often bump into them. But just so you know what it is if and when you see it, here goes:

In special years, when the weather is right, Alsatian winemakers may decide to produce a special wine called *Vendange Tardive* (literally, "late harvest"). The wines are not necessarily sweet; they may be off-dry. To be called Vendange Tardive, the wine must also be made from one of the four grape varieties above, all harvested in the same year, and the grapes have to have a certain level of sugar when they're picked. How does anyone know? The wine police actually come and check the sugar levels in the vineyards!

Next comes *Sélection des Grains Nobles*. To be called this, the grapes have to have even higher levels of sugar, and these wines will be sweet. Remember botrytis, the noble rot that makes Sauternes special? Sometimes the *Sélection des Grains Nobles* grapes are affected by it as well.

The *grand crus* and regular bottlings of Alsatian wines go wonderfully well with food, they're well priced, and despite their unusual skinny tall green bottles, they're not scary at all.

Here are some reliable producers:

Zind-Humbrecht
Hugel
Schlumberger
Trimbach
Josmeyer

Champagne

Guess what—there's not really much you need to know about champagne. Surprised? So much mystique and romanticism surrounds this famous wine that people think there's more to it than there really is. The champagne houses, of course, want us to think that. Why? So we'll continue thinking of it as a super-luxury item, and continue paying through the nose for it. (If you want

Easy Champagne Pronunciation Key

Champagne: shahm-*pahn*-yuh
Blanc de Blancs: *blahn* duh *blahn*
Blanc de Noirs: *blahn* duh *nwar*
Méthode champenoise: may-toad shahm-pun-*wahs*
Moët et Chandon: mwet-tay-shahn-*doh*
Dom Pérignon: *dome*-pay-ree-*nyoh*
Roederer: roh-duh-*ruhr*
Taittinger: tay-tahn-*zhay*
Bollinger: boh-lahn-*zhay*
Piper-Hiedsieck: pee-*puhr*-eed-sake
Veuve Clicquot: *vuhv*-klee-koh
Tête de cuvée: tett duh keu-*vay*

to read a scathing exposé of the champagne industry, read Andrew Barr's *Wine Snobbery*.)

However . . . we have to admit that there's nothing like champagne! It's ultrafestive, and while nothing can match it for celebrating, it also goes well with a wide variety of food and it makes a most marvelous apéritif.

Champagne is usually blended from three grapes: Pinot Noir, Chardonnay, and Pinot Meunier; though there are champagnes made from 100 percent Chardonnay (called Blanc de Blanc), 100 percent Pinot Noir (called Blanc de Noir) or a combination of only Pinot Noir and Pinot Meunier (also called Blanc de Noir). Some firms produce a rosé champagne, usually made by adding

TIP FROM CABERNET FRANK
Champagne is ready to drink as soon as it's released—even the fancy stuff. It's already been aged, sometimes for a long time, at the winery. While it may keep in the bottle for some time, it won't continue to improve, so drink up!

a small amount of red wine into the blend, but sometimes by using the black grapes (Pinot Noir and Pinot Meunier) and leaving the skins in for a little longer. These are a little fruitier, but they're still dry.

If you read Chapter Four, you'll remember the *méthode champenoise*, which is the way champagnes are made. Wines made this way have very tiny bubbles compared with sparkling wines made any other way, and the bubbles stay in the wine long after opening it—days, even!

Your basic champagne is what's known as *non-vintage brut*. This

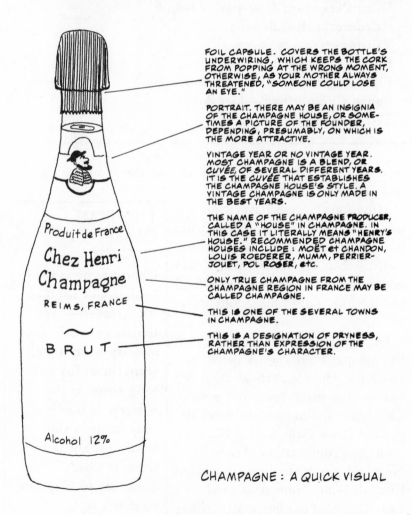

FOIL CAPSULE. COVERS THE BOTTLE'S UNDERWIRING, WHICH KEEPS THE CORK FROM POPPING AT THE WRONG MOMENT, OTHERWISE, AS YOUR MOTHER ALWAYS THREATENED, "SOMEONE COULD LOSE AN EYE."

PORTRAIT. THERE MAY BE AN INSIGNIA OF THE CHAMPAGNE HOUSE, OR SOMETIMES A PICTURE OF THE FOUNDER, DEPENDING, PRESUMABLY, ON WHICH IS THE MORE ATTRACTIVE.

VINTAGE YEAR OR NO VINTAGE YEAR. MOST CHAMPAGNE IS A BLEND, OR CUVÉE, OF SEVERAL DIFFERENT YEARS. IT IS THE CUVÉE THAT ESTABLISHES THE CHAMPAGNE HOUSE'S STYLE. A VINTAGE CHAMPAGNE IS ONLY MADE IN THE BEST YEARS.

THE NAME OF THE CHAMPAGNE PRODUCER, CALLED A "HOUSE" IN CHAMPAGNE. IN THIS CASE IT LITERALLY MEANS "HENRY'S HOUSE." RECOMMENDED CHAMPAGNE HOUSES INCLUDE : MOËT et CHANDON, LOUIS ROEDERER, MUMM, PERRIER-JOUET, POL ROGER, etc.

ONLY TRUE CHAMPAGNE FROM THE CHAMPAGNE REGION IN FRANCE MAY BE CALLED CHAMPAGNE.

THIS IS ONE OF THE SEVERAL TOWNS IN CHAMPAGNE.

THIS IS A DESIGNATION OF DRYNESS, RATHER THAN EXPRESSION OF THE CHAMPAGNE'S CHARACTER.

CHAMPAGNE : A QUICK VISUAL

The fashion for brut champagne is relatively new. Up until fairly recently, people (including the French) would drink champagnes of varying sweetness—from *demi-sec* (half-dry, which of course also means half-sweet), to *sec*, to extra dry, *brut*, and *extra brut*. Brut literally means "crude" or "raw." In olden days the French drank their champagne on the sweeter side, but they were exporting a lot of it to England and the English liked it as dry as possible. The French thought that was weird, and that's why they used such an odd word for it. It's also why "extra dry" appears in English when it appears on champagne bottles.

means there's no date on the label: the various champagne houses blend the wines from several years together in order to keep a consistent "house style." "Brut" simply means very very dry.

In very good vintages, which come three or four times a decade, certain champagne houses produce a special *vintage champagne.* This means that all the grapes were harvested the year indicated on the bottle; there was no blending of years involved. These wines attempt to capture the essential character of that particular harvest year.

Some of the firms also produce an extra fancy-schmancy bottling called *tête de cuvée* or *prestige cuvée.* You may know some of these: Moët et Chandon's Dom Perignon, Roederer's Cristal, Taittinger's Comtes de Champagne, Perrier-Jouet's Fleur de Champagne, Krug's Clos de Mesnil, and Bollinger's RD.

TIP FROM CABERNET FRANK
Many people are surprised to learn that *brut* champagne is drier than extra dry.

What's that you say? All champagnes taste pretty much the same to you? Well, don't be embarrassed—compared with other types of wine, the distinctions between champagne are pretty subtle indeed.

When the champagne firms blend their *cuvée* to achieve their

house style every year, there is something particular they're going for. Some champagnes are blended in a more delicate style, some are very full and rich, and some are in between. Here are how a few familiar names fall into that continuum:

- Light and fairly delicate: Taittinger, Mumm, Perrier-Jouet, Deutz, Laurent-Perrier, Pol Roger
- Medium: Moët et Chandon, Piper-Hiedsieck, Charles Hiedsieck, Joseph Perrier
- Rich and full: Louis Roederer, Veuve Clicquot, Krug, Bollinger

Now you know enough to enjoy champagne. (As if you didn't already!)

The Loire Valley

The Loire Valley, which runs just to the left of Paris on any map of France, is home to a wide range of wines made from many different grape varieties. Though better known for its whites (both sparkling and still), the Loire Valley also produces respectable reds. The whites are traditionally kept away from new oak, so if you're a fan of vanilla and butter notes in your wine, this ain't the place for you. If you like crispness, and if you don't want to bother with any hierarchy of *crus,* you'll love the Loire.

UPPER LOIRE VALLEY

The wines of the upper Loire Valley, those closest to Paris, are probably the most famous. The whites here are made from Sauvignon Blanc; the reds and rosés from Pinot Noir and Pinot Gris. Here are the two best known:

Sancerre, a dry crisp white wine, made to drink young. Sancerre is known for gooseberries and nettles on the nose. Not only does that sound painful, but who the hell knows what nettles smell like anyway? Drink it very young, a year or three after bottling. It also comes in red and rosé.

Pouilly-Fumé is very similar to the white Sancerre, but it's sometimes said to have a smoky nose. (*Fumé* means "smoked.") It can take a little more bottle age than Sancerre—it drinks well from about two to six years.

Easy Loire Pronunciation Key

Loire: l'war
Pouilly-Fumé: poo-yee-feu-*may*
Moelleux: m'weh-luh
Liquoreux: lee-kurh-uh
Rosé d'Anjou: ro-*zay*-dahn-*zhoo*
Savennières: sah-vuh-*nyehr*
Muscadet: meuh-skah-*day*

VOUVRAY CAN BE A MIDDLE-
OF-THE-ROAD WINE

LOOK, IF YOU DON'T DECIDE ONE WAY OR THE OTHER, IT'LL BE VOUVRAY AGAIN TONIGHT.

TOURAINE

This is the area in and around the city of Tours, best known for the white wines of Vouvray. Light red Cabernet Franc–based wines of Bourgueil and Chinon are also found here, but they're not exported much. Try them if you should be lucky enough to find yourself traveling in the Loire Valley.

Vouvray, made from Chenin Blanc, comes in a wide range of styles. Some Vouvray is made dry and still. The very high acid of the Chenin Blanc grape means that Vouvrays need to age longer than other whites: about ten years for the dry ones. The sparkling Vouvray, called Vouvray Mousseux, has a wonderful frothiness unlike the plain old bubbles in other sparkling wines.

Just as in Alsace, the winemakers of Vouvray can make late-harvest wines in the very best years. They are described as *moelleux* (which means "soft and sweet") or *liquoreux* (even thicker and sweeter). Sometimes they're botrytis-affected (remember that mold that grows on the grapes in Sauternes?). These need to age for twenty or more years in the bottle.

But since there are a lot of mediocre Vouvrays running around out there, make sure to get one from a reliable producer. Marc Brédif, Huet, and Champalou are a few highly regarded ones.

ANJOU

Farther along the Loire river, toward the Atlantic Ocean, Anjou is famous for its pink wine *Rosé d'Anjou,* which is often pretty sweet. But it also produces *Savennières,* a dry white wine that is one of the better wines made from Chenin Blanc.

PAYS NANTAIS

This means the countryside around Nantes, which is pretty close to the intersection of the Loire River and the Atlantic Ocean. (There's a really long stoplight there, so why not stop and have a glass of wine?) Here you'll find plenty of *Muscadet,* which is made from a white grape variety called Melon de Bourgogne. Stick with the appellations that say "Appellation Muscadet de Sèvre-et-Maine." This wine is known for going really well with—you got it: seafood. It should be drunk as young and fresh as possible.

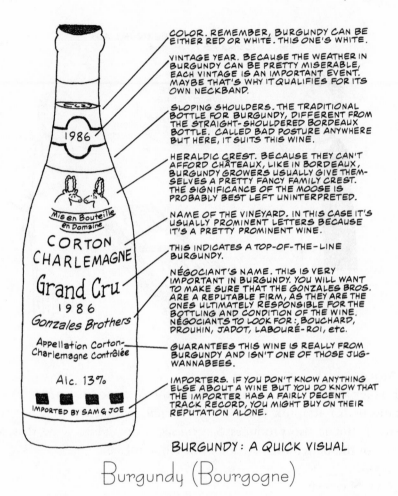

COLOR. REMEMBER, BURGUNDY CAN BE EITHER RED OR WHITE. THIS ONE'S WHITE.

VINTAGE YEAR. BECAUSE THE WEATHER IN BURGUNDY CAN BE PRETTY MISERABLE, EACH VINTAGE IS AN IMPORTANT EVENT. MAYBE THAT'S WHY IT QUALIFIES FOR ITS OWN NECKBAND.

SLOPING SHOULDERS. THE TRADITIONAL BOTTLE FOR BURGUNDY, DIFFERENT FROM THE STRAIGHT-SHOULDERED BORDEAUX BOTTLE. CALLED BAD POSTURE ANYWHERE BUT HERE, IT SUITS THIS WINE.

HERALDIC CREST. BECAUSE THEY CAN'T AFFORD CHÂTEAUX, LIKE IN BORDEAUX, BURGUNDY GROWERS USUALLY GIVE THEM-SELVES A PRETTY FANCY FAMILY CREST. THE SIGNIFICANCE OF THE MOOSE IS PROBABLY BEST LEFT UNINTERPRETED.

NAME OF THE VINEYARD. IN THIS CASE IT'S USUALLY PROMINENT LETTERS BECAUSE IT'S A PRETTY PROMINENT WINE.

THIS INDICATES A TOP-OF-THE-LINE BURGUNDY.

NÉGOCIANT'S NAME. THIS IS VERY IMPORTANT IN BURGUNDY. YOU WILL WANT TO MAKE SURE THAT THE GONZALES BROS. ARE A REPUTABLE FIRM, AS THEY ARE THE ONES ULTIMATELY RESPONSIBLE FOR THE BOTTLING AND CONDITION OF THE WINE. NÉGOCIANTS TO LOOK FOR: BOUCHARD, DROUHIN, JADOT, LABOURÉ-ROI, etc.

GUARANTEES THIS WINE IS REALLY FROM BURGUNDY AND ISN'T ONE OF THOSE JUG-WANNABEES.

IMPORTERS. IF YOU DON'T KNOW ANYTHING ELSE ABOUT A WINE BUT YOU DO KNOW THAT THE IMPORTER HAS A FAIRLY DECENT TRACK RECORD, YOU MIGHT BUY ON THEIR REPUTATION ALONE.

BURGUNDY: A QUICK VISUAL

Burgundy (Bourgogne)

Lots of people, even seasoned wine lovers, are afraid to attack the Burgundy region, for a good reason: if you try to learn all the vineyards and wine producers, it's unbelievably confusing. Most books start at the top or the bottom of the region (southeast of Paris, between Dijon to the north and Lyons to the south) and discuss each village, expecting you to remember the names and the hierarchy of wines you can find in each.

Let's dispense with the formality, since it's hard to memorize this stuff unless you are lucky enough to go to Burgundy to visit. Here's what you need to know:

Burgundy makes red and white wines, and is equally famous for both. Red Burgundies are made from the Pinot Noir grape; white ones are made from Chardonnay. In the bottom part of the region, which is called Beaujolais, the red grape is the Gamay, and throughout the region there is some Pinot Blanc planted as well.

There are five subregions of Burgundy:

Chablis
Côte d'Or (divided into Côte de Nuits and Côte de Beaune)
Côte Chalonnaise
Mâconnais
Beaujolais

TIP FROM CABERNET FRANK
The French make fun of Nouveau Beaujolais by calling it "Beaujol-pif." *Pif* is slang for nose. Using this expression is a good way to crack up a Frenchman.

The reason so many of these have the word "Côte" in their names is that *côte* means "slope" in French, and much of this area, which follows the Saone River, is hilly. However, when people talk about "Burgundy," they may or may not mean the whole official region that includes these five areas. They may be referring

Carbonic Maceration

Nouveau Beaujolais, like light red wines meant to be drunk very young from other countries, is made a little differently than other red wines. Instead of regular fermentation, a technique called *carbonic maceration* is used to convert the sugars into alcohol. No yeast is added: the grapes are left in bunches; carbon dioxide is pumped in to eliminate any oxygen. The grapes below are crushed merely by the weight of the grapes above, and fermentation actually takes place within each grape. The process makes them lose a lot of their harsh malic acid, and gives them a little boost in alcohol, while adding nice flavors.

to just the middle part of the region, the Côte d'Or, which includes the Côte de Nuits and Côte de Beaune. Chablis is often discussed completely separately, and sometimes listed separately on wine lists, as is Beaujolais.

BEAUJOLAIS

This most southerly part of official Bourgogne has little to do with what we normally think of as Burgundy, so let's get this out of the way first. The grape used for the wines, all of which are red, is a different one from Burgundy—the Gamay. Beaujolais produces a tremendous amount of wine, and it's widely available all over the U.S.

Wines with the appellation "Beaujolais," and "Beaujolais Supérieur" are simple, fruity, juicy, refreshing wines.

Beaujolais-Villages, which comes from a specific part of the region, represents a little step up in quality. Take an even bigger step up with what are called *Beaujolais Cru* wines. These wines might not even say "Beaujolais" on the label, since they're identified by the particular commune in which the *cru* is located. For example, one might say "Appellation Fleurie Contrôlée." Besides Fleurie, other Beaujolais Cru wines you might find: Morgon, Juliénas, Moulin-à-Vent, Brouilly, Côte de Brouilly, Chénas, St. Amour, and Régnié.

Nouveau Beaujolais: Literally "New Beaujolais," this is the stuff that everybody gets all excited about every November. Nouveau Beaujolais (or *Nouveau Beaujolais-Villages*) simply means Beaujolais that is released as soon as it is bottled, without any aging whatsoever. The day it arrives by air to the U.S. (just in time for Thanksgiving) and Japan, the Nouveau Beaujolais fanatics go nuts. Much of this is marketing hype.

> **TIP FROM CABERNET FRANK**
> **Montrachet is known as the greatest of all the white Burgundies.**

Easy Burgundy Pronunciation Key

Bourgogne: bour-*gun*-yuh
Côte d'Or: coat-door
Côte de Nuits: coat-duh-*nwee*
Beaune: bone
Chalonnaise: sha-lo-*nezz*
Mâconnais: mah-co-*nay*
Beaujolais: boh-zhoh-*lay*
Beaujolais-Villages: boh-zhoh-lay-vee-*lahzhe*
Terroir: tehr-wahr
Louis Jadot: loo-*wee*-zhah-doh
Bouchard Père et Fils: boo-*shar* pehr-eh-*feese*
Joseph Drouhin: zhoh-*zeff* droo-*eah*
Gevrey-Chambertin: zhev-*ray*-sham-bur-*teh*
Chassagne-Montrachet: sha-*sah*-nyuh mon-trah*shay*
Pommard: poh-*mar*
Pouilly-Fuissé: poo-yee fwee-*say*
Meursault: mur-*soh*

While it's true that it's something of a tradition in the region to celebrate the bottling, it's been blown totally out of proportion around much of the world. Nouveau Beaujolais is fruity and refreshing, a fun wine—what the wine pros call "a quaffing wine." This means you can slurp it down without worrying much about it. To me it's like fruit punch. But hey—I like fruit punch.

CHABLIS
Jumping over the main part of Burgundy, to a little winemaking islet, we land in *Chablis*. Chablis, as you probably know, is famous for its white wines, which are bone-dry, crisp, and elegant, with citrus and mineral aromas.

Mercifully, Chablis is easy to learn. Just remember that its vineyards divide into *grand cru* (the tippety top, the best), *premier cru* (damn good), plain old Chablis (respectable), and Petit Chablis (better than nothing, but none too interesting).

CÔTE D'OR
Okay, onward and downward—toward the heart of Burgundy.

The big deal about Burgundy is the *terroir* (the taste of the earth—turn back to Chapter Four, and shame on you if you forgot what it is). Both Pinot Noir and Chardonnay are neutral enough to let the *terroir* find expression in the wines—this is what everybody's trying to do here. The fancy-schmancy technical side of winemaking takes a backseat to grape growing; that's where all the action is. The reason people make so much noise about the different villages and vineyards is that *terroir* means much more than just something physical in the soil. It's really an expression of place: the soil, the climate, the people, the spirit of the land. It probably helps to be French to completely understand this.

See, land has always been a major issue in France. Remember the French Revolution? It was about land. Before the Revolution, when a landowner died, the law required him to pass his land holdings on to his eldest son. What did the daughters and younger sons get? Diddly-squat. However, this was okay with everybody since it kept the land parcels in nice big powerful pieces. After the Revolution, things changed. Now landowners were required to divide their land equally among their children.

You can imagine what happened: If one guy had three kids, his land got divided into thirds; if each of those had three kids, the original land was now in ninths; another generation of three kids each and you've got twenty-seven tiny little pieces of land, all owned by someone different.

That's why Burgundy is such a pain in the ass. The vineyards are carved up into such tiny little parcels that lots of people own just a row or two of vines. Now, if you want to go out and try to keep track of that, be my guest. But be forewarned that Matt Kramer devotes more than 130 pages of his excellent book *Making Sense of Burgundy* solely to listing vineyard ownership. That's why they don't have châteaux there—imagine what teeny, tiny little châteaux they would be!

Since many of the vineyard holdings are so minuscule, many grape growers don't make their own wine, either. Often they sell their grapes to a *négociant*, which is a company that buys up grapes and wine from particular growers and makes wine from them. On such bottles, the name of the *négociant* will look like a brand name. But there are also growers who make and bottle their own wine; these are called *domaines*. On the label or wine

list, it will appear as "Domaine So-and-So." Although the *négociants* often have more up-to-date winemaking equipment and technical skill, one type of producer isn't necessarily better than the other. In recent years the *négociants* have been buying vineyards so they can bottle wine grown on their own property.

Following are the names of some Burgundy *négociants* that you might notice on wine lists and in shops.

Labouré-Roi
Louis Jadot
Bouchard Père et Fils
Joseph Faiveley
Joseph Drouhin
Hospices de Beaune (a famous wine-producing charity
    hospital)

If you don't want to be bothered with doing a lot of research before purchasing a Burgundy, find a *négociant* whose wines you like, and try the different appellations it offers. Or if a sommelier or wine merchant you trust recommends a particular domaine, you might want to give it a try.

> Q: Why are Burgundies so expensive?
> A: Because the region is so tiny and because people will pay the sky-high prices asked. No matter the quality of the wines coming out of it, Burgundy can never produce enough. Demand will always exceed supply.

The wines in Burgundy are divided officially into three levels. In ascending level of geographic specificity and expense, they are:

- Village wines (also known as commune wines)
- Premiers crus
- Grands crus

If you see something on a wine list and it doesn't say whether it's a village wine, a *premier cru,* or a *grand cru,* go right ahead and

ask the waiter or wine steward. It's not a dumb question—believe it or not, just asking will earn you a little respect.

The village (commune) wines are the simplest wines, from the vineyards that are not considered to be the choicest ones. They can still be very good. These wines cost much less than the other two categories; if you see a Burgundy on a wine list, and you don't gasp audibly when you look at the price, it's probably a village wine. If you're in a wineshop, take a look at the label: if you're looking at a *premier cru* or *grand cru*, it'll always say so right on the label, since it means people will pay more for it.

Here are some village wines from Bourgogne that appear often on wine lists (see map, page 123):

Red Wines:	White Wines:
Gevrey-Chambertin	Pouilly-Fuissé
Morey-Saint-Denis	Puligny-Montrachet
Chambolle-Musigny	Chassagne-Montrachet
Nuits-Saint-Georges	Meursault
Chassagne-Montrachet	Aloxe-Corton
Aloxe-Corton	Beaune
Beaune	
Pommard	
Volnay	
Santenay	
Mercurey	
Côte de Beaune-Villages	

Although the village wines can be very nice, if you want the transcendent kind of experience that people talk about with

---

**Q: Why isn't wine produced everywhere in the world?
A: Many climates are either too warm or too cold to grow grapes that will make good wine. Grapes need a certain amount of heat to ripen, but if there's too much unrelenting heat, the resulting wine will lack finesse.**

Burgundies, you'll have to spend more than a few bucks, and try out some *premier cru* and *grand cru* wines. These wines are not cheap; nor are they always fabulous. There's some risk involved. But if you become a serious enthusiast, you might just be the kind of person who's up for the challenge that Burgundy offers.

I could give you a list of all the *premier cru* and *grand cru* vineyards and ask you to memorize them, but that particular exercise in futility would be a waste of valuable wood pulp. Instead, place your trust in someone who has spent years thinking about this stuff: a trusted wine merchant or savvy sommelier. If you want the Burgundy bug to bite you, invest in a copy of Matt Kramer's *Making Sense of Burgundy,* and then get ready to sell off some of your stocks. For those so inclined, the rewards may be great.

BURGUNDY VINTAGES
Most of the whites should be consumed when they're between three and five years old; some of the finer bottles can age longer. The reds are usually best at five to eight years old, but of course the heavy hitters want much, much longer in the bottle. For the reds, 1988, 1989, and 1990 are excellent years (in fact, 1990 is

killer), and 1991 and 1992 are very good. For the whites, you almost can't go wrong. Starting with 1985, all vintages are at least excellent; 1985, 1989, 1990 and 1992 even rate as classic.

Other French Wines

You may also run into a few wines that don't have "Appellation Contrôlée" written anywhere on them. These will probably say "Vin de Pays," which means "country wines." There is a movement afoot in certain regions to produce better than the usual *vins de pays,* and you might want to investigate.

Also, a new wave of winemakers in the Languedoc and elsewhere have started producing wines from grapes that are not traditional in those regions. Plus, they're labeled as varietals. *Quelle horreur!* How un-French! Therefore, they can never achieve AC status, since in order to be *appellation contrôlée,* a wine can only be made from certain grape varieties in specific regions.

Some of them are worth trying anyway, especially because they're inexpensive. Fortant de France, the pioneer in the area and the largest of the firms, offers palatable Chardonnay, Sauvignon Blanc, Viognier, Cabernet Sauvignon, and Merlot at very reasonable prices. Les Jamelles and Reserve St. Martin also offer drinkable varietal wines from France.

IF YOU FORGET EVERYTHING ELSE
YOU'VE READ IN CHAPTER SIX,
JUST REMEMBER THIS:

1. The words *premier, grand,* and *classé,* when attached to the word *cru,* can only mean something good.
2. Red Bordeaux is made from Cabernet and/or Merlot.
3. White Bordeaux is made from Sauvignon Blanc and Sémillon.
4. Red Burgundy is made from Pinot Noir.
5. White Burgundy is made from Chardonnay.

6. Reds from the northern Rhône (Hermitage, Crozes-Hermitage, Côte-Rôtie, etc.) are made from Syrah.
7. Côtes du Rhône and other reds from the southern Rhône are made from a Grenache-based blend.
8. Vintage champagne is generally fancier than non-vintage champagne.
9. While non-vintage champagne expresses the house style of the champagne firm, vintage champagne expresses the particular character of that harvest year.

Chapter Seven

OTHER OLD WORLD WINES—
ITALY, GERMANY, SPAIN, AND MORE

Some people (they're usually French) act as though the only wines to come out of Europe are from France. How wrong they are! Wines come from many European countries—what wine professionals refer to as the "Old World." You probably know that Italy, Germany, Spain, and Portugal produce wine. But have you thought about England (yes, England!), Switzerland, Austria, Hungary, or Greece? Not much from these last few lands finds its way onto our shelves, so we'll just touch on a few high points.

Italy

Italy produces a whole lot of wine—more than any other country, even France—and for a long time, much of it wasn't very good. Not so these days: Italy's really on a roll, producing some of the most wonderful wines in the world.

What do you think of when you think of Italian wine? Let me guess—red, right? Well, Italy does produce fabulous red wines, and it's true that Italian whites used to be unimpressive, but that's changing, too.

So don't think of Italy as a place to look for cheap rotgut reds; if you don't have much to spend, you might want to stick closer to home. However, more and more Italian (and other) restaurants are offering wide-ranging Italian selections, and you'll surely want to try them out.

In Italy, subregions are referred to as zones. All of this is regu-

---

Wine's Middlemen

You already know about grape growers and winemakers, and you've surely had some contact with wine merchants. But how do the wines get from the winery—especially if that winery is across an ocean—to your local wineshop? The answer, of course, is middlemen.

- *Importer:* **A firm that buys wine direct from the winery and brings it into another country, the U.S., for instance. This firm will sell the wine to distributors and/or retail outlets.**
- *Distributor:* **A firm that buys wine from the importers (or, in the case of domestic wines, direct from the winery), and sells it to restaurants and retail outlets.**
- *Négociant:* **A firm that buys wine in barrels from wineries before it's bottled, or even buys grapes from growers and makes its own wine. In either case, it's bottled under the *négociant's* own label, and it's sold to importers and distributors. This is most common in the Burgundy and Rhône Valley regions of France.**

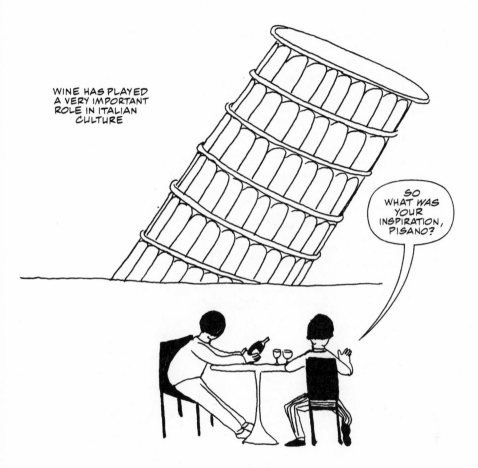

lated, and strings of initials are given out, such as D.O.C., D.O.C.G., but you don't have to worry about this—it's more confusing than helpful, especially since the system keeps changing, and some of the best Italian wines can only be labeled "Vino da Tavola" (table wine), since they don't conform to an old approved and regulated recipe.

For the most part, Italian wines are named after the zones they're from—for instance, Barolo is a zone in Piedmont; Chianti Classico is a zone in Tuscany. However, there are exceptions, in which a wine is named after its grape variety, such as Nebbiolo d'Alba—Nebbiolo is a grape variety, and Alba is the zone it's from.

ITALY

Also, the last dozen years or so have seen a rise in the number of French grape varieties grown and vinified in Italy, labeled as varietals. Since you'll know what those are if you see them, we'll mostly stick to wines made from the traditional Italian grape varieties.

Vintages: 1988 was an excellent year for Italian reds; 1989 was excellent in Piedmont (Barolo, Barbaresco, Dolcetto, etc.), but not great for Tuscany (Chianti, Brunello, etc.). 1990 was fabulous all around—many refer to it as the vintage of the century. 1991 and 1992 were nothing to write home about;1993 was pretty good in Piedmont, so-so in Tuscany.

Here are some of the Italian wines you're most likely to bump into.

Chianti: The thing that confuses the most people is the difference between Chianti and Chianti Classico—an important distinction, since Chianti Classico is the best zone in all of Chianti. Chianti, a pretty large area within Tuscany, includes seven different zones: Chianti Classico, Chianti Montalbano, Chianti Colli Fiorentini, Chianti Rufina, Colli Senesi, Colline Pisane. If it just says "Chianti," it can be from any one of the seven, though if it's from one of the better ones, such as Classico or Rufina, the label will brag about that. Wines belonging to the Chianti Classico "Consorzio" will sport a black rooster, though that's not necessarily an indication of quality.

Chianti has been made traditionally according to a recipe, which was actually "invented" in the 1870s. It calls for 75 to 90 percent Sangiovese, 5 to 10 percent Canaiolo (another red variety) and up to 10 percent "other," usually Trebbiano and/or Malvasia. Since then, many winemakers have been leaving out the

MEMBERS OF THE OFFICIAL CHIANTI CLASSICO "CONSORZIO" USE A BLACK ROOSTER AS THEIR SYMBOL

TIP FROM CABERNET FRANK **Even though Chianti seems like something that's probably been around forever, it was actually only "invented" in the 1870s!**

Canaiolo and white wine, and the official requirement for them will soon be dropped.

Chiantis have changed a lot in the last twenty-five years: they used to be sort of thin and fruity, and not that interesting. Now winemakers are making deeper, darker, more intense Chiantis with more body, wines that can age longer.

D.O.C.G. Chianti, whether it be Chianti Classico or any other Chianti, may also be labeled "Riserva," which means that the wine has been aged for at least three years, and must not include any white wine grapes.

A few reliable Chianti producers: Badia e Coltobuono, Brolio, Ruffino Riserva Ducale, Santa Cristina, Antinori, Felsina Berardinga, Fontodi, Castellodei, Isole Olena, Rampolla.

Supertuscans: In the 1960s and 1970s, Tuscan winemakers started blending Cabernet Sauvignon into the Sangiovese for

THE MAKERS OF CABERNET-BASED TUSCAN WINES, CALLED "SUPERTUSCANS" HAVE ADOPTED AGGRESSIVE MARKETING TACTICS

Sassicaia

Sassicaia, a 100 percent Tuscan Cabernet created for the first time by winemaker Piero Antinori from the 1968 vintage, has, up until recently, been simply labeled "Vino da Tavola." But lately it's been granted its own appellation: Bolgheri Rosso. Since the appellation calls for at least 80 percent Cabernet Sauvignon, with additions of Sangiovese or Merlot allowed, several other neighboring Supertuscans will be eligible as well.

added depth, and it worked so well they called them "Supertuscans." Today, Supertuscans may be Sangiovese blended with Cabernet, Merlot, or Syrah—or they may even contain 100 percent Cabernet. Since Chiantis can't contain more than 10% of grapes other than Sangiovese and Canaiolo, those with more Cabernet or Merlot can't be called "Chianti." That's why Supertuscans may be labeled "Vino da Tavola" (table wine), even though they may be top quality.

Brunello di Montalcino: Sangiovese grapes do their best in this zone, and Brunellos, made of 100 percent Sangiovese, are to many people the very best wines of Italy. Brunellos must be aged at least four years, three of them spent in oak. When they're good, they're rich, deep, delicious, unforgettable wines. *Rosso di Montalcino:* Also 100 percent Sangiovese, but these only have to be aged for one year. They're nowhere near as interesting as the Brunellos, but they're widely available and much less expensive. Reliable Brunello producers: Biondi-Santi, Altesino, Barbi, Col d'Orcia, Val di Suga.

Some Supertuscans

Sassicaia	**Solaia**
Tignanello	**Ornelaia**

TIP FROM
CABERNET
FRANK
**Biondi-Santi
Riserva is
known as the
Rolls-Royce of
Brunello di
Montalcinos.**

Vino Nobile di Montepulciano: The blend is the same as the traditional Chianti, but with a maximum of 80 percent Sangiovese, which is called "Prugnolo Gentile" in this zone. (Winemakers often ignore the maximum, and make them with 100 percent Sangiovese.) These wines used to be really prestigious (hence the word *nobile*), but they've had some ups and downs over the decades. They're similar to Chiantis,

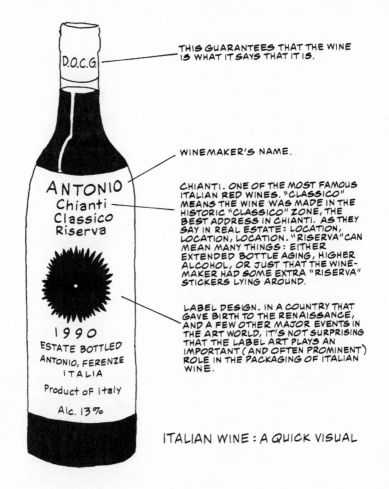

D.O.C.G.

THIS GUARANTEES THAT THE WINE
IS WHAT IT SAYS THAT IT IS.

WINEMAKER'S NAME.

ANTONIO
Chianti
Classico
Riserva

CHIANTI. ONE OF THE MOST FAMOUS
ITALIAN RED WINES. "CLASSICO"
MEANS THE WINE WAS MADE IN THE
HISTORIC "CLASSICO" ZONE, THE
BEST ADDRESS IN CHIANTI. AS THEY
SAY IN REAL ESTATE: LOCATION,
LOCATION, LOCATION. "RISERVA" CAN
MEAN MANY THINGS: EITHER
EXTENDED BOTTLE AGING, HIGHER
ALCOHOL, OR JUST THAT THE WINE-
MAKER HAD SOME EXTRA "RISERVA"
STICKERS LYING AROUND.

LABEL DESIGN. IN A COUNTRY THAT
GAVE BIRTH TO THE RENAISSANCE,
AND A FEW OTHER MAJOR EVENTS IN
THE ART WORLD, IT'S NOT SURPRISING
THAT THE LABEL ART PLAYS AN
IMPORTANT (AND OFTEN PROMINENT)
ROLE IN THE PACKAGING OF ITALIAN
WINE.

1990
ESTATE BOTTLED
ANTONIO, FERENZE
ITALIA
Product of Italy
Alc. 13%

ITALIAN WINE: A QUICK VISUAL

but not as elegant as the better ones. *Rosso di Montepulciano:* The same recipe, but not aged as long.

Galestro: This new white Tuscan wine was created in the 1970s as a blend of Trebbiano and Malvasia, two varieties that wine-makers stopped using in Chianti and had to find a use for. It may also contain Vernaccia, or even Chardonnay, Pinot Blanc, or Riesling. Offered by fourteen different Tuscan producers, Galestro is very light, low in alcohol, and unpretentious (in fact not too serious), meant to be drunk with very casual food.

Vin Santo: Although Tuscany is its traditional home, this sweet wine is also produced in Umbria and Trentino. It's made by drying Trebbiano and Malvasia grapes on straw mats in the rafters, and then aging the resulting wine for a very long time (three to ten years) in barrels. Everybody and their cousin in Tuscany make Vin Santo, and they range from the pitiful to the sublime. The best ones are intensely flavored: orange peel and nuts; they can be almost sherrylike. Many are very sweet, but occasionally they're dry.

Vernaccia di San Gimignano (also known simply as "Vernaccia," though there are also other types of Vernaccia): A dry white wine from Tuscany, made from a blend of Trebbiano and Malvasia, a higher-quality version of a blend that is very common in Tuscany. Although it's usually of a pretty unimpressive commercial quality, there are several producers, such as Terruzi & Puthod, striving to do a good job with this wine.

Vino Novello: Found in many different regions of Italy, especially Bardolino, but also in Piedmont and Tuscany, *vini novelli* are literally "new wines." Bottled and sold in the winter after harvest, *vini novelli* are made to be consumed very young and fresh. They're very light and fruity, similar in style to French Nouveau Beaujolais.

Barolo: One of the most famous and delicious wines of Italy, made from the Nebbiolo grape in the Piedmont region. These dry red wines are big, deep, rich, and complex, with pretty high alcohol (over 13 percent) and plenty of tannin. They're aged at least three years, two of them in oak. *Barolo Riserva* must be aged at least four years; *Barolo Riserva Speciale* at least five.

Good Barolos are always expensive, sometimes outrageously so,

TIP FROM CABERNET FRANK
Tradition calls Barolo "the wine of kings, and the king of wines."

since production is limited. Some dependable producers: Angelo Gaja, Elio Altare, Aldo Conterno, Fontanafredda, Franco Fiorina, Marchesi di Barolo, Alfredo Prunotto, Bruno Giacosa, Ceretto, Marchesi di Gresy.

Barbaresco: Like Barolo, Barbaresco is made from the Nebbiolo grape in the Piedmont region, yet it's softer and gentler than Barolo, a little less alcoholic, and not aged quite as long (at least two years). Riserva means it has spent three years in

ITALIANS LEARN ABOUT WINE AT AN EARLY AGE.

ONCE UPON A TIME THERE WERE THREE ITALIAN WINE PRINCESSES: BAROLO, WHO WAS THE OLDEST, AND VERY BIG AND POWERFUL; BARBARESCO, WHO WAS THE SECOND OLDEST, A LITTLE SMALLER AND MORE DELICATE; BARDOLINO, WHO WAS THE YOUNGEST, AND A LITTLE LIGHT AND SILLY.

FRASCATI IS MADE IN THE SUBURBS OF ROME

wood, and Riserva Speciale means four years. Some reliable producers: Fontanafredda, Franco Fiorina, Alfredo Prunotto, Angelo
Gaja.

Barbera (Barbera d'Alba, Barbera d'Asti, and *Barbera del Monfer-
rato):* Barbera is a grape variety that grows in any of these three
zones. This dry red wine has lots of fruit and bright acidity, not
too much tannin. Some reliable producers: Elio Altare, Alfredo
Prunotto, Angelo Gaja.

Dolcetto: A rich, deeply fruity dry red wine from several zones
in Piedmont; it should be drunk young. Look for wines from
Angelo Gaja, Elio Altare, Pio Cesare, Bruno Ceretto, and Franco
Fiorina.

Valpolicella: Many of the examples we get in the U.S. of this dry
red wine from the Veneto region (near Venice) are lousy—thin
and uninteresting. It's made from the grapes Corvino, Rondinella,
and Molinara. Look for wines labeled "Valpolicella Superiore,"
which are a little better.

Amarone: This dried grape wine is made from the same grapes
as Valpolicella, and in the same zone in Veneto, but with much
different (read: more delicious) results. Sometimes the grapes are
botrytis-affected, sometimes not. It's a rich, dry, heady red wine

"FRIZZANTE" IS A SEMI-
SPARKLING ITALIAN WINE,
NOT A HAIR CONDITION

with a character all its own: you either love it or hate it. Amarone ages long; ten to fifteen years is not unusual. Masi is the most famous.

Bardolino: A light, simple, dry red wine, made from the same grapes as Valpolicella, but often of somewhat higher quality.

Pinot Grigio: A crisp, pale dry white wine made from the Pinot Gris grape in the Veneto region. It's usually high in acid and pretty boring, especially when compared with Pinot Gris from Alsace or even the Pacific Northwest of the United States.

TIP FROM CABERNET FRANK
The straw basket that used to encase a lot of Chianti is called a "fiasco." In fact lots of Italian wine used to be a fiasco!

Prosecco: Both the name of the grape and the name of the wine, this white wine from the hills near Venice is usually fizzy (*frizzante* in Italian) or sparkling *(spumante)*. Charming and unpretentious, it's usually off-dry, often with a faintly bitter aftertaste.

Moscato: Aromatic wines made from

the Muscat grape can be found all over Italy—the most famous is Moscato d'Asti. They can be still, *frizzante,* or *spumante,* and they're usually delicate and a little sweet.

Soave: A very popular dry white wine from the Veneto region, much of which is watery and dull. It's traditionally been made from the Garganega grape, with Trebbiano or Pinot Blanc added in. Since 1992, winemakers are allowed to use Chardonnay in the mix, improving things somewhat. If you come across Soaves from producers Anselmi, Masi, or Pieropan, you might want to give them a try.

Gavi: A crisp dry white wine, made from the Cortese grape in the Piedmont region. Quality is mixed, and it's not cheap.

Frascati: This undistinguished dry white wine, a blend of Trebbiano and Malvasia, comes from the Castelli Romani zone, a suburb of Rome.

Germany

If you can get past the labels, Germany's pretty easy. Unlike most of the Old World, German wine labels will usually tell you the varietal and often how sweet you can expect the wine to be. The only possible problem you might have is that there's also so much geographical and other information on the label, frequently in an intimidating Gothic script, that you might easily overlook the obvious—the essential information.

But do yourself a favor and get past that, since German wines not only go wonderfully well with food, they're also inexpensive (except, of course, for the expensive ones), and delightful on their own as an apéritif or dessert wine. German wines suffer from a reputation of being sickeningly sweet thanks to certain commercial brands, but they're actually some of the finest wines of the world. Although in general (and historically) sweetness is a thing to be desired in these wines, what makes them wonderful is their balance between sweetness and acidity. And even when sweet, they're light (low in alcohol), beautifully aromatic, and elegant.

DR. HEGER, DR. LOOSEN, DR.
WEIL, DR. MÜLLER-BERGHOFF...
EVER NOTICE HOW MANY GERMAN
WINES ARE MADE BY DOCTORS?

MAYBE THAT'S WHY
GERMAN WINE
LABELS ARE SO
HARD TO READ

Also, in recent years, winemakers have begun making more and more dry wines.

The best way to get at German wines is to examine a label. The first line tells you the region. Although there are thirteen regions in Germany, most of the wines you find here will be from a few of them: Mosel-Saar-Ruwer, Rheingau, Pflaz, and Rheinhessen, all of which are in the southwest, near the Rhine River and the French border. Just so you know, the other regions are Ahr, Mittelrhein, Nahe, Franken, Hessische Bergstrasse, Würtemberg, Baden, Saale/Unstrut, and Sachsen. Don't worry right now about the differences between all the regions, or you'll go nuts.

Next you'll find the vintage year. That part's easy.

Below that, you'll find where the grapes were grown. This is the part that may look the most foreign and confusing, but it's easy after a few tries. This may be either the town (which has the suffix *er* attached to it, meaning from that place), and possibly the vineyard. Examples: Münsterer Kapellenberg (which means from the town of Münster, Kapellenberg vineyard); Niersteiner Oelberg (which means from the town of Nierstein, Oelberg vineyard). Or you might see "Weingut," which means "estate," such as "Weingut St. Antony" (meaning the St. Antony Estate) or "Weingut Freiherr Heyl zu Herrnsheim" (meaning the Freiherr Heyl zu Herrnsheim estate).

Next you'll find the grape variety (assuming the wine contains at least 85 percent of it). The most famous and prized German wines are *Rieslings,* but there are other varieties as well: *Gewürztraminer; Pinot Blanc* (which is *Weisser Burgunder* in German, being a white grape from Burgundy); *Pinot Gris* (which is *Ruländer* or *Grauer Burgunder* in German); *Silvaner* (a lesser variety); *Müller-Thurgau* (widely planted, but used for cheaper wines); *Kerner* and *Scheurebe.* The red you're most likely to encounter is *Pinot Noir* (*Spätburgunder* in German).

Next to the grape variety, you'll usually see one or two other words, which describe the style of the wine. You may see either *"Trocken,"* which means "dry," or *"Halbtrocken,"* which means "half-dry," or "off-dry," meaning just a little bit sweet. If it doesn't say either, you can pretty much assume it will have at least some sweetness to it.

Then you'll see, either below that or next to the grape variety, some assessment of the quality level, which may also relate to sweetness.

After that, you'll find some pronouncement about the quality level of wine.

The lowest level is *Tafelwein* (ordinary table wine). This may appear on the label as either "Deutscher Tafelwein" or "Deutscher Landwein." (*Deutscher* means "German"—if it doesn't say it, it may not be from Germany at all.) *Landwein* is a little better.

TIP FROM CABERNET FRANK
If someone offers to share their Beerenauslese with you, act suitably impressed, even if you don't remember what it is. If they offer to share a Trockenbeerenauslese, consider kissing their feet.

CERTAIN COMMERCIAL GERMAN WINES USE RELIGIOUS IMAGERY ON THEIR LABELS

Next up is what you'll see the most of: *Qualitätswein* (quality wine). This comes in two levels: either *Qualitätswein bestimmter Anbaugebiete* (QbA), the lower of the two, which includes a whole slew of everyday wines, or *Qualitätswein mit Prädikat* (quality wines of special distinction), the fancier stuff that you'll want to look for. These are also known as QmP or simply *Prädikat*.

Within QmP, there are six possible levels of sweetness. These refer to exactly how ripe the grapes were when they were har-

> **Q: Where do Liebfraumilchs (such as Blue Nun) fall into the overall German picture?**
> **A: Hopefully, they fall into the sink. Liebfraumilchs are the sticky-sweet, commercial beverages that gave German wines a bad name.**

vested—and in general, the further along this scale a wine is, the more prestigious, rare, and expensive (although a Kabinett from a great producer will be better than an Auslese from a lesser producer).

Kabinett: Generally the driest of all the levels, although it can range from bone-dry to off-dry. Kabinett means the grapes were normally ripe when harvested. Great for an apéritif, or with food.

Spätlese: Usually a hint or more of sweetness, but they can also be dry; they have lots of concentration and flavor. These are late harvested grapes (picked at least a week after the start of the regular harvest); the reason they're not necessarily sweet is that sometimes the winemaker lets all the sugar ferment into alcohol. Also meant to be drunk with a meal.

Auslese: Usually sweet, with intense aromas and concentrated flavors. The very ripe grapes for wines labeled "Auslese" were handpicked in bunches, and must meet a minimum sugar content. Sometimes they're botrytis-affected. Auslese wines are usu-

GERMAN WINES ARE RANKED ACCORDING TO SWEETNESS: FROM THE SWEETEST (TROCKENBEERNAUSLESE) TO THE DRIEST (KABINETT)

GERMAN WINES CAN BE DIFFICULT TO PRONOUNCE

WE'D LIKE A BOTTLE OF THE SCHLOSSBOCKELHEIMER DONNOF.

CERTAINLY, SIR. WOULD THAT BE THE BEERENAUSLESE OR THE TROCKENBEERENAUSLESE?

ally drunk as dessert wines or apéritifs. Auslese, and the three that follow it, may all be aged for decades.

> **TIP FROM CABERNET FRANK**
> In general, the more words that are strung together to describe a QmP wine, the sweeter and more expensive it will be.

Beerenauslese: Sweet, rich, and intense, and only possible in exceptional vintages. Made from overripe grapes, often botrytis-affected, harvested individually (one grape at a time), Beerenauslese wines are rare and expensive, to be served for dessert, as are the two following.

Eiswein: The grapes for Eiswein must meet the same criteria as those for Beerenauslese, and then they are allowed to freeze on the vine. The wine is pressed out of the frozen grapes, and

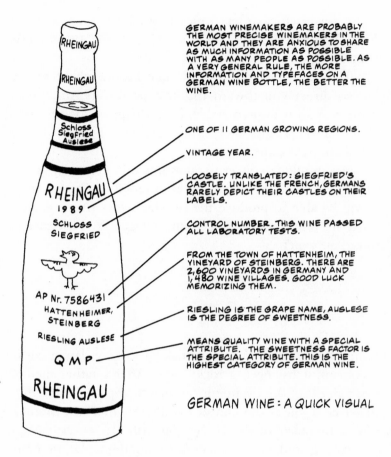

GERMAN WINEMAKERS ARE PROBABLY THE MOST PRECISE WINEMAKERS IN THE WORLD AND THEY ARE ANXIOUS TO SHARE AS MUCH INFORMATION AS POSSIBLE WITH AS MANY PEOPLE AS POSSIBLE. AS A VERY GENERAL RULE, THE MORE INFORMATION AND TYPEFACES ON A GERMAN WINE BOTTLE, THE BETTER THE WINE.

ONE OF 11 GERMAN GROWING REGIONS.

VINTAGE YEAR.

LOOSELY TRANSLATED: SIEGFRIED'S CASTLE. UNLIKE THE FRENCH, GERMANS RARELY DEPICT THEIR CASTLES ON THEIR LABELS.

CONTROL NUMBER. THIS WINE PASSED ALL LABORATORY TESTS.

FROM THE TOWN OF HATTENHEIM, THE VINEYARD OF STEINBERG. THERE ARE 2,600 VINEYARDS IN GERMANY AND 1,480 WINE VILLAGES. GOOD LUCK MEMORIZING THEM.

RIESLING IS THE GRAPE NAME, AUSLESE IS THE DEGREE OF SWEETNESS.

MEANS QUALITY WINE WITH A SPECIAL ATTRIBUTE. THE SWEETNESS FACTOR IS THE SPECIAL ATTRIBUTE. THIS IS THE HIGHEST CATEGORY OF GERMAN WINE.

GERMAN WINE: A QUICK VISUAL

it's therefore incredibly concentrated and rich, while the acidity is still preserved.

Trockenbeerenauslese: The grapes are even riper and therefore higher in sugar than those required for Beerenauslese; in fact they may be almost raisins, and they're usually botrytis-affected. These are the rarest and most expensive of all the German wines.

Rather than cramming a lot of information about all the German regions, at this point the best thing to do is simply to see what you can find, either in wineshops or in restaurants, and start tasting. When tasting German wines, look in particular for the acid-sugar balance, the body and texture of the wine, and floral, mineral, and fruit aromas. You may find, if you keep tasting them, that you prefer one sweetness level

(Spätlese, for instance, offers a nice hint of sweetness with crisp acidity). You may decide you're a Spätlese type, or an Auslese type, etc.

You'll need to rely on a knowledgeable merchant or sommelier to direct you toward the best producers, since what's available to you is unpredictable. If you happen to see a bottle that says "Terry Theise Selections," grab it. Theise is an importer with great taste.

Vintages shouldn't concern you as much in Germany as many other regions, since the major question raised is whether the estates will be able to produce the sweeter wines (Auslese, and so on) that are only possible in certain vintages. You'll either find them or you won't.

Spain

Although Spain has a long winemaking history dating back to the Romans, it has been a rocky one. After a rather mediocre first two thirds of the twentieth century, the Spanish wine industry received a jolt at the end of the 1970s. In 1979, Miguel A. Torres, winemaker of the *bodega* (Spanish for winery) Miguel Torres, having studied winemaking techniques in Dijon, France, had put them to such good use that he managed to win first prize for his 1970 Tempranillo-Cabernet blend Gran Coronas Black Label in a big Cabernet competition in France.

After that, Spain started seeing improved technology in winemaking and more concentration on estate bottlings as opposed to bulk production.

The big deal about Spanish wines is how long they're aged in oak. The Spanish attitude tends to be "the more oak, the better," which you might or might not agree with. One nice result is that the wines are just about always drinkable on release, since the *bodega* has already held it for you until it's ready. In any case, several adjectives are applied across the board to the different red wines of Spain, depending on how long they spend aging in oak:

Jovén (literally "young") wines are not required to spend any time aging in casks before release.

Crianza wines spend, in most regions, a year in oak casks, and another two years aging in bottle or tank. More of these are exported than any other category.

Reserva wines, selected from better vintages, spend at least a year in oak, and two years aging in bottle.

Gran Reserva, from outstanding vintages, spend at least two years aging in oak, and another three years in bottle.

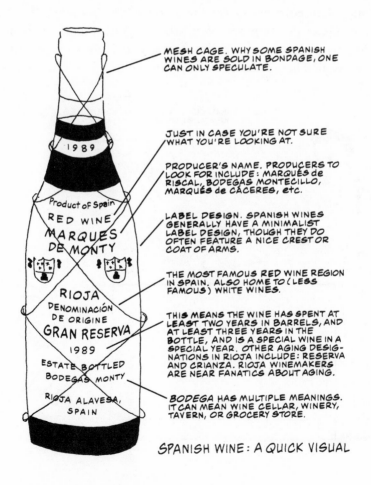

MESH CAGE. WHY SOME SPANISH WINES ARE SOLD IN BONDAGE, ONE CAN ONLY SPECULATE.

JUST IN CASE YOU'RE NOT SURE WHAT YOU'RE LOOKING AT.

PRODUCER'S NAME. PRODUCERS TO LOOK FOR INCLUDE: MARQUÉS de RISCAL, BODEGAS MONTECILLO, MARQUÉS de CÁCERES, etc.

LABEL DESIGN. SPANISH WINES GENERALLY HAVE A MINIMALIST LABEL DESIGN, THOUGH THEY DO OFTEN FEATURE A NICE CREST OR COAT OF ARMS.

THE MOST FAMOUS RED WINE REGION IN SPAIN. ALSO HOME TO (LESS FAMOUS) WHITE WINES.

THIS MEANS THE WINE HAS SPENT AT LEAST TWO YEARS IN BARRELS, AND AT LEAST THREE YEARS IN THE BOTTLE, AND IS A SPECIAL WINE IN A SPECIAL YEAR. OTHER AGING DESIGNATIONS IN RIOJA INCLUDE: RESERVA AND CRIANZA. RIOJA WINEMAKERS ARE NEAR FANATICS ABOUT AGING.

BODEGA HAS MULTIPLE MEANINGS. IT CAN MEAN WINE CELLAR, WINERY, TAVERN, OR GROCERY STORE.

SPANISH WINE: A QUICK VISUAL

Vintages: 1982 and 1987 were excellent years in Spain. All
other vintages (*cosechas* in Spanish) from 1985 through 1993 were
at least pretty good.

Spanish wines, like those from France, are named after their
regions, which are scattered throughout the country. The officially recognized ones are called *denominaciones*. The most interesting, accessible Spanish wines at this point in history are red
wines from the north, and sherries, of course, which you'll read
about in Chapter Nine. If you familiarize yourself with the few
wines that follow, you'll be pretty well covered.

Rioja: The best known *denominación,* Rioja sits in the central
part of northern Spain. Red Riojas, usually Tempranillo-based
and blended with Garnacha (Grenache), Mazuelo (Carignan),
and Graciano varieties, offer attractive fruit, making them good
for drinking on release, but enough structure to allow them to
age well. There's a trend toward increased use of Graciano, which

SPANISH WINEMAKERS HOLD ON TO THEIR WINES MUCH LONGER
THAN MOST OTHER WINEMAKERS

had fallen out of favor, but is now seen as adding wonderful aromatic elements. Although some Riojas, especially Gran Reservas, are expensive, there are also many excellent values here, including those from Marqués de Cáceres, Bodegas Montecillo, and Marqués de Riscal. For a little more dough, look for wines from Bodegas Muga and CVNE.

The region also produces oaked white Riojas, young, unoaked white Riojas, and some charming, inexpensive rosés.

Penedès: This Catalan region, along the eastern coast just below Barcelona, is home of Miguel Torres and his famous Gran Coronas. These are good wines, but in my humble opinion, overpriced (about thirty-four dollars for the current release of Gran Coronas Black Label). You may know Torres's Sangre de Toro by the little red plastic bull attached to the neck. Red wines cover a wide range of quality and price, and more expensive isn't necessarily better.

Ribera del Duero: This *denominación* in the northern-central part of Spain, southwest of Rioja, runs along the Duero River. This is sort of the *denominación* of the moment—it was only named officially in 1982, and the wines it's producing (Pesquera, made from Tinto Fino, a type of Tempranillo, and Vega Sicilia, a Cabernet-Merlot blend) are some of the best in Spain.

Cava: Spain's own sparkling wine offers an inexpensive, if not incredibly interesting, alternative to champagne. Made from a blend of Parellada, Macabeo, and Xarel-lo grapes, most of this *méthode champenoise* wine is produced in the Penedès region. Freixenet (pronounced Fresh-en-*ette*) and Codorniu are widely available in the U.S., and you can pick them up from between six and ten dollars a bottle.

Albariño: Probably Spain's most interesting white wine (also its most expensive), an attractive, young, crisp, aromatic Albariño (look for peaches and apricots in the nose) is a good wine for impressing Spain-o-philes. Unusually for Spain, the wine is varietally named after the grape it's made from rather than its region, Galicia. Bodegas Vilariño-Cambados's Martín Codax is the top-selling Albariño, but I have preferred those from Bodegas Morgadío, Bodegas Valdamor, and Pazo de Señorans.

ALBARIÑO, PARELLADA, TEMPRANILLO... SPANISH GRAPE VARIETIES SOUND LIKE THE NAMES OF EXOTIC DANCES

DEAR, IT'S OUR SONG, THE TEMPRANILLO!

Sherry (Xérès): See Chapter Nine for the lowdown on Spain's famous fortified wine.

Portugal

Although Portugal is better known for its famous fortified wine, port (see Chapter Nine), it also produces a wide variety of table wines. If you're old enough, you may remember the huge fashion for Mateus and Lancer's in the 1960s and 1970s. These are Portuguese wines: fairly sweet, slightly fizzy rosés.

But a wide variety of white wines and red wines come from Portugal, too. Several wineries, including Caves Aliança, Sogrape (owner of Mateus), and Fonseca Successores, are leading efforts to update winemaking technology, which should result in improved wines in several regions that grow very good grapes.

Vinho Verde: Literally "green wine," Portugal's well-known white wine is only green in the metaphorical sense: it's consumed young. Actually it comes in both white and red, though the red version isn't much exported. It's tough to characterize it exactly, since it comes from six different regions in Portugal and it may be made from several different grape varieties, but some are floral, some fruity. All white Vinho Verdes are pale straw color, fairly acidic wines; most are slightly fizzy. Most are

THE MAKERS OF MATEUS BOUGHT THE IMAGE OF THE CASTLE ON THE LABEL FOR A SINGLE PAYMENT, RATHER THAN A ROYALTY FOR EACH OF THE MILLIONS OF BOTTLES SOLD

TAKE THE MONEY, YOU SAID! IT'S ONLY A STUPID PICTURE, YOU SAID! I HOPE YOU'RE HAPPY!

also pretty low in alcohol, except for those made from the Alvarinho grape (Albariño in Spain).

Dão: Red wines named for this northern-central region must contain at least 20 percent Touriga Nacional, which is one of the grape varieties used for port, along with any combination of eight other varieties, including Tinta Roriz, known in Spain as Tempranillo. Dão enjoys a reputation as Portugal's longest-lived red wine. Winemaking techniques are a little behind the times in the region, and the wines can be disappointing, though it's a region to watch in the future since growing conditions are ideal.

Bairrada: This region just to the west of Dão produces red wines from the Baga grape variety, known for often being overly tannic, due, again, to outdated winemaking technology. But like Dão, Bairrada wines are likely to improve in the near future.

Austria

If you weren't sleeping through the Germany section, you'll be able to make your way pretty easily around Austrian wines, since they play by similar rules, and the words describing the different levels of wine are similar. I won't go into detail, though, since the better Austrian wines aren't widely exported. You may bump into some imported by Terry Theise Selections, in which case, grab 'em and you'll have something worthwhile.

Hungary

Though it has a long and distinguished winemaking history, Hungary's wine industry sort of crept to a halt under communist rule, but now it's once again on the rise, and exports will probably increase dramatically, which means you'll start seeing them on merchants' shelves—especially those made from French varieties. Wines are usually labeled varietally, with some exceptions.

The Cabernets and Merlots are mostly undistinguished, and not particularly well made. The whites I've tasted have been better, particularly those from the Etyek region. Chardonnay and Sauvignon Blanc produced by Tibor Bathori at the Vinum Bonum winery from this region are very attractive wines for under ten dollars, and should be increasingly available (imported by Hungarian Cellars).

You may have seen *Bulls Blood (Egri Bikavér)* in a wineshop at some point in your life. It's an inexpensive, deep red wine, none too interesting.

Tokaji Asú (also known as *Tokay*), made from the Furmint grape variety, and blended with two other varieties, Hárslevelu and perhaps Muscat, is Hungary's most famous wine. There are other Tokays from Hungary, but the one labeled "Asú" is the special one. Botrytis-affected grapes are handpicked, fermented, made into a paste, and added to wine. Sweetness is measured in *puttonyos*—from three to six, six being the sweetest, and it's balanced by acidity. It can be weirdly delicious. In exceptional years, an even sweeter one, *Essencia,* is produced.

IF YOU FORGET EVERYTHING ELSE
YOU'VE READ IN CHAPTER SEVEN,
JUST REMEMBER THIS:

1. Italy is famous for reds. Brunello, Chianti, Barolo, and Barbaresco are biggies.

2. Barolo and Barbaresco are made from Nebbiolo.
3. Chianti and Brunello are made from Sangiovese.
4. Supertuscans are Sangiovese blended with Cabernet, or even 100 percent Cabernet.
5. In Germany sweetness is the big deal. After *Auslese,* the longer the word the sweeter the wine.
6. Riesling is Germany's noble grape.
7. In Spain, long aging in oak is the big deal: Crianza, Reserva, Gran Reserva, in order of length of aging.

Chapter Eight

OTHER NEW WORLD WINES—

AUSTRALIA, NEW ZEALAND, CHILE, ARGENTINA, AND SOUTH AFRICA

Wine professionals call just about everything outside of Europe the "New World," but that doesn't mean that people haven't been making wine in some of these regions for centuries. Spanish conquistadores brought vines to Chile, for instance, in the mid-sixteenth century, while South African winemaking dates back to the mid-seventeenth century.

This should cheer you up: If Old World wines are a tangled web of zones, regions, *denominaciones,* and zillions of different grape varieties, New World wines are a piece of cake. Why? The most important wines in all these regions will be made from by-now-familiar grape varieties (Cabernet, Chardonnay, Riesling, etc.), and they're almost all labeled as varietals. You can tackle this chapter with your eyes closed.

Australia

This very important wine region (which has been making wine for 150 years) produces many accessible, friendly wines with ex-

AUSTRALIAN WINEMAKERS GENERALLY MAKE MANY MORE KINDS OF
WINE THAN ANY OTHER WINEMAKERS IN THE WORLD

cellent value, though it takes a little hunting around to find real
stars. Since wines produced in any region down under may contain grapes from any other region, you don't have to go crazy
memorizing them. Just keep in mind these few place names, all
of which are in the southeastern states of South Australia and
New South Wales. Although the quality is generally good in
Australia, it does help to know some of the better producers.

The main difference between Australia and the U.S. is that
Australia produces a lot of Syrah (which it calls *Shiraz*), Riesling
(which it calls *Rhine Riesling*), and Sémillon, as well as Cabernet-
Shiraz blends, and Sémillon-Chardonnay blends. Lots of Cabernet Sauvignon, known for mint and eucalyptus aromas, comes
out of Australia as well. Chardonnay tends not to rely as much
on oak as those from California tend to. Excellent Sauvignon
Blancs are produced as well, as are dessert wines made from Muscat. (See Chapter Nine for Australian ports.)

Internationally, the Australian wine industry comes under fire for concentrating too much effort on producing wines that will win prizes at shows but that may not be very subtle. It's well-known that bigger, more obvious wines do better in blind tastings. They also don't age as well as less self-conscious wines.

Hunter Valley: Probably the best-known wine district in Australia, located in New South Wales, north and inland from Sydney. Produces Sémillon, Chardonnay, Shiraz (known for its "sweaty saddle" aroma), and Cabernet.

Barossa Valley: This beautiful, well-known region in South Australia, an hour's drive inland from Adelaide, was settled by German immigrants in the nineteenth century; for that reason, the

THE WINE PRODUCER. ENGLISH CULTURAL INFLUENCE MEETS FRENCH VITICULTURAL INFLUENCE. A SURPRISING NUMBER OF AUSTRALIAN WINE PRODUCERS ARE NAMED CHÂTEAU SOMETHING.

GROWING REGION.

GRAPE NAME(S). SOMETIMES IT'S A TWO-GRAPE NAME AS SHOWN HERE, AND SO THE PREDOMINANT GRAPE WILL BE LISTED FIRST.

AUSTRALIANS ARE MORE GIVEN TO ORDER THAN POETRY.

PROBABLY THE MOST IMPORTANT INFORMATION ON THE LABEL. TO AN AUSTRALIAN. AWARDS; HIGHLY VALUED STATUS SYMBOLS FOR AUSSIE WINE DRINKERS. THEREFORE, THINK OF THIS INFORMATION AS YOU WOULD THE COLLEGE GPA OF A PROSPECTIVE BLIND DATE. IT'S INTERESTING INFORMATION, BUT HARDLY THE WHOLE STORY.

CHATEAU NIGAL
Hunter Valley
CABERNET
SAUVIGNON
SHIRAZ
BIN 709
SHOW AWARDS:
1 GOLD
2 SILVER
Product of Australia
Alcohol 12.5%

AUSTRALIAN WINE: A QUICK VISUAL

AUSTRALIAN WINE SHOWS
ARE FIERCELY COMPETITIVE

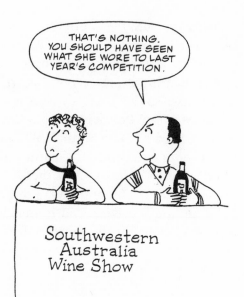

THAT'S NOTHING.
YOU SHOULD HAVE SEEN
WHAT SHE WORE TO LAST
YEAR'S COMPETITION.

Southwestern
Australia
Wine Show

Riesling grape is prized here, and some excellent Rieslings, usually aromatic, dry, and mouthwatering, are produced, as well as Shiraz, and many other varieties. It's also where many of the most famous Australian wineries are. If you happen to find yourself in Australia, touring the Barossa Valley is a wonderful treat—as gorgeous and friendly as Napa but entirely without the crowds of tourists.

Eden and Clare Valleys: Near the Barossa Valley, both valleys are known for outstanding vineyards. Eden Valley grows Riesling, Chardonnay, and Pinot Noir; Clare Valley is known for Cabernet as well as Riesling and Chardonnay. Also great for touring.

McLaren Vale: Lots of assorted small wineries here.

Coonawarra: A region off the coast, southeast of Adelaide, famous for its Cabernet.

Producers worth seeking out:

Penfold's
Peter Lehmann
Lindemans
Seppelts

Yalumba
Mitchelton
Hardy's
Brown Brothers
Rockford (small, but fabulous)
Château Reynella
Rosemount

Grange Hermitage

Penfold's, Australia's largest winery, produces Australia's most famous and expensive wine, Grange Hermitage. In fact, Grange is one of the greatest wines in the world, though it was only invented in 1951 by winemaker Max Schubert. Made from 100 percent Syrah (hence the name "Hermitage"), these wines are made for long aging—up to thirty years or more. Beginning with the 1994 vintage, Penfold's will drop "Hermitage" from the name, in deference to the French region.

Australian Wine Trend: "Basket Press" Wines

"Basket Press" on an Australian wine label means the grapes were pressed using an old-fashioned wooden contraption that looks like a cross between a huge basket and a barrel, with a large screw in the middle. Lots of wineries have these quaint-looking presses strategically placed where visitors will see them.

New Zealand

Although still a fledging in terms of the world wine picture, New Zealand is already known for excellent Sauvignon Blancs in a style that brings out the distinctive varietal character of the grape—the vegetal, cat-pee nose, which you either love or hate. Oak is a dirty word when it comes to Sauvignon Blanc in New Zealand—this spiffy new wine industry believes in stainless steel for exactly that reason: Winemakers want to taste the grape, not the wood.

Chardonnays are up-and-coming, especially from a winery called Cloudy Bay, which makes commendable Sauvignon Blanc as well.

As in the United States, winemakers in New Zealand are accorded celebrity status, which Europeans chalk up to the fact that the industry's new and no one's figured out *terroir* yet.

Chile

According to Fanor Velasco, export manager for Chile's largest winery, Viña Concha y Toro, Chile's premium varietal wines are made specifically with the export market in mind. "When you go to dinner at a nice restaurant in Santiago," he says, "the wine

IN NEW ZEALAND, AS IN CALIFORNIA, WINEMAKERS ARE
TREATED LIKE CELEBRITIES

list will have two choices: red wine and white wine." Quality wine is simply not part of the culture yet, but that doesn't stop Chilean winemakers from making some pretty good wine, at very reasonable prices. Since they're making them primarily for the export market, most of what they offer is Chardonnay, Sauvignon Blanc, Cabernet, and Merlot.

The French influence in Chile is pretty strong: the Rothschild family (of Château Lafite Rothschild fame) owns half of Chilean winery Los Vascos, one of the two or three best respected, and their familiarity with the Cabernet grape hasn't been for nought. Chilean-owned Concha y Toro has put a French winemaker, Gaetane Carron, in charge of its prized Puente Alto Winery.

Chilean Cabernets and Merlots tend to be well made, flavorful, balanced, very drinkable wines. The main complaint

oenophiles have about them is that they don't age well. But who cares when you're paying between six and twelve dollars—not for the bargain bottles, but for the top scorers in the wine mags!

Respectable low-priced Chardonnays abound from Chile, but Sauvignon Blanc is where the real white wine action is.

Best Chilean producers:

Santa Rita
Los Vascos
Cousino-Macul
Concha y Toro (look for bottlings from specific vineyards)
Undurraga (Sauvignon Blanc)

Argentina

Although Argentina produces way more wine than Chile, fewer high-quality/great-value bottles make their way out of the country. One particular winery, however, blows the Chilean reds out of the water: Cavas de Weinert. Weinert makes a *Carrascal,* which is an oddly configured blend of 50 percent Malbec, 30 percent Cabernet Sauvignon, and 20 percent Merlot; a very nice wine indeed for around nine dollars. But the killer is Weinert's Cabernet Sauvignon—a complex, elegant, concentrated Cab; the 1985 seriously rivals some of Bordeaux's (and California's) best—really! It ain't cheap, but I've rarely been more satisfied after forking over sixteen to nineteen dollars for a bottle of wine. Trapiche is also very good, and a great value.

South Africa

Wine has been produced in this part of Africa for more than three hundred years—in fact, in the late seventeenth century, a couple hundred French Huguenots immigrated to the Cape of Good Hope to escape religious persecution, and they happened to know a thing or two about wine. A red dessert wine called Costancia was one of the most prized wines in the world in the

CASABLANCA IS A WHITE WINE REGION IN CHILE

POUR IT AGAIN, SAM. YOU POURED IT FOR HER, YOU CAN POUR IT FOR ME.

early eighteenth century. However, for most of this century South Africa's wines weren't looking so hot, until the late 1980s, that is, when improvements in technology and in the selection of vine varieties did wonders. However, sanctions against the apartheid regime kept people around the world from buying these wines (or even wanting to!).

Today, with the recent abolishment of apartheid, the climate has suddenly changed, and we'll be getting more and more wines from this country. According to Ronn Wiegand, M.W., a specialist in South African wines, "As more arrives here, it will become apparent that an extremely serious wine-producing nation is back in the spotlight."

Most of the high-quality wines that you'll want come from the Coastal Region near Cape Town. Within that region, the four place names you'll want to look for are Costancia, Stellenbosch, Paarl, and Franschhoek Valley. The first three are what are referred to as *districts,* and the fourth, Franschhoek Valley, is a subdistrict of Paarl.

South African wines are usually varietally labeled, though sometimes the varietal name is different from what we're used to. The country also produces unusual blends, which may be labeled with proprietary names.

Steen: This is what they call Chenin Blanc, and it's the most widely planted grape in the country, but much of it goes into cheap bag-in-a-box wine, which is called, oddly, Stein.

Chardonnay: Increased plantings make this and up-and-coming variety.

Pinotage: South Africa's very own crossing of Pinot Noir and Cinsault produces big, chewy flavorful wines that some people love and some people think are over-the-top. They remind me of a rustic rendition of the Syrah grape, which I find pleasant.

Shiraz: Just as in Australia, in South Africa, Syrah is called "Shiraz."

Our familiar friends Sauvignon Blanc, Cabernet Sauvignon, and Merlot are all on the rise here, which is a pretty new development. As this country gets the hang of it, we may be in for some nice surprises. Sparkling wines have also jumped into the forefront; the best ones use the *méthode champenoise,* which they call the "Methode Cap Classique."

Many fortified wines, including a sherry-style fortified wine, are produced here, but almost none of it has been exported so far.

There isn't a whole lot of anything from South Africa on the shelves yet, but the majority of those you'll see are bottled by one of the big cooperatives (KWV, the Bergkelder, or Stellenbosch Farmers' Winery). There are also a small number of wine estates. To buy South African wines, look for selections from specific estate wineries from the districts listed above. The 1990 La Motte Estate from Franschhoek Valley, labeled simply as "Red Wine," is very attractive, refined and Bordeaux-esque. 1988 Stellenrych Cabernet Sauvignon and 1987 Meerlust Rubicon, both from the Bergkelder cooperative, are also appealing, as are 1989 Nederburg Edelrood and 1989 Nederburg Baronne, both blends of Cabernet, Shiraz, and Merlot.

IF YOU FORGET EVERYTHING ELSE YOU'VE READ IN CHAPTER EIGHT, JUST REMEMBER THIS:

1. Australia produces tons of good quality wine for very reasonable prices.
2. Syrah is called "Shiraz" in Australia.
3. In Australia and South Africa, they blend grape varieties that aren't blended elsewhere, such as Cabernet-Shiraz and Sémillon-Chardonnay.
4. New Zealand is the place for Sauvignon Blanc.
5. Look for great values and good quality from Chile.
6. Cavas de Weinert and Trapiche are the names to remember from Argentina.
7. South African wines will become more and more available and quality should continue improving.

Chapter Nine

FORTIFIED WINES FROM AROUND THE WORLD

In the course of our little trip around the world, we've already looked at a number of regular dessert wines, wines which are sweet because the grapes that made them were either late-harvested, botrytis-affected, frozen on the vine, or allowed to turn into raisins. A few of the great ones: French Sauternes, Alsatian Vendange Tardive, German Beerenauslese, Italian Vin Santo, Hungarian Essencia.

Yet don't think for a minute that dessert wines and fortified wines are one and the same. Sure, lots of dessert wines, such as port or Muscat de Beaumes-de-Venise, happen to be fortified wine, but many are not. On the other hand, not all fortified wines are necessarily dessert wines: vermouth, for instance, is an apéritif. Nor are they even necessarily sweet—dry sherries are the exception to the rule.

What the hell *is* a fortified wine, anyway?

Okay, remember how wine is made? The sugars from the ripe grapes are fermented into alcohol. Imagine stopping the fermentation halfway through. Even if the grapes weren't overripe, you'd still be left with some sugar that didn't turn to alcohol. That's exactly what happens with fortified wine: One day, someone discovered that if you add a neutral spirit halfway through the fermentation, you're left with a wine that is still *sweet,* and also strong, from the added spirit.

With most of the high-quality fortified wines we'll be looking at (and if we're lucky, tasting), the neutral spirit that's added halfway through the fermentation is a spirit distilled from grapes, like a flavorless brandy.

> **TIP FROM CABERNET FRANK**
> **The root of the word "fortified" is *fort,* which means "strong." Therefore you can think of fortified wines as "strengthened."**

So, what are some of these alleged fortified wines? The most famous ones are port, sherry, vermouth, and Madeira. But there are many others, including many local *vins doux naturels* and *vins de liqueur* from France. Let's look at some of the biggies:

Port

One might imagine Portugal's famous fortified wine is called port because it's from Portugal. Actually it's because all the port makers, or *shippers,* as they're called, are located in Oporto, a city at the mouth of the Duoro River in the north of Portugal (where, by the way, they call port *porto*). The vineyards that grow the grapes that go into the port cover the terraced hills along the banks of that lovely river.

Port is usually made with six or seven different varieties of grapes, though up to eighty are allowed. They are crushed at the various *quintas,* or estates. After the must ferments for two or three days, it's poured into a vat containing a grape spirit, stopping the fermentation. (It's done a little differently at some of the larger, more commercial *quintas,* or for must not destined to become top-end port, but the technique is way too boring to go into.)

After the wine has been fortified, it ages for six months or so at the *quinta,* then it's sent down the river to what are called the *port lodges,* which are all located right across the river from Oporto. Here the fortified wine is further aged (often in wood casks). Then it can go one of a few ways. In any case, it'll wind up being sweet, thick, and about 18 percent alcohol. Here are the different types of port:

Ruby port: This is one of the two inexpensive, simple styles of port. This port is bottled after a couple years of aging and is ready to drink once you buy it.

Tawny port: Here's where people get a little confused, because "tawny" has two different meanings. With very inexpensive ports, it refers only to the color: lighter-color grapes have been used. Like ruby port, it's a simple drink. In any case, it has very little in common with serious wood-aged tawny ports.

Okay, now that we've gotten the penny-ante players out of the way, let's get to the good stuff.

Vintage port: In exceptional years (no more than three or four a decade), the port shippers decide to "declare" a vintage, just as

---

"I Love Lucy" Goes to Portugal

At the better port *quintas*, the grapes are crushed by foot, à la "I Love Lucy." This technique is usually reserved for the best portion of the harvest that will, hopefully, become vintage port. I didn't believe it either until I went there and saw it (and did it) myself.

Why, you may ask, would they use human feet to crush the grapes when everything could be mechanized? It's because the wine doesn't ferment very long before the spirit is added and fermentation is stopped (only two or three days). Thus, the winemaker has a problem: how to get as much color and flavorful extract out of the grape skins in a short time. The beauty of the human foot is that it can really crush the berries well; yet the foot is still soft enough not to pulverize the seeds and stems, which would make the port too bitter and tannic.

PORT SHIPPERS AT AN EARLY AGE

they do in Champagne. When this happens, they take their best stuff, blend the wines from the different grapes until they have just the right mix for their "house style," age it in wood for two or three years, then bottle it (without filtering) and let it age in the bottle.

The best vintage ports benefit from aging in the bottle for twenty or thirty years, or even more! Since it wasn't filtered, the port "throws a deposit" as it ages. Therefore, when you store it, you have to be careful always to keep the label up, so the sediment falls on the other side. That's why it must be decanted before serving. In general, this is the most expensive kind of port. It winds up being a very deep, dark purple color, with big fruit and spice character and a gorgeous satiny texture.

The other style of high-end port is called wood-aged *tawny port* (this is the *serious* tawny). As with vintage port, the wines are carefully blended, then aged for at least six years. Usually what you'll see in wineshops are tawnies labeled "10 year," "20 year," "30 year," or "40 year," with prices to match. Tawny port is a dif-

> **At formal dinners in Portugal, white port is usually served as an apéritif, then everybody rushes through the food so they can get to dessert, at which point tawny is served, followed by vintage.**

ferent color than vintage port—much browner. Rather than fruit and spice aromas and flavors, it features caramel, vanilla, butterscotch, hazelnuts, that sort of thing. If vintage port is like satin, tawny port is like velvet.

Just as the wine world is divided into people who like Bordeaux and people who like Burgundy, the port world is divided into those who like vintage and those who'd sell their mother for tawny. In other words, one is not inherently better than the other.

If you want to try the vintage style of port, but can't afford them, have no place to cellar them, or don't have the patience, you might want to check out a *single-quinta vintage port*. To produce this, the port shipper takes wine from a harvest year that wasn't quite good enough to be declared vintage, and makes a blend of wines from grapes only from one particular *quinta*. Then they age it in wood for two or three years, just like vintage port, bottle it, slap the harvest year on the label, and then age it in bottle a few years. One of the nice things about single-*quinta* vintages is that they're ready to drink upon release, and they're less expensive than true vintage port.

Q: How long should you age a vintage port before drinking it?
A: It depends totally on the particular year and shipper. For instance, I recently had a bottle of vintage 1976 Fonseca that was ready to drink, while a 1977 Taylor Fladgate won't be at its best for some years yet. It's best to consult a reliable source for any particular example, either a trusted wine merchant or a book with comprehensive tasting notes for port.

Late bottled vintage (LBV): These are ports made from single vintages, also that weren't quite as good as "declared" vintages, and bottled between four and six years after harvest, at which point, they're ready to drink.

White port: We don't see a whole lot of it in the United States, but you can occasionally pick up a bottle of this port made from several white-grape varieties. It's made in a simple style, but it's lovely as an apéritif, especially served with green olives or almonds, as they do in Portugal.

Q: Why do so many of the port shippers have English-sounding names?
A: Historically, the English bought French wine. But when England and France went to war in the 1600s, England started looking to Portugal for wine. The two countries became pals, port was invented as a way to preserve the wine for easier shipping, and lots of English people moved to Portugal and set up shop in the fledgling port trade.

Sherry

Sherry is Spain's famous fortified wine. It is known in Spain as Jerez, after its hometown of Jerez de la Frontera; in France it is called Xérès. Bottles of sherry list all three names on the label.

However, just because Spain and Portugal are next-door neighbors doesn't mean that port and sherry have much in common, other than that they're both fortified. They don't! Except for one type of dessert sherry, most sherry is much less viscous than port, much less sweet—some of it is totally dry—and it never has a year on the label.

Unfortunately, one of the most fascinating wines in the world has gotten a bum rap in this country because when most people hear the word "sherry" they think of sweet cream sherries, which, by the way, people in Spain pretty much ignore. However, they do enjoy a glass of crisp, cold, very dry fino sherry every day—it's what everyone drinks with the omnipresent early-evening snack of tapas. I'm predicting a rise in popularity here.

Sherry, in case you're wondering, is made mostly from the Palomino grape along the southwest coast of Spain. Unlike table wine, for which winemakers keep the oxygen out of the barrels, for sherries, barrels are filled only partway, to let a lot of oxygen in. This is why sherry has a slightly oxidized taste, which is desirable in sherry (and Madeira) and not in other wines. (When other wines smell like sherry we call them *maderized,* and throw them out.) But depending on the quality of the grapes, in what kind of soil they were grown, and even the location of the *bodega,* many different styles of sherry will be possible.

FINO, AMONTILLADO, AND MANZANILLA: THREE TYPES OF FINO

Fino: After the grapes are pressed and the must has fermented, sometimes a yeast starts to grow on the surface of the wine, one that feeds on the young wine and the oxygen. This is called a *flor.* Once this starts happening, the winemaker knows the wine will be a fino of some sort. The wine is left to develop in cask, then

TIP FROM CABERNET FRANK
Fino-type sherries should be consumed shortly after they're opened—don't keep them for much more than a week in the fridge. Oloroso-type sherries may be kept, unrefrigerated, several weeks after opening, sometimes longer.

it is racked, and fortified to 15 1/2% alcohol, if it hasn't reached that on its own. If the flor continues to thrive on top of the wine after that, it will remain a fino, and be bottled and sold as such while it's still fresh. Fino is pale, dry, and delicate, and the *flor* gives it a very unusual characteristic aroma and flavor. It's delicious chilled, either as an apéritif or with soups or seafood.

Some finos will be left to age in oak casks—these will become *amontillados.* A true amontillado requires eight additional years of aging in cask, so it can be more expensive than fino. But true amontillado is a rare treat; most of what you'll see in stores is commercial amontillado, made by using a shortcut "aging" process. Amontillado is golden, dry, and somewhat fuller and richer than fino with a more complex, often nutty aroma. Also good as an apéritif.

Another type of fino is called *manzanilla*. This is made exactly the same way as a fino (with *flor*); it can even be made from grapes from the same vineyard. However, instead of making the wine at a *bodega* in Jerez, the winemaker brings the grapes to a neighboring town called Sanlúcar. Sanlúcar is cooler and damper than Jerez, and the *flor* grows thicker there. The resulting manzanilla-style sherry takes on a lovely seaside-y, almost briny flavor.

OLOROSO SHERRIES
(OLOROSO, CREAM, AND PX)

For *oloroso*-type sherries, the winemaker decides ahead of time that he or she wants to make a wine in a different style than fino. The grapes, either Palomino or a different variety called Pedro Ximénez (also known as PX), may be dried to make a sweet style, or not. These are fortified to 18 percent, so no *flor* can possibly develop. Regular olorosos, aged with more air in the barrel, will be darker and more alcoholic. They can be luxuriously rich and dry at the same time. If a lot of PX grapes or dried Palomino grapes are used, the resulting sherry will be a *cream* sherry (you've probably heard of Harvey's Bristol Cream). These are sweet sherries, silky and rich, best drunk after dinner. For sherry labeled PX or Pedro Ximénez, only sun-dried PX grapes are used. This sherry, drunk for dessert, or even poured on top of ice cream, turns out thick, almost black, and sweet, and tastes raisiny.

THE *SOLERA* SYSTEM

Partly to control the growth of the *flor,* and partly to keep a consistent house style, sherries are aged in an elaborate system of barrels, easiest to understand if you picture them as rows stacked on top of each other. Each row is called a *criadera*.

TIP FROM CABERNET FRANK
There's no such thing as vintage sherry.

The wine in the bottom row (the solera) is the oldest. To work the system, a couple times a year the winemaker takes some wine out of the solera, puts it into the barrels in the second level, and replaces it with some of the younger wine. Then he takes some out of the second level, and puts it into the third level, etc., all the way to the top row, which is the newest. The barrels are never more than two-thirds full, since they need the oxygen to develop *flor* and to acquire the oxidized flavor peculiar to sherry. The *flor* needs to keep eating fresh wine, so that's also periodically added to the system.

Why do you need to know this incredibly boring and technical winemaking information? It will remind you why there's no vintage year on a bottle of sherry. You may see something that looks like a year, such as 1729, but that is the date that the particular *solera* was established.

Madeira

This fortified wine from an island off Portugal used to be incredibly popular in the United States. In fact, before Prohibition, it was probably the most popular wine for the upper classes on the East Coast. It has now fallen somewhat out of favor.

Madeira may be labeled dry, medium dry, medium sweet, rich, or sweet. If the bottle sports one of those descriptors, it means the wine didn't contain at least 85 percent of a particular grape, so it couldn't be labeled varietally. If it does contain 85 percent of one variety, it'll be labeled *Sercial, Verdelho, Bual,* or *Malmsey,* with Sercial being the driest and Malmsey the sweetest.

Then you'll see some indication of how long the wine has been aged. "Granel," the cheapest, is aged about eighteen months. Next comes "Finest" (three years), "Reserve" (five years), "Special Reserve" (about ten years), "Extra Reserve" (fifteen years). "Vintage" Madeira is aged at least twenty years in cask and two more in bottle.

Madeira can age for an incredibly long time, some for even a hundred years. *"Rancio,"* a sort of rich oxidized taste that people describe either as "cheesy" or weirdly fruity, is a taste to look for.

Vermouth

I've been fond of vermouth, a fortified wine flavored with herbs, for as long as I can remember, though lots of people can't stand the slightly bitter flavor. These days, it seems it's making a bit of a comeback. Vermouth got its name from wormwood, which was one of the original flavorings.

Today vermouth represents a wide range of herb-flavored fortified wines. They can be totally dry, slightly sweet, more than slightly sweet; white, red, or yellow; and they're generally French or Italian. Vermouth is made from very simple table wine, then fortified and usually sweetened.

Vermouth is a simple drink, more like a cocktail than a wine, so people don't stand around swirling it and discussing the aromas they find. It's used as an ingredient in many cocktails (such as martinis and Manhattans), but vermouth is delicious on its own as an apéritif.

Vin Doux Naturel

This category of French wine, usually made from either Muscat or Grenache, translates literally as "natural sweet wine." However,

---

Some Vermouths You May Know

Dry, White Cinzano (Italy)
Cinzano Bianco (slightly sweet)
Red Cinzano
Punt e Mes (Italy)
Lillet (France, both red and white, slightly sweet)
Boissière (France, dry white)
Martini & Rossi (Italy, red or white, sweet or dry)

---

it actually refers to a wine fortified with a neutral grape spirit. Go figure. In any case, the result is sweet.

Banyuls is regarded as the best of France's *vins doux naturels*. This wine, from the Languedoc-Roussillon region in the southeast of France, is made from Grenache, fortified, and either bottled (red) or aged in wood (tawny). The appellations are either "Banyuls," "Banyuls Grand Cru," or "Banyuls Rancio," which means the barrels were left out in the sun to oxidize partially, giving it the *rancio* taste sometimes associated with Madeira. It's not on a lot of wine lists at the moment, but since it's becoming more popular in France, we may start to see it.

Muscat de Beaumes-de-Venise: You've heard about this one, made from the Muscat Blanc à Petits Grains variety in the Rhône. This golden wine has a gorgeous, floral, orangey nose and a velvety texture. It's great for dessert (I like it instead of, rather than with).

Other *vins doux naturels*, which you'll probably never bump into unless you travel in France: *Maury, Rasteau, Rivesaltes.*

Vin de Liqueur

These are similar to *vins doux naturels*, but they have to be fortified with a spirit that comes from their own region.

Pineau des Charentes, from the Cognac region, is the only one

I've ever seen in the U.S. Legend in Cognac has it that it was created by accident, when someone poured some cognac into a barrel containing grape juice. In any case, they take red or white wine and fortify it with cognac, the famous brandy made in the region. Both red and wine Pineau are charming as apéritifs, served chilled.

Floc de Gascogne: Basically the Armagnac version of the same thing, but it only comes in white. In case you're not familiar with armagnac, it's a famous brandy, similar to cognac, but from the Armagnac region.

Ratafia de Champagne: This *vin de liqueur* from the Champagne region is made by adding a local brandy made from the same grapes as champagne to champagne that has just started fermenting.

Australian Fortified Wines

Australians love fortified wines, and they make some pretty good ones.

Liqueur Muscat, made from our friend the Muscat grape, left to dry on the vine, then long-aged in wood, is much darker than Muscat de Beaumes-de-Venise.

Liqueur Tokay: Same technique, but made from the Muscadelle variety, which the Australians conveniently call Tokay.

American Fortified Wines

In California, there are several:

Ficklin Vineyards makes vintage and nonvintage California port.

Quady Winery makes Essencia, a luscious fortified orange Muscat, and Elysium, a fortified black Muscat.

Preston makes a delicious fortified Muscat, called Muscat Brûlé.

IF YOU FORGET EVERYTHING ELSE
YOU'VE READ IN CHAPTER NINE,
JUST REMEMBER THIS:

1. Fortified wines aren't necessarily dessert wines.
2. Vintage port and aged tawny port are the fanciest two ports.
3. Single-*quinta* port is a great alternative to vintage port.
4. Sherry can be dry or sweet, and never has a vintage date.
5. Sherry gets its distinctive flavor from contact with oxygen.
6. Vermouth is a fortified wine.

Part III

HOW TO BUY AND ORDER WINE

Chapter Ten

IN A RESTAURANT

By now you know quite a bit about wine: gone are the days of walking into a restaurant, only to freeze up when you're handed the wine list. Watch how your quality of life will soar!

But wait—you may find that you've just traded in one kind of restaurant angst for another. For those of us who enjoy wine, dining in a restaurant can be fraught with a new kind of peril.

Here's the way it goes: You waltz into a restaurant, your table is ready, you sit down, and the server hands menus all around. And walks away.

Where's the wine list? Do I look like someone who definitely won't want to order a bottle of wine? Do I look cheap? Am I so poorly dressed that I look like I don't even belong in the restaurant? Just when I'm considering psychotherapy, I step back and say, "Hey, wait a minute. Isn't it much better for the restaurant if I *do* order wine? Then why do they make it so difficult?"

If you should find yourself in this predicament, now is the time to take action. "Excuse me," you'll insist as the server swooshes by, on his way to somewhere else. "Can we please please please please please see a wine list?"

Okay, the list lands on your lap. Now what?

You have two choices: the first is to make your way through the list with absolutely no help—which assumes that the listings for all the wines are complete, vintages aren't left out, etc. Make your decision, and order.

The second is to ask for some help. The kind of help you get depends on the kind of restaurant you're in. If it's a first-class restaurant, you may ask to see the wine steward (sommelier). If the restaurant purports to be a swanky joint, and they laugh when you ask for the wine steward, turn up your nose and say, "Is there anyone—a wine director, or anyone at all—who's familiar with the wine list?"

If it's not a very fancy place, they probably won't have a sommelier, in which case you'll have to depend on your waiter. Good luck.

DOPING THE WINE LIST

Before the waiter or wine steward gets here, however, there are several judgments we can make simply by looking at how the list is put together. By looking for a few things, we'll be able to predict, without even recognizing most of the wines on the list,

whether the restaurant cares about wine, whether the wines are likely to be served properly, whether the house is likely to pull the old switcheroo and bring an inferior bottle or vintage, what the general quality level of the wines will be, and how reasonable or unreasonable the markup is. Why is all this important? Because it will let you know whether or not you can feel confident simply placing yourself in the restaurant's hands by randomly picking something or seeking the staff's advice, in which case it won't matter if you don't know the wines on the list.

All this just by looking at the list?

You bet. Here goes:

Look at the list, and ask yourself the following questions:

How is it organized? Many lists are separated initially into white wines and red wines and then, within those categories, into regions (i.e., French white wines, California white wines, Italian white wines, etc.). Other lists will be organized first into regions and then separated into white and red (and sometimes "sparkling") within those regions. Sometimes there are two separate lists—a regular list, and a "reserve" list, containing special, usually more prestigious and expensive, offerings. Once you've figured out how they've organized it, ask yourself this: Does the organization seem to make sense?

Are there selections from different regions? If so, does the list identify those regions? Do the regions chosen make sense for the restaurant? Every restaurant does not need to stock wines from many different regions just to prove that it cares about wine, but if it is a very long and comprehensive list, it's nice to see different regions represented. If an Italian restaurant decides to offer mostly (or even all) Italian wines, that's probably reasonable. Many California restaurants offer only California wines, which makes sense if you believe that it's best to drink the local wines of whatever region you're in. (If you travel in Europe, for instance, the local wines often go best with the local cuisine.) But say you're in a German restaurant, and there are no German wines, or very few; only French and California selections. Isn't that kind of strange and disappointing?

Is the information complete for each listing? Are vintage years, for

instance, listed for all the wines? Is the producer clearly identified? Is the region, district, AVA, or commune listed?

Do any obvious mistakes jump out at you? Is Nouveau Beaujolais
listed under the Bordeaux section? Are California sparkling wines
or Spanish cavas listed as "champagne"? Incomplete or inaccurate
information indicates that the restaurant probably doesn't care
much about wine. (Competent wine directors are usually pretty
anal characters.) In this case, you can surmise that just randomly
picking one or relying on the waiter's advice won't be a good
idea—chances are the restaurant hasn't bothered to train its staff
about its wines. If you decide to order something, you'll have to
ask the server to bring out bottles so you can see exactly what they
are yourself before you order one. If this seems to upset the server,
tell her that she should urge the manager to make sure the wine
list is accurate and complete. You should also remember when you
leave the tip that it's not the server's fault if the management can't
get its act together when it comes to wine.

On the other hand, if listings seem very complete, you may be
in a restaurant wine haven. You may notice, for instance, that the
different districts within a region are broken down into sublist-
ings. California will be broken down into Sonoma, Napa, Mendocino, etc., or Bordeaux will be broken down into Médoc,
Pomerol, Graves, etc. Particular wine and food pairings may be
suggested somewhere, and you may recognize interesting or unusual bottles. All this suggests that someone will be able to help
you further, if necessary.

Is the list long or short? If it's long, it can mean a number of
things. Restaurants with a lot of money sometimes use this tactic
to impress us. Sometimes it *is* impressive—perhaps the restaurant
offers interesting selections in a wide variety of styles that have
obviously been cellared for a long time, at reasonable prices, and
presents them completely and well. But sometimes a long list is
not impressive. After all, anyone who has a fortune can hire a
consultant, put together a fabulous cellar, and then ask patrons to
pay through the nose for it.

Sometimes a small, well-selected list can be the most impressive of all. Imagine: You're a restaurateur or the wine director of a modest restaurant, and you have to pick about thirty wines, all of which will fit on one page. Think of all the different wines you've read about in this book. How would you even begin to go about choosing? Would you concentrate on only one region, or cover a few? Don't forget that you have to include wines over a broad price range that also go with a range of food.

Are there half bottles or by-the-glass offerings? If so, are there more than one or two? Are they, as far as you can tell, well chosen? If there are several interesting offerings in this area, it probably means the restaurant cares about wine.

> **TIP FROM CABERNET FRANK**
> "Sommelier" comes from the French word *somme,* one of the meanings of which is "burden." The original meaning of *sommelier* was "butler."

Now look at the pricing. (I'll bet you have already!) Are there a good number of affordable selections? What if you feel like something more celebratory—can you find more special wines? And does the price of the more special wines actually reflect something of greater value?

Find a wine for which you know the price. To do this, you may have to memorize the store-bought price for a few bottles commonly found on wine lists. Make sure you don't apply a regular bottling price for a wine listed as a "reserve."

For French wines, consider a bottle that you happen to know is an inexpensive *cru bourgeois* Bordeaux. Since it probably won't indicate *cru bourgeois* right on the list, keep a few of them in mind: Château Larose-Trintaudon, Château Greysac, Château Puy Blanquet. If you see relatively young wines in these categories (five years old or less) priced over twenty-five or thirty dollars, you may be in for a rip-off. The same holds true for a Côtes du Rhône, or a Beaujolais Cru: these are inexpensive wines, and you shouldn't be asked to pay too much for them in a restaurant.

226

How to Spot an Overpriced Wine List

Here are some wholesale prices—in other words, what the restaurant pays—for a few California wines (and one Italian) that often turn up on wine lists. Prices may vary slightly throughout the country depending on distributor, and the restaurant may get a further discount for buying in bulk, but they'll never cost much more than this. Cut out this page, or photocopy it, and keep a copy in your wallet so you can surreptitiously whip it out to check out wine lists. Note that these are the prices at press time.

1992 Robert Mondavi Chardonnay Napa Valley—
wholesale $11
1992 Robert Mondavi Chardonnay Carneros—
wholesale $15.50
1992 Sonoma-Cutrer Chardonnay "Russian River Ranches"—wholesale $9.58
1992 Kistler Chardonnay—wholesale $16.58
1992 Beringer Chardonnay Napa Valley Private Reserve—wholesale $13.33
1993 Saintsbury Pinot Noir, Carneros—wholesale $12
1992 Saintsbury Pinot Noir, Carneros Garnet—
wholesale $7.33
1990 B.V. Pinot Noir Carneros Napa Valley Reserve—wholesale $10.08
1990 Robert Mondavi Cabernet Sauvignon—
wholesale $12.50
1991 Caymus Cabernet Sauvignon—wholesale $14.75
1992 Antinori Santa Cristina—wholesale $6

If a restaurant is charging more than two and a half times their cost, they may be overcharging you.

Now look at what the restaurant charges for the wine. Don't forget that the restaurant pays wholesale prices, generally 65 to 75 percent of suggested retail. Restaurants commonly say that their average markup is two and a half times (250 percent) of wholesale, yet it's very common to see markups of 300 or even 400 or 500 percent of wholesale. Take a 1990 Robert Mondavi Cabernet Sauvignon, which I recently saw on a wine list for forty dollars. As you can see from the sidebar, wholesale on that bottle is $12.50. That means the restaurant marked it up 3.2 times (40 divided by 12.50 is 3.2), which is 320 percent. Is that reasonable? You be the judge.

On the other hand, it's usually the least expensive wines on the list that suffer from the highest percentage of markup. The same list that had the 1990 Mondavi Cab also offers a 1982 Château Haut-Brion for $160; a discount retail price for the same bottle is $119.99, and one wholesaler offers it for $94.50. That means that if the restaurant bought it from a wholesaler today, at the going rate the markup would be around 70 percent, compared with a 320 percent markup for the less expensive wine. Nevertheless, the house is still making $65.50 profit just on that one bottle.

Don't forget to figure in the equation that the restaurant may be cellaring the wine. In other words, the restaurant is buying it upon release, and holding it until it has aged enough to serve, which means it pays less for it when it's younger. It still incurs costs, however, in maintaining a cellar, which in some areas can be rather expensive.

In California and other wine areas, markup routinely may be much less than the allegedly average 250 percent—more like 50 to 75 percent over what they pay. Bravo for those restaurants: they help the wineries sell wine, they help their customers afford it, and they help themselves by making it inexpensive for people to educate themselves. The more people grow accustomed to having wine with dinner, of course, the more wine restaurants will ultimately sell.

Wine Bargains in New York City Restaurants

In New York City, which is not in the heart of wine country by any stretch, markups can be outrageous, as they are in most American cities. However, there are a couple of restaurants with innovative wine programs that make it easy for patrons to try new wines, and they've proven to be lucrative for the restaurants.

Cité restaurant stunned the Big Apple in 1994 and 1995 by offering unlimited glasses of four different high-quality wines for no extra charge with its fixed-price three-course dinner, after eight P.M. The wines change every quarter; at press time they include a nonvintage Jordan "J" sparkling wine from California, a Puligny-Montrachet 1992 from Vochet, a Gevrey-Chambertin 1991 from Labouré-Roi, and a Heitz Cellars 1989 Cabernet. What madness possesses them to do this? Since Cité is located in the theater district, it is always busy before eight o'clock, but it used to empty out when all the shows started. By offering a wine special after eight, the restaurant hoped to draw in non-theatergoers. Did it work? You bet. The place has been packed ever since. Let's hope Cité keeps the wine special.

Century Café, also in NYC's theater district, offered great wines for one dollar over wholesale for a year and a half, which went a long way toward getting people to try things they wouldn't have been able to afford otherwise. They recently changed their program, and are now limiting markup to a maximum of fifteen dollars over cost. A bottle that costs them forty dollars will be available for fifty-five dollars on the list, which is about what it would cost you in a store. Kudos to brave restaurants such as these! Such bold approaches wind up generating more business for the restaurant, a new generation of wine lovers, and everybody wins!

Okay, smarty-pants: maybe the restaurant cares about wine. But does it care about food and wine? After all, it's a restaurant. Think about how these wines will probably go with whatever you know about the food. I recently went to a seafood restaurant, and the wine list consisted of about half whites and half reds. Okay, fine—but the reds were all, without exception, California Cabernets! Did you ever try to drink California Cabernet with filet of sole? These wines didn't go with anything on the menu.

On the other hand, if a simple French bistro offers a few simple French wines, that's great. And if you're in a restaurant on the West Coast specializing in Pacific Rim cuisine, and the restaurant happens to list a few Rieslings, you can figure right away that you're in fat city. You get the idea.

Okay, now let's put our wine-list questions into practice.

Take a look at the list (on pages 232–233) from Joe's Restaurant, a popular eatery in Venice, California, and read through the questions one by one.

How is it organized? First come by-the-glass selections, divided into white, red, and sparkling. Then come bottle selections. Whites come first—California, then French. Next, reds—California, then French. Then come half bottles, then champagne and sparkling wine. No problem there.

Are there wines from different regions? Of the thirty-four bottle selections, thirty are American, and four French. Germany, Italy, Spain, Australia, etc., aren't represented. Is this appropriate? Well, considering that Joe's is a restaurant specializing in California cuisine with some French influence, I think so. Where two prices are listed, one is for wine served by the glass, one for wine served by the bottle.

Is each listing complete? Yes. Or almost. The column on the left dutifully lists the vintage years. Now look at the first wine listed under "California White Wines." 1993 is the vintage, Ojai Vineyards is the producer, Sauvignon Blanc is the varietal, Santa Barbara County is the AVA. That's complete! Now look under "French Red Wines." 1990 is the vintage and Châteauneuf-du-Pape is the region, which as we know in France signifies the type of wine. Domaine du Haut des Terres Blanches is the producer.

There's only one listing that's not complete, and that's under the "Wines by the Glass" sparkling category. See it? N/V means "non-vintage," that's fine, Bouvet is the producer, fine, *brut* is the style, fine. But then, instead of a region it says "Sparkling Wine." Well, we knew it was a sparkling wine, but where is it from? France? California? As it turns out, Bouvet-Ladubay is a Loire Valley producer of sparkling wine owned by Taittinger, the famous champagne house; this one is from the Saumur appellation.

Are there any obvious mistakes? No.

Is the list long or short? This is what I consider to be a small yet very well-chosen wine list. It's totally appropriate for the size and feeling of Joe's menu, which is also small and personal, casual, yet serious and elegant at the same time.

Are there half bottles or by-the-glass selections? Yes to both. Joe's offers three whites, three reds, plus the sparkling wine by the glass. Lots of restaurants would offer three Chardonnays, but Joe's has more imagination and gives us a Chenin Blanc. How refreshing! As for the reds, we get a Cab from Napa, a Merlot from Santa Barbara, and a Bonny Doon proprietary red (which happens to contain a combination of Rhône and Italian varieties). Something for everyone! Among the half bottles, there's a Gewürztraminer, three Chardonnays, a Cabernet, a Sangiovese, and a champagne.

The beauty of wine by the glass is that if two people are dining and one doesn't drink, the other, the wine lover, can enjoy wine with dinner and not have to polish off a whole bottle. When I'm in this situation, I often have a glass of white with my first course and a glass of red with my main course. Half bottles are great for two people dining together. That way the couple can start with a half bottle of white with their first course and then a bottle (or even a half) of red with the main course.

How is the pricing? Bottles run between nineteen and fifty-five dollars. There are fourteen bottles for twenty-five dollars and under, which is pretty good; about two fifths of the list. Now let's look for something for which we know a price: How about the B.V. Pinot Noir Carneros Reserve at thirty

RESTAURANT

WINES BY THE GLASS

WHITE	Glass	Bottle
1993 Navarro Vineyards—Chardonnay—Mendocino	5.00	19.00
1993 Bonny Doon Vineyards—Pacific Rim Chenin Blanc	4.00	16.00
1992 Qupé—Chardonnay—Santa Barbara County	6.50	25.00

RED		
1991 Glass Mountain—Cabernet Sauvignon—Napa Valley	5.00	19.00
1992 Brander—Merlot—Santa Barbara County	5.50	22.00
1993 Bonny Doon Vineyards—Ca' del Solo Big House Red	4.00	16.00

SPARKLING		
N/V Bouvet—Brut—Sparkling Wine	5.00	20.00

CALIFORNIA WHITE WINES	Bottle
1993 Ojai Vineyards—Sauvignon Blanc—Santa Barbara County	21.00
1992 Buttonwood Farm—Sauvignon Blanc—Santa Barbara County	20.00
1992 Silverado Vineyards—Chardonnay—Napa Valley	26.00
1992 Markham Vineyards—Barrel-Fermented Chardonnay —Napa Valley	25.00
1992 Mount Veeder Winery—Chardonnay—Napa Valley	30.00
1993 Byron Vineyards—Chardonnay—Santa Barbara County	28.00
1993 Acacia Winery—Chardonnay "Carneros"—Napa Valley	29.00
1993 Patz & Hall—Chardonnay—Napa Valley	39.00
1991 Thomas Hsi—Chardonnay—Napa Valley	33.00
1992 Long Vineyards—Chardonnay—Napa Valley	42.00
1992 Sanford Winery—Chardonnay Barrel Select "Unfiltered"— Santa Barbara	45.00

FRENCH WHITE WINES

1992 Mâcon Villages—Prisse	19.00
1992 Sancerre—"Chavignol"—Paul Cotat	36.00

CALIFORNIA RED WINES

1991 Cain Cellars "Cuvée"—Meritage Blend—Napa Valley	22.00
1991 Morgan Winery—Cabernet Sauvignon—Carmel Valley	26.00
1988 Carmenet Vineyard—Cabernet Sauvignon—Sonoma Valley	27.00
1990 B. R. Cohn Winery—Cabernet Sauvignon—Olive Hill Vineyard—Sonoma Valley	34.00
1992 Silverado Vineyards—Merlot—Napa Valley	28.00
1992 Ojai Vineyards—Syrah—Santa Barbara County	27.00
1990 B.V.—Pinot Noir—Carneros Reserve	30.00
1987 Stags' Leap Winery—Petite Sirah—Napa Valley	35.00
1988 Stags' Leap Winery—Reserve Petite Sirah—Napa Valley	45.00

OREGON RED WINES

1992 Benton Lane—Pinot Noir—Oregon	22.00
1992 Adelsheim Vineyard—Pinot Noir—Yamhill County	25.00

FRENCH RED WINES

1990 Châteauneuf-du-Pape—Domaine du Haut des Terres Blanches	
	26.00

CHAMPAGNE & SPARKLING WINE

1991 Iron Horse Vineyards—"Wedding Cuvée"	33.00
N/V Veuve Clicquot—France	55.00

WINES BY THE HALF BOTTLE

1992 Navarro Vineyards—Gewürztraminer—Anderson Valley	12.00
1991 Silverado Vineyards—Chardonnay—Napa Valley	14.00
1993 Qupé—Chardonnay—Santa Barbara County	15.00
1992 Acacia Winery—Chardonnay "Carneros"—Napa Valley	16.00
1989 Carmenet Vineyard—Cabernet Sauvignon—Sonoma Valley	16.00
1992 Noceto—Sangiovese—Shenandoah Valley	11.00
N/V Veuve Clicquot—Champagne—France	29.00

dollars. Wholesale on that, as you can see from our chart, is
$10.08, which is 297 percent markup. As we know 250 per-
cent is the purported average. It might bother me more that
the restaurant pockets almost twenty dollars here, even considering they have to cellar it, open it, provide glasses, etc.,
but as you can see on pages 259–260, food prices are so reasonable (thirty dollars for a four-course fixed-price menu)
that I can't get too upset about it.

Do the wines make sense for the kinds of food on the menu? On the
wine list, there are an awful lot of Chardonnays under "California Whites"—nine, compared with two Sauvignon Blancs. This
is probably because they are so popular.

But there's a second reason as well. Flip to pages 259–260 in
the next chapter, and take a look at Joe's menu, along with an explanation of which of the wines would complement them. After
reading the next chapter, you'll start to understand exactly why
Chardonnay is so well represented. Many of the first and second
courses, such as Belgian endive salad with roasted pears, walnuts,
and Fourme d'Ambert cheese; grilled shrimp on creamy polenta,
crispy leeks, lobster sauce; roasted quail filled with pears and apple bacon, are rich enough to stand up to Chardonnay, which is a
very rich wine. Several of the main courses would work with
Chardonnay, too. However, it's nice that there are Sauvignon
Blancs as well, since Joe's also offers a nice selection of fairly light
or grilled first courses.

Now look under reds. Three Cabernets, plus a Meritage,
which is mostly Cabernet, from three different AVAs. Two Merlots from Napa. Two Pinot Noirs from Oregon and one from
Carneros (both great regions for Pinot). One Syrah, two Petite
Sirahs, and one Châteauneuf. Lots of big reds here! That's appropriate for this restaurant, though; the menu features hearty
main courses such as roasted venison and grilled rib-eye steak.
And the three Pinots go really well with lots of crossover items
the restaurant serves as the second course of its four-course
fixed-price menu, or main courses such as the roasted pork tenderloin (a signature dish at Joe's), grilled salmon, dorade with red
wine sauce, and so on.

So? If you're very satisfied with the answers to most of these questions, you can fairly safely conclude that you're probably looking at a pretty good wine list. This makes it safer just to randomly pick something you don't know.

THE BEST OF ALL POSSIBLE WORLDS
Of course there is occasionally, in the best restaurants, entirely another scenario. You waltz in, get seated, the captain hands you menus *and* a wine list, gives you time to ponder your dinner order, then a wine steward comes over in a friendly and unintimidating manner and says, "May I be of any assistance in your wine selection?"

People with oenophobia regard such a character with suspicion. "I know," they think to themselves, "that jerk just wants to make me look dumb in front of my friends." Or, "That broad thinks I'm cheap, and she wants to make sure I'm bullied into ordering *something*." How wrong they are! The wine steward is there to *help* you. He or she often doesn't really care whether you order anything or not. If you don't want wine, "just say no." If you *do* want help, the wine steward's job is to make life easier—not harder—for you.

NOW WHAT?
The moment has come: it's time to choose. If the wine steward has shown his face before you've really had a chance to look at the menu, tell him to bug off for a minute. If you feel like ordering something right away, you might have a glass of champagne or sparkling wine, always a perfect, elegant apéritif. Most good restaurants will offer at least one by the glass. Or be a trailblazer and try a glass of fino sherry.

After everyone's had a chance to look at the menu, ask what they're having. Think about the kind of wine that goes well with the first course. Usually, it will be white, as first courses tend to be a little lighter—salad, seafood, or vegetable-oriented. (Chapter Eleven will help you further in matching wines with the flavors of the food that you order.)

In most cases, unless everyone's having seafood or grilled or lightly sauced poultry, you'll want a red for the main course. A typical main-course scenario in a group of four people, however, could include a wide range of wine needs. One person might be having lamb or beef. That's easy—they'll want a big red. One person is having roast chicken. Easy, especially if the sauce is robust—they could have just about any red or a rich white. One person might be having a pasta, which can often go with red or white, though a big red might overwhelm it, depending on the ingredients. The last person might be having seafood.

Youch! What do you do? You could start by saying to the seafood person, are you sure that's really what you want? If you're not the manipulative, bullying type, however, take another tack. If the seafood person is having something very delicate—say, sole meunière—I'd probably see if they'd be willing to go for an appropriate white by the glass or the half bottle, because then your job with the other three is pretty easy. If the seafood is something like roast salmon in red wine sauce, you're in luck. In these types of cases—a lamb chop, roast chicken, pasta, salmon, there is one kind of wine that goes with all: anything made from Pinot Noir. Pinot Noirs and Burgundies are delicate enough not to overpower the salmon or pasta, yet bold enough to stand up to red meat. To my mind, it's the grape variety that goes best with the widest range of foods.

If you're dining just with one other person, you might well be close enough to that person to talk about a wine after you've both thought about a couple of possible main courses, but haven't quite decided. Say you're trying to decide between the duck breast in blackberry sauce and the braised lamb shank, and your pal is deciding between the filet mignon with green peppercorn sauce and the grilled tuna with olives and roast tomatoes. Maybe you ought to look at the wine list. If there's a Pinot Noir from Oregon you're dying to try, you should have the duck breast and the tuna. If it's a red Bordeaux you're after, stick with the lamb shank and the filet mignon. Or you could go with the duck and the Bordeaux, because the blackberry sauce will pick up the wonderful black-fruit character of the Cabernet and/or Merlot grape variety. Get it? Just think of them as combos.

All right—we're almost there. If you can zero in on the list with a producer you want to try and can afford, great—you're ready to roll. If you need some help, motion your friendly wine steward over again.

In fine restaurants, usually the wine steward will only approach after you've ordered so she can look at what you'll be eating and use your chosen dishes as a guide. But you might want to select a wine before you've made that final decision. If so, just say something like this: "We'd like to start out with a Sauvignon Blanc for our first course, but I'm not familiar with these producers." You might tell her what you are considering from the menu.

The question of price can be sticky, but it doesn't have to be. If you're among people you're close to, you can add, "We'd like something in the eighteen-to-twenty-two-dollar range." If that's not comfortable, you might point to the part of the wine list that lists the producers and say, "I was wondering about this one." The sensitive sommelier will usually suggest something in approximately the same range. If not, she's a jerk. Try not to point to the price column, however, or the steward will think you're ordering by price alone without regard to the wines.

Next the sommelier might ask you, "What style of Sauvignon Blanc do you prefer?" That's sort of putting you on the spot, so it's much more polite if she says, "Do you prefer a particular style of Sauvignon Blanc—oaked or unoaked?" If you don't know, tell her that, and she'll help guide you to one. Or if you're embarrassed to say you don't know, just say that you like both styles, that you're just interested in a good example of either. Regardless, don't forget that this person is here to help you, albeit with your guidance.

This kind of conversation is how you elicit help. It all becomes much easier if it's a return visit to a restaurant where you've received good wine advice before—you'll be more comfortable relying on the wine steward or knowledgeable waiter.

Here are two pages—the Bordeaux section—from the wine list at Le Chantilly, one of New York City's most elegant French restaurants.

Le Chantilly

RED BORDEAUX — (1)

			Full Bottle		Half Bottle	
(2)	30	Château Le Pontet, Saint-Emilion	1986	26.– (4)		
	31	Château La Cardonne, Médoc	1989	29.–		
	32	Château Greysac, Médoc	1988	28.–		
	33	Château Martinet, Saint-Emilion	1989	32.–		
	34	Château Simard, Saint-Emilion	1985	39.–	1985	20.–
(5)	35	Château Fourcas-Hosten, Médoc	1989	32.–		
	36	Château Bouscaut, Graves	1989	42.–		
	37	Château La Loup, Saint-Emilion	1988	35.–		
	38	Château Haut-Faugères	1990	38.–		
	39	Château Citran, Haut-Médoc	1989	46.–		
(6)	40	Château Calon-Ségur, Saint-Estèphe	1989	58.–		
	41	Château La Lagune, Haut-Médoc	1990	58.–		
(7)	42	Château Gruaud Larose, St. Julien	1985	75.– (8)		
	43	Château de Sales, Pomerol	1989	42.– (9)		
	44	Château Beychevelle, St. Julien	1984	45.–		
	44A	Château Brane-Cantenac, Margaux	1988	58.–		
(10)	45	Château Carruades de Lafite Rothschild, Pauillac	1986	65.–		
	46	Château Talbot, St. Julien	1988	62.–	1989	33.–
	47	Château Prieuré-Lichine, Margaux	1990	55.–		
	48	Château Raussan-Ségla, Margaux	1985	75.–		

(11) 49   Château Lynch–Bages, Pauillac   1988   88.-
     50   Château La Conseillante, Pomerol   1988   85.-
     50A   Château La Mission Haut-Brion,
             Graves   1981   90.-
                                                    1990   88.-

     51A   Château La Mission Haut-Brion,
(13)   Graves   1986   98.- (12)
     51   Château Cheval Blanc, Saint-Emilion   1987   110.-
     52   Château Margaux   1983   230.-
(14) 53   Château Latour, Pauillac   1981   170.-
     54   Château Haut-Brion, Graves   (15)
             (magnum)   1974   160.-

     55   Château Haut-Brion, Graves   1981   140.-
     56   Château Mouton Rothschild, Pauillac   1981   190.-
     58   Château Lafite Rothschild, Pauillac   1983   190.-
     59   Château Pétrus, Pomerol   1981   580.-

              (16)   WHITE BORDEAUX —(17)

     60   Château Olivier, Graves   1990   46.-
     61   Château Carbonnieux, Graves   1992   45.- (18)
     62   Château Bouscaut, Graves   1989   32.-
     63   Château Margaux, Pavillon Blanc   1990   78.-
     64   Château Haut-Brion Blanc   1987   95.-
(19) 65   Château La Tour Blanche, Sauternes   1989   78.-   (20)
     66   Château Rieussec, Sauternes   1985   65.-   1986   35.-
     67   Château d'Yquem, Sauternes   1987   280.- 1987   150.-
     (21)

NOTES ON LE CHANTILLY LIST

1. This list starts with the largest, most general appellations,
   becoming more and more specific, and generally more
   and more expensive, although it does not tell you
   whether or not each wine is a *cru classé*. As it turns out,
   the first ten wines are not. All of the rest are *crus classés,*

except for the Pomerols, which have never been classified, and a few others noted below. Many of the wines on this list are popular choices for the lists of fine restaurants in America.

2. Refers to the bin number. This is the way many restaurants keep track of their inventory; it helps the server pull out the bottle from the right place in the cellar. If you don't feel like struggling with a difficult pronunciation, you can certainly order by bin number.

3. Producer

4. District

5. All of the Médocs included in the first ten wines are *crus bourgeois,* all from either 1988, an excellent year, or 1989, an outstanding year.

6. Château Citran is also a *cru bourgeois* Médoc. The immodest price tag reflects the widely held opinion that it's one of the best.

7. This is the first *cru classé* bottle on the list. This one is a *troisième cru classé* (third growth); you can see the jump in price from the previous bottle.

8. A *deuxième cru* (second growth). Although 1985 was not as great a vintage as 1989, this one is mature and drinking well, while a 1989 from a *cru classé* is still in its youth.

9. Pomerols have never been classified. Like #50, Château de Sales is a well-known and well-regarded Pomerol.

10. This "second wine" of the *premier cru* Château Lafite is actually called Moulin des Carruades. It's not *cru classé.*

11. This *cinquième cru* (fifth growth) is widely considered to be way underrated in the 1855 classification.

12. A second château owned by the proprietors of Château Haut-Brion, the *premier cru* Graves, though this one is simply *cru classé.*

13. A *premier grand cru classé* and widely considered to be one of the two best Saint-Emilions. 1987 was a difficult year, so ask the sommelier about the particular wine before blindly forking over this kind of dough.

14. All five of the *premier crus* are represented here.

15. A magnum is twice as large as a regular bottle, holding 1,500 ml instead of 750 ml.

16. As we know, Pomerol was never classified, but this is the most expensive—and one of the most famous of all Bordeaux.

17. The first five are all dry white wines; the last three are all sweet wines usually served with dessert or foie gras.

18. Unlike #60, 61, 62, and 64, which are all *cru classé* white Graves, this white wine is from the Médoc, Château Margaux, the *premier cru* from the Margaux commune. Since only red wines were classified in 1855, this wine is called simply a "Bordeaux blanc."

19. A *premier cru* Sauternes.

20. Another *premier cru* Sauternes. Restaurants often feature Sauternes in half bottles; it's so rich and sweet that a little goes a long way.

21. The granddaddy of all Sauternes; the one in a class by itself: *grand premier cru*. 1987 is not one of the best years, though it is ready to drink. A better year might not be.

HOW TO TELL IF YOU'VE BEEN BITTEN BY THE "WINE BUG"

1. NEW WORDS OR PHRASES ENTER YOUR VOCABULARY

2. YOU BEGIN TALKING ABOUT THE WEATHER IN PARTS OF THE WORLD YOU'VE NEVER BEEN TO

3. YOUR "INVESTMENT ADVISER" IS A WINE RETAILER

MALOLACTIC FERMENTATION, *etc. etc.* RESIDUAL SUGAR, *etc. etc.* DEGREES BRIX.

YOU KNOW, THERE'S A SEVERE DROUGHT IN THE BAROSSA VALLEY THIS YEAR.

I'M READY TO TAKE A MORE AGGRESSIVE POSITION ON LAFITE.

> **TIP FROM CABERNET FRANK**
>
> If a sommelier ceremoniously hands you the cork after opening a bottle of wine, don't smell it—it won't tell you anything! You can look at it, and see if there's a vintage date on it, or simply move it out of your way, as though it were just a piece of bark on the table. Which it is.

WHEN THE WINE ARRIVES

Now the bottle appears, and the series of events that so many people view as an intimidating, elaborate ritual begins. Here's the way it should go; watch carefully to make sure that it does. It's your moment in the sun, so smile. And breathe through the nose.

1. The server arrives with the bottle, and shows you the label. Look at it to make sure it's exactly the same bottle that you chose, including the year, the producer, the type of wine. If you order a reserve, it had better say "Reserve" on the label. If the wine list said a Burgundy was *premier cru,* and you don't see those words on the label, beware. If it was a Robert Mondavi Pinot Noir Carneros and they bring you a Robert Mondavi Pinot Noir Napa Valley, do not accept it. It's a less expensive wine that is not as fine.

This is where unscrupulous or ignorant restaurants can pull the old switcheroo. The most common ruse is to give you the same producer, but a different region, vineyard, or year. Often it's because they're out of what you ordered, and either they're trying to get away with giving you a lesser bottle or they figure a different vintage or vineyard doesn't matter. If the server does happen to be presenting you with a slightly different bottle, it's his or her responsibility to point that out, otherwise you should suspect them of foul play.

2. Once you've accepted that the bottle is correct, watch as the server cuts the foil, pulls the cork, and wipes the rim of the bottle. It can be very disconcerting to see some crud on the rim go into your glass.

3. Usually the server will hand you the cork. If it makes you feel better, you can look at it, feel that it's damp on one side and dry on the other, which means there's been no leakage. But the cork really won't tell you much, and smelling it won't tell you *anything*. Just put it down and keep watching.

4. Now the server should pour a small sample for you, since you're the one who ordered. This is required, even if you're a woman! (Incredibly, in this day and age, some people still think only men are equipped to judge wine.)

5. Look at the wine in your glass, checking to see that it's not murky or inappropriately fizzy. In *very* rare cases it is, meaning there may be something wrong. If so, proceed with caution. When a white wine looks brownish, this is also a very bad sign. It could be oxidized.

Now swirl the wine, and take a good whiff. This is where you really make your judgment. Your job is not to decide whether you like the wine; it's to determine whether the wine is faulty or not. Here are the possibilities:

a) The wine can smell "clean." This means no obvious faults. Taste it, and nod that it's okay. The server doesn't want to hear what you think of the wine at this point, only whether there's something objectively wrong with it or not.

b) The wine can smell "corked." This is the most common fault. Corked wines result when the bleaching of the cork leads to the development of the chemical 246-TCA (2, 4, 6-trichloroanisole) in the wine. This problem is more common than lots of people think: it afflicts up to 5 percent of all wines. A corked wine smells like a musty, mildewy cork or wet, decomposing newspapers. Some people are more sensitive to the smell than others. Once you know that smell, you're not likely to be unsure about it.

However, some wines—for instance, red wines from Graves in Bordeaux—can occasionally smell a little corked even when they're not. Often a smell like that will "blow off."

If you smell anything that you think might be corky, tell the server or wine steward. You can have him smell it, and you might want to suggest that since it might blow off, he should wait before pouring the rest of it. Leave it in their hands. If you wait fifteen minutes, and it still smells off, then it is corked. Have the server verify your assessment. If the server doesn't know what you're talking about or gives you a rough time about it, ask to see the wine director, wine steward, or manager. If nobody knows what a corked wine is, do not return to that restaurant, since they have big fat nerve to mark up their wines if they don't know how to serve them. Period.

c) The wine could smell "maderized." This means it has been exposed to air somehow, and has oxidized. It will smell almost like a sherry. If you don't know how sherry smells and tastes, you might want to buy an inexpensive bottle and try it. Maderized wines are pretty rare.

In any case, if you suspect a fault in the wine, tell the server or wine steward exactly what you think it is, and ask them to smell and taste it. If they insist there's nothing wrong, and you know there is, do not accept the bottle.

TIP FROM CABERNET FRANK

If you want to know for certain exactly how 246-TCA smells in a "corked" or "corky" wine, you can order a sample of it. Send three dollars to: The Wine Trader, Attn: "Corky," PO Box 1598, Carson City, NV 89702. They will include instructions on how to dissolve a few granules of 246-TCA in a glass of wine.

SENDING A BOTTLE BACK

This brings me to something that mystifies many people. When is it okay to send back a bottle and when is it not?

You may only send back a bottle if it is faulty—in other words, corked or maderized or oxidized.

You may not send back a bottle just because you don't like it, or it's not exactly what you expected. That's not fair to the restaurant. There are some very good restaurants that will routinely take back a bottle simply because you're not happy with it, especially if their sommelier recommended it. But it's really a lot to ask of a restaurant, and those that have a take-back-anything policy do it solely to maintain good customer relations.

DECANTING AND BREATHING

In some cases, after you taste the wine

TIP FROM CABERNET FRANK

A crumbly cork doesn't mean the wine is faulty, nor does a cork that's gooey on top. And don't be alarmed if you see something that looks like little pieces of glass in your white wine—they're just harmless tartrate crystals caused by a reaction of potassium and tartaric acid. They're actually a good sign: they mean the wine wasn't excessively filtered.

---

and make sure it's okay, the server may suggest decanting it. As you know, this could be for one of two reasons. Either the wine is very young and would benefit from lots of contact with air, or it's a fairly old big red wine that is likely to have thrown a deposit.

If the server doesn't suggest it, you may ask to have it decanted. Flip back to Chapter Three to remind yourself how it should be done. If they say they can't decant it—they don't know how or don't have time—you may ask to decant it yourself. In that case, again, you may want to question what right the restaurant has to charge four times what they're paying for the wine if they can't

OPENING THE WINE AND LETTING IT "BREATHE" IS STANDARD PRACTICE FOR MANY WAITERS

HEY, SIT BACK. GIVE THE WINE SOME AIR.

> Some restaurants are so well-known for their fabulous wine lists
> that oenophiles make pilgrimages just to read their selections.
> Montrachet restaurant in New York City is one such place.
> Named for the most exalted white Burgundy, probably the
> most famous white wine in the world, Montrachet specializes
> in wines from Burgundy. Here is one page of its list.

1. This entire page of *grand cru* Montrachets represents a
   tiny slice of the list.
2. Montrachet (or Le Montrachet) is a *grand cru* vineyard
   in the Côte d'Or, specifically in the Côte de Beaune
   district. It's only about twenty acres; part of it is in the
   Puligny commune and part is in the Chassagne
   commune. It's safe to say that Le Montrachet is the
   fanciest Chardonnay in the world. Other *grands crus*
   nearby include Bâtard-Montrachet, Bienvenue-
   Montrachet, Chevalier-Montrachet, and Corton-
   Montrachet. They're all fabulous, too, but Le
   Montrachet is the ultimate.
3. The Producer. Domaine de la Romanée-Conti is the
   most famous producer of this wine, and in fact one of
   the most famous and prestigious wine producers in the
   world.
4. As you can see, these wines ain't cheap.
5. As in many other regions of France, 1989 was a
   fabulous vintage for white Burgundies.
6. Domaine Ramonet is another important producer.
7. Since Le Montrachet is one vineyard, it is split up
   between a number of different owners, some of whom
   may just own a row or two of vines. Marquis de
   Laguich owns the part of the vineyard from which this
   wine comes.
8. *Négociant* Joseph Drouhin makes the wine for Marquis
   de Laguiche.
9. This may seem pretty old for a white wine, but *grand
   cru* Montrachets from the best years can age for up to
   twenty or thirty years.

MONTRACHET

(1) WHITE BURGUNDIES
GRAND CRUS

(2) Le Montrachet • Romanée Conti 1991	750.
Le Montrachet • Romanée Conti 1983	1000.
(3) Le Montrachet • Romanée Conti 1982	1000.
Le Montrachet • Ramonet 1992	900.
(4) Le Montrachet • Ramonet 1991	700.
Le Montrachet • Ramonet 1990	900.
Le Montrachet • Ramonet 1989	1000.
(5) Le Montrachet • Ramonet 1986	1200.
Le Montrachet • Ramonet 1985	900.
Le Montrachet • Ramonet 1984	650.
(6) Le Montrachet • Ramonet 1983	1000.
Le Montrachet • Ramonet 1982	1200.
Le Montrachet • Ramonet 1981	800.
Le Montrachet • Ramonet 1979	1200.
Le Montrachet • Ramonet 1978	1200.
Le Montrachet • Domaine Leflaive 1991	600.
Le Montrachet • Marquis de Laguiche • Drouhin 1985	500.
(7) Le Montrachet • Marquis de Laguiche • Drouhin 1976	650.
(8) Le Montrachet • Prieur 1992	275.
Le Montrachet • Marc Colin 1983	375.
Le Montrachet • Marc Colin 1982	350.
Le Montrachet • Marc Colin 1978	450.
Le Montrachet • Morey 1985	300.
Le Montrachet • Gagnard Delagrange 1990	375.
Le Montrachet • Gagnard Delagrange 1988	400.
Le Montrachet • Latour 1986	275.
(9) Le Montrachet • Latour 1982	325.
Le Montrachet • Latour 1981	225.

serve it appropriately. And you should say so to the manager. If no one complains, they think no one notices or no one cares.

Sometimes the server (or you) may suggest pouring a red wine into the glasses to breathe—perhaps while you eat your first course. This can be a very good idea.

TEMPERATURE

You may feel that the wine being served is a little too cold or too warm. Most reds should be served just under comfortable room temperature. If the restaurant's cellar is kept at the proper temperature, it won't be too warm. If it is, ask the server to give it a quick whirl in an ice bucket filled halfway with ice, and the rest of the way with water. Five minutes should bring it down to where you want it.

White wine should be served refreshingly cool, but not too cold. If it isn't cold enough, again, an ice bucket with ice and water should do the trick quickly. If it's a little too warm, ten minutes in the glass should bring it up to the proper temperature, and by the time you get to the rest of the bottle, that'll be fine, too.

RESTAURANT GLASSWARE

A word about restaurant wineglasses—my pet peeve. They should be large enough—at least 12 ounces—and filled no more than half-full. I'm usually disappointed, even in very fine restaurants, that the glasses used to serve their fabulous wines aren't large enough to allow you to swirl them around and fully enjoy them. One of the most common errors in wine service is to pour

the glasses too full. If you see this happening, ask the server to pour them no more than half-full next time around.

Once you've started drinking the wine, it's the server's job to refill the glasses. If he's on top of things, he'll periodically look to see that no one's glass is empty. However, if he's not doing his job, by all means you may pour it yourself!

BRINGING YOUR OWN WINE

In most parts of the country, most restaurants will not allow you to bring your own wine. The exceptions are restaurants that have just opened and await their liquor license (in some states this takes months), or they have no liquor licenses at all.

However, some enlightened restaurants will allow you to bring your own wine, and for this privilege, they will charge you what's called a *corkage fee*. Corkage is usually between five and fifteen dollars; in return, the restaurant will open the wine for you, pour it, and give you the use of its glassware.

This practice is much more common in California than in other parts of the country—perhaps because residents there are more likely to have cellars at home.

In any case, when restaurants are good enough to allow their patrons to bring their own wine, many patrons pay them back by abusing the privilege. There are several unwritten rules:

1. Try not to bring a wine that's on the restaurant's list.
2. Don't bring an ordinary bottle. A restaurant will understand if you want to open something special, whether it's something unusual, something extravagant, or something with some sentimental value. The bottle doesn't have to be expensive to be special.
3. If you're unsure of the restaurant's policy, call in advance and ask. Even if there's generally a no-bringing-your-own rule, the management may bend it if you have a special bottle for a special occasion. In any case, *do not* show up with bottles without checking first.

In addition, it will be appreciated if, when bringing one bottle of your own, you then perhaps order another bottle off the list. Say you brought a Pinot Noir; then you might order a Riesling off the list to start off your meal. You may want to offer your server a taste of what you've brought.

If restaurant patrons show some sensitivity about bringing in bottles, perhaps more restaurant owners will be encouraged to allow the practice. Of course, if the owners showed more sensitivity when it came to pricing the bottles on their lists, perhaps we wouldn't be so *inclined* to bring our own bottles!

TIPPING

Finally, be sure to reward good wine service in your gratuity. A server often has to go out of his or her way to know the wines, and this should be reflected in the tip.

We all know that good service should be rewarded with a tip of 15 to 20 percent of the total bill before taxes. But many people are stumped when they have to figure out tipping when dinner included an expensive bottle of wine. Current etiquette requires that you calculate the tip on the entire bill, including the wine.

If you've brought your own wine, be certain to leave a larger tip than you normally would, since the server has to do a lot of extra work to serve it. In fact, you might tack on 15 percent of what a reasonable restaurant price for the wine would be.

IF YOU FORGET EVERYTHING ELSE YOU'VE READ IN CHAPTER TEN, JUST REMEMBER THIS:

1. The sommelier is there to help you.
2. Check the label to make sure it's exactly what you ordered.

3. Don't smell the cork.
4. When tasting a wine you've ordered, you're not deciding whether you like it or not, only whether the wine is flawed or acceptable.
5. If you think the wine may be corked or maderized, tell the server, and don't accept it.
6. Reward good wine service by tipping well.
7. If you've brought your own wine, remember to add a little extra to the tip.

Chapter Eleven

WINE AND FOOD

While there's a time and place for the serious tasting of wine, that's not in fact what wine is made for. Wine is meant to be drunk with food, as part of a meal. Many French people find it odd that we Americans will have a glass of wine by itself—for instance before dinner. In France, people generally only open a bottle of wine at mealtime. The only exceptions are champagne, which is often enjoyed as an apéritif, kir (white wine with cassis), and fortified wines (port, vermouth, and sherry).

As I've mentioned, wine enhances food, and food enhances wine—and winemakers are the first to admit it. Sure, they'll *taste* first—take a moment to concentrate, check out the aromas, the color, the body, the texture, the finish, the length. Then they'll pour themselves a glass, pick up their knife and fork, and enjoy. That's the fun part, the part that actually improves the quality of life.

But when people start to think about which wines they should serve or order with foods, suddenly, once again, they panic. Ye olde fear of wine kicks in, even for many who are not

otherwise oenophobic. They're dying to try that California Zinfandel they picked up last week, but what on earth should they
make to go with it?

Well, to put it mildly, people get worked up into a much bigger tizzy than they ought to about all this. In Bordeaux, for instance, people at home usually have the everyday wine they're
accustomed to drinking, and whatever they decide to have for
dinner or lunch will just automatically "go." No one loses any
sleep over the notion that red Bordeaux is better suited to lamb
than pork. If they have pork, they'll drink what they drink: red
Bordeaux. Another Bordeaux example: It's commonly said that
Roquefort (and other strong blue cheeses) don't work with red
wine. And yes, if you sit down and really pay attention to that
particular flavor combination in your mouth, it might not be the
best idea. But try telling that to the Bordelais who make a regular
habit of it! One of the reasons the French love a cheese course at
the end of a meal is that they still have a little red wine left, and
they love it with the cheese. They're not about to say, wait a
minute, red Bordeaux really goes better with a Camembert.

Yet anyone who looks into the issue of food and wine matching will inevitably get bombarded with dogmatic proclamations

that seem inviolable. Part of the confusion is this: A lot of those rules are meant to be applied to really fine (and expensive) mature wines. So, okay—if you happen to be lucky enough to find yourself at the same dinner table with a 1961 Château Margaux, you'd be nuts to overwhelm such a fabulously delicate treasure with a fumingly ripe Gorgonzola. But how often do we have *cru classé* Bordeaux, let alone a *premier cru* from a stellar year? Not often enough, I'll venture . . .

As far as I'm concerned, unless you're drinking something very special, don't worry too much about the food and wine combination. If you like the food, and like the wine, that's all that's important.

MATCHING FOOD AND WINE

That said, there are a few old "rules" you may want to know about. I'll lay them out, tell you what's wrong or right about them, and then give you some more reasonable general guidelines.

Serve white wine with fish: This is the food-and-wine matching cliché. There are a few reasons behind it. First, white wines tend to

THE ART OF MATCHING FOOD WITH WINE HAS BECOME A SUBJECT OF SERIOUS STUDY

I JUST GOT MY MASTERS IN QUANTUM PHYSICS.

WHAT A COINCIDENCE! I JUST GOT MY MASTERS IN "MATCHING FOOD AND WINE"!

be more acidic than red, and we tend to like a little acid (for instance, lemon) with our fish. Second, fish is said to impart a weird taste to red wine. And third, red wines tend to have bigger flavors than whites, and fish tends to be milder tasting than meat, leading to the conclusion that red wines overwhelm fish.

While all this *can* be true, there are so many exceptions that it almost seems silly to have a rule at all. First, plenty of red wines have some acidity (Chianti, for example). Second, although I've heard the idea that fish imparts a weird taste to red wine, the only actual explanation I've read is that it's because fish can be oily. Okay, fine— but many types of fish are not oily! And one of the fattier fish we commonly eat, salmon, works fabulously well with red wine. Third, much fish *is* very mild, but the rule doesn't take *sauce* into account.

The truth is that a lot of this depends on the preparation—and not only where fish is concerned. Cooking fish in red wine has become more and more popular in recent years, and serving the same kind of red wine to drink will *always* be a good idea.

Don't serve wine with salad: The reasoning behind this is that the acid in the salad dressing will make the acid in the wine seem dull. For many wines, this is true, but if you serve a salad with a wine with crisp acid, such as a Riesling or a Sauvignon Blanc, it will be just fine.

Serve red wine with meat: The tannins in a young red wine are softened, as we know, by the protein in the meat. The tannins eat the protein in the meat rather than the protein in your mouth, making the wine seem softer. This is not such an issue with more mature reds, or reds that aren't as tannic. But with a California Cabernet, or a young Bordeaux or Barolo, there's certainly a lot of truth to the maxim. That doesn't mean that vegetarians can't enjoy these wines: cheese, butter, and other dairy products serve the same function. A steaming plate of pasta with just about any kind of sauce and some cheese will work just as well.

Here are some more basic, easy-to-follow guidelines. I'm going to list the food item first, then wines that work with them, since that's how most of us plan our meals. Some are dishes you might prepare at home; others are more often seen on restaurant menus.

Smoked salmon: champagne, brut sparkling wine, Riesling, Sauvignon Blanc, white Burgundy, Pouilly-Fumé, white Bordeaux.

Grilled or sautéed foie gras (goose liver): Viognier, California Chardonnay, Condrieu, Château-Grillet, red Bordeaux, Meritage, Pinot Noir, red Burgundy, Merlot.

Simply prepared grilled fish: Crisp, refreshing white wines, such as Sauvignon Blanc, Sancerre, Pouilly-Fumé, Kabinett Riesling, Alsatian Riesling, champagne, or brut sparkling wine are ideal. Rosés with some acidity and slightly chilled Beaujolais are fine, too.

Fish with red wine sauce: the same wine as is in the sauce, or Pinot Noir, Burgundy, Chianti, or Beaujolais.

Seared tuna: Riesling (especially if wasabi is involved), Pinot Noir, Beaujolais.

Fresh salmon: Chardonnay, white Burgundy, Pinot Noir, Beaujolais, Rioja.

Artichokes: A chemical in artichokes makes wines taste sweeter to many people, so this is a difficult match. A Rhône Ranger rosé or dry French rosé often does quite well.

Salade niçoise: Rhône Ranger rosé or Châteauneuf-type blend, red Côtes du Rhône.

Roast portobello mushrooms or other wild-mushroom dishes: light reds or rich whites: Pinot Noir, Chianti, Beaujolais, Chardonnay.

Crab, lobster, or other crustaceans: These are rich enough to enjoy with a white Burgundy, Chablis, white Graves, or California Chardonnay.

Fish in a creamy or buttery white sauce: rich whites such as white Burgundy, Chardonnay, white Bordeaux, Sémillon.

Grilled chicken: just about any dry white wine, Beaujolais, red Côtes du Rhône, Chianti.

Grilled chicken with rosemary: fabulous with red Châteauneuf-du-Pape or a Rhône Ranger Châteauneuf-type blend, or serve with any of the above listed for grilled chicken.

Pasta with fresh tomato-based sauce, and other light pasta dishes: fresh-tasting wines, such as Sauvignon Blanc, Chianti, Dolcetto, Barbera, Zinfandel, Pinot Noir, Beaujolais.

Pasta al pesto: The heady combination of pine nuts, Parmesan, basil, and garlic can stand up to Chardonnay, Sauvignon Blanc, Beaujolais, Pinot Noir, Dolcetto, Chianti, Zinfandel.

Pasta with meat sauce or lasagna: any kind of red wine.

Simply prepared veal or pork (sautéed or roasted, with no sauce or a light sauce): Pinot Noir, Beaujolais, Chianti, Dolcetto, Côtes du Rhône.

Pacific Rim cuisine (light and a little spicy): Riesling.

Lamb (grilled, roast, or chops, etc.): Cabernet, Merlot, Meritage, red Bordeaux, Zinfandel, any Rhône Valley reds, Barolo, Barbaresco, Chianti Classico Riserva, Spanish Crianzas or Reservas, South African reds, Chilean or Argentine reds.

Beef, cooked plain (steak, filet mignon, roast beef etc.): red Burgundy, plus anything listed for lamb.

Beef stew: red Burgundy, plus anything listed for lamb.

Roast chicken with no sauce: Pinot Noir, Beaujolais, Dolcetto, Chianti, red or white Burgundy. (See below for roast chicken with sauce.)

Sautéed chicken pieces with a tomato-based sauce: same as roast chicken.

Chicken curry: Pinot Gris, Côtes du Rhône, Rhône Ranger Châteauneuf-type blends, Riesling, Sancerre.

Roast turkey with gravy or sauce: any of the wines for roast chicken, plus red Bordeaux, red Burgundy, Châteauneuf-du-Pape, Côtes du Rhône, Barbaresco.

If you can cook a little bit, there are plenty of ways to make a dish match a wine at home. For instance, I love roast chicken with a big red wine, such as a young Bordeaux. To make them match, you just need something that will let them make sense together—a sauce, either with red wine or meat stock in it, or one with chicken stock, and a little butter swirled in at the end. It's easy to make a pan sauce when the chicken's out of the pan by pouring out most of the fat, adding red wine, placing it on a burner, and scraping all the browned bits up from the pan as the wine reduces down. After about three minutes, adjust seasoning, and you've got a great little sauce. This kind of thinking can help you find lots of matches where you wouldn't think of them.

If you're making a light pasta dish that you want to go with a bigger red wine, just add some chopped meat or wild mushrooms or olives—anything that will give it a little more depth.

Another way to go about the whole thing is to say, "Okay, I have this fabulous red Burgundy. Now what can I make to go with it?" If you want to go that route, take a look at the classic food and wine combinations below. Many of them came about as the best way to show off a particular wine, so they're worth trying. A lot of them are from France, since the French are very organized about that sort of thing.

Muscadet and oysters
Alsatian Riesling and smoked salmon
Alsatian Riesling or Sylvaner and onion tart
Sauternes and foie gras (Bordeaux)
Fino sherry and green olives (Spain)
Champagne and caviar with toast points
Red Burgundy and beef (for example, beef Bourguignon)
Pauillac (or other red Bordeaux) and roast lamb
Red Côtes du Rhône and roast pork with sage
Sauternes and Roquefort
Vintage port and Stilton (England)
Biscotti and Vin Santo (Tuscany)
Chardonnay and Dungeness crab (California)

MATCHING FOOD AND WINE IN AMERICAN RESTAURANTS

I know what you're thinking: all these classic, mostly French, food and wine combos may be well and good, but we don't eat in classic French restaurants more than once in a blue moon. In everyday life, these pairings are pretty esoteric. What about matching wines with American food?

For your enlightenment, here is the menu of Joe's Restaurant. It's annotated with good wine choices from Joe's wine list, as well as other good matches, too. After you take a look, you might want to flip back to the wine list on pages 232–233, and make your own selections.

RESTAURANT

Prix-Fixe Menu

MENU # 1

(**1**) Grilled scallops wrapped in apple-smoked bacon, arugula salad
or
Chicken and spinach raviolis, tomato coulis & basil (**2**)

———

Green salad
or
Soup of today

———

(**3**) Chilean seabass with an onion crust, snap peas, tomatoes & pearl onions,
red onion juice
or
Roasted pork tenderloin with mashed potatoes, wild mushrooms (**4**)
& roasted garlic

Cranberry apple crisp
(PLEASE ORDER WITH YOUR ENTRÉE)

$30.00

MENU # 2

(**5**) Salad of arugula, grilled eggplant & dried tomatoes,
ovilina cheese, balsamic vinegar
or
Belgian endive salad, roasted pears & walnuts, (**6**)
Fourme d'Ambert cheese

———

(**7**) Grilled tuna & seared foie gras, rosti potato, red wine sauce
or
Grilled shrimp on creamy polenta, crispy leeks, lobster sauce (**8**)

———

(9) Roasted venison with wild mushroom raviolis, julienne of vegetables,
red wine game sauce

or

Barbecued monkfish with lobster homefries, lobster sauce & basil oil (10)

Warm chocolate soufflé cake with vanilla ice cream
(PLEASE ORDER WITH YOUR ENTRÉE)

$38.00

Mixed lettuces, tomatoes, red onions, avocado & mushrooms $6.

Grilled eggplant with Chèvre, pine nuts, & dry tomato vinaigrette $7.

(11) Warm onion tart with gravlax & chive crème fraîche $9.

Tuna tartar with preserved lemons, cucumbers & tomatoes $8.

(12) Roasted quail filled with pears & apple bacon, cornbread salad $10.

Chanterelle mushroom raviolis, wild mushroom broth & parsley $8.

Grilled vegetables with saffron risotto, tomato coulis $8.

Sea scallops with herb mashed potatoes, chanterelle mushrooms $10.

B.B.Q. monkfish with lobster homefries & roast garlic juice $16.

(13) Dorade with potato scales, salsify, spinach & red wine $15.

Chilean seabass, onion crust, snap peas, tomatoes & pearl onions $14.

(14) Grilled salmon, basil mashed potatoes, tomato olive vinaigrette $16.

(15) Grilled rib-eye steak, roasted potatoes & garlic, spinach salad $20.

Crispy chicken, Parmesan stuffed potato & spinach with garlic $14.

Pork tenderloin with mashed potatoes & wild mushrooms $16.

1. **Grilled scallops wrapped in apple-smoked bacon, arugula salad:** Light seafood such as scallops, especially when grilled without a heavy sauce, goes well with refreshing, crisp white wines such as Sauvignon Blanc. The smokiness of the bacon would be nice with this wine, which is also known as "Fumé" (smoked). Joe's list offers several from California, plus a 1992 Sancerre (Loire Valley) from Paul Cotat. 1992 is a good year, and Sancerre should be drunk within two to three years of harvest. Sauvignon Blancs from Australia, New Zealand, or Chile would also work well. California Chardonnay would be a little rich for this dish, though the fattiness of the bacon would let you get away with it.

2. **Chicken and spinach raviolis, tomato coulis, and basil:** again, a pretty light dish. Tomato coulis is fairly acidic, so you'd want a white wine with crisp acidity. Again, Sauvignon Blanc would be your ticket.

3. **Chilean seabass with an onion crust, snap peas, tomatoes and pearl onions, red onion juice:** Chilean seabass is fairly light, though the onion crust would permit a wine with a little more richness. Either a Sauvignon Blanc or a Chardonnay would probably work here.

4. **Roasted pork tenderloin with mashed potatoes, wild mushrooms, and roasted garlic:** Pork is a white meat, and the wild mushrooms and roasted garlic add some deep, rich flavors. If you want to go with a white, try something with some depth. On Joe's list, that would be mostly California Chardonnays. I'd look for one that's fairly Burgundian in style; that is, not too fruity or sweet. The 1993 Byron would be a good choice, but lots of them would work fine. Here's where you might ask the staff's assistance in finding one that isn't too fruity.

However, you might prefer to match this with a red. Pinot Noir, lighter than Cabernet Sauvignon and Merlot, would be a great choice. A Chianti Classico or Barbaresco would also work well (you could try Joe's half-bottle offering of a 1992 Noceto Sangiovese from California), as would a good Côtes du Rhône, since these are all flavorful yet not intense.

5. **Salad of arugula, grilled eggplant, and dried toma-**

toes, ovilina cheese, balsamic vinegar: Most salads need some crisp acidity to stand up to the vinegar in the salad. Here it shouldn't be too much of a problem, since balsamic vinegar has fairly soft acid; still, I'd go with a Sauvignon Blanc.

6. **Belgian endive salad, roasted pears and walnuts, Fourme d'Ambert cheese:** Yes, this is a salad, but Fourme d'Ambert cheese is a very rich blue cheese, so you'd want a fairly rich wine. Try a Chardonnay.

7. **Grilled tuna and seared foie gras, rosti potato, red wine sauce:** You might remember that Sauternes, as well as other sweet, rich wines, are classic matches with foie gras. This is true in particular for foie gras prepared in the traditional way— marinated and baked very briefly—which results in slices of an ultrarich delicacy, almost pâtélike in consistency. Most foie gras we see on American menus is seared, as it is here, and has a completely different texture than the traditional version. In combination with tuna, probably cooked rare, and the red wine sauce, you'd want a red wine to accompany this dish. Best bet? A Pinot Noir. If the list offered red Burgundies, or *cru* Beaujolais such as Fleurie or Moulin-à-Vent, they'd be worth considering, too.

8. **Grilled shrimp on creamy polenta, crispy leeks, lobster sauce:** The word "creamy" indicates this dish is probably on the rich side. In the best of all possible worlds, a fabulous white Burgundy such as a Meursault or Montrachet would be swell. But a good California Chardonnay could be fine, too. Again, you don't want lots of fruit.

9. **Roasted venison with wild-mushroom raviolis, julienne of vegetables, red wine game sauce:** Rich meats such as roasted venison provide the perfect opportunity to go for the big reds; California Cabernets are the obvious choice. Merlots would be fine, too, as long as they're not too flabby—a Washington State Merlot would be great, though Joe's menu doesn't offer one. Red Bordeaux is another obvious choice—just about any would be great here. And what about the Rhône Valley? Joe's offers a 1990 Châteauneuf-du-Pape, Domaine du Haut des Terres Blanches. If it's a substantial Châteauneuf, that would be good. Any northern Rhône red—Hermitage, Crozes-Hermitage, Cor-

nas, etc., would be great, as would a good California Rhône Ranger red—Joe's has a 1992 Ojai Vineyards Syrah. Big-gun Italian reds, such as Barolo or Brunello di Montalcino, would be fabulous, too, or a California Petite Sirah.

10. **Barbecued monkfish with lobster homefries, lobster sauce, and basil oil:** Certainly this would work with a Chardonnay, but since it's a main course, chances are others at the table might want a red, producing a fairly typical dining quandary. A great solution here? A Pinot Noir.

11. **Warm onion tart with gravlax and chive crème fraîche:** Remember the classic combos listed above? If you take a look at it again, with this dish in mind, surely one wine will scream out to be ordered: a Riesling! Joe's, unfortunately, doesn't offer any, probably because the menu features California wines and cuisine.

12. **Roasted quail filled with pears & apple bacon, cornbread salad:** a perfect California Chardonnay dish. Why? California Chardonnay is known for its apple and pear aromas. Here's where you might ask the staff if one of their Chardonnays in particular would offer these flavors. A Pinot Noir would also work very well—it's great with game birds such as quail.

13. **Dorade with potato scales, salsify, spinach, and red wine:** red wine with fish! The people have spoken! Why am I so sure? Because it has a red wine sauce. Ask the server what kind of red wine the dorade was cooked in, order the same varietal, and you'll be golden.

14. **Grilled salmon, basil mashed potatoes, tomato-olive vinaigrette:** Of course you could have a Chardonnay with this, but Pinot Noir also goes wonderfully well with grilled salmon. A tomato-olive vinaigrette throws a little bit of a wrench in the works wine-wise, since as we know, the presence of vinegar means you want a wine with crisp acidity. Yet the olives, along with the basil, bring to mind a sort of Provençal, southern-French feeling. Perhaps a Côtes du Rhône Villages, or even a lighter-style Châteauneuf-du-Pape would do nicely.

15. **Grilled rib-eye steak, roasted potatoes and garlic, spinach salad:** A steak can always stand up to just about any big

red wine. Joe's list offers a plethora of California Cabs, along with two Petite Sirahs. Syrah would also work well, either from France (a northern Rhône), California, or on a wider-ranging menu, Australia. Any red Bordeaux or big rich, red Burgundy (this you'll have to *pay* for), Cabernets from Argentina or South Africa, or Barolos or Brunellos from Italy would stand up to the steak.

SERVING WINE WITH FOOD

Now that you know how to match wine with food, exactly *how* do you serve it?

First, you need to consider the proper order if you want to serve more than one wine. In general, the rules are: whites before red, young wines before old, dry before sweet. Let's break it down a little.

Apéritif: This is any drink, including wine, that you have before dinner. Ideally, it should be accompanied by a little hors d'oeuvre tidbit. Sherry, white port, vermouth, and champagne (all well chilled) are the most classic; Riesling and Sauvignon Blanc are nice, too.

First course: At home, when having a dinner party, most people will serve a first course, whether it be a soup, salad, shellfish, what-have-you. Most of these will call for a white wine of some sort, though traditionally soup calls for sherry. If so, think about glasses: Do you want to have two glasses on the table, one for white and one for red? Otherwise you'll have to either wash them, or wait until everyone's done with their white before you move on to the red. Pour around the table for your guests, remembering not to pour the glasses more than half-full. Keep the bottle near you so you can pour for people when you see they need more.

Main course: Let's say, for the sake of argument, that you'll be having a red

TIP FROM CABERNET FRANK
The four most difficult foods to match with wine: artichokes (try a rosé), asparagus (Muscat d'Alsace), anchovies (dry rosé or Alsatian Sylvaner), and chocolate (don't even bother).

GAMES WINE SNOBS PLAY

wine with this course. It might be your second course at a more formal dinner, or perhaps your only course for a casual dinner at home. If you are serving two different red wines of the same type during this course, you'll usually serve the younger one first. If they're two different kinds, most people will serve the lighter one first. (Wine geeks always get into arguments about whether to serve a very mature Burgundy or a younger Bordeaux first. If you have that problem, I hope it's the worst thing that ever happens to you.) In any case, make sure your guests' glasses are filled: it's your responsibility as host, especially since many people are uncomfortable pouring for themselves at someone else's home.

Before dessert: This is the part of the meal that often stumps wine lovers—especially those accustomed to drinking wine with food. And it's why the cheese course is such a great idea! While everyone has some red wine left in their glass, finishing it up with a little bread and cheese is the height of gracious living!

Dessert: If you serve a dessert wine, the general rule is it has to be at least as sweet as the dessert, otherwise the wine will taste awful. Champagne doesn't work well for dessert since it's *not* sweet. For that reason, you'll have an easier time if your dessert isn't over-

Food and Wine Menus

Restaurants that take as much pride in their wine lists as they do in their menus will often be happy to make wine suggestions—sometimes even printed alongside the names of dishes, especially with multicourse fixed-price menus. Many such restaurants have a wide selection of wines by the glass.

Jean Louis at the Watergate Hotel in Washington, D.C., which holds a *Wine Spectator* Grand Award for its wine cellar, offers fifteen by-the-glass selections (and by the way, only one American Chardonnay among them!). Since the menu, which changes daily, consists of a choice between three fixed-price multicourse menus, the very approachable and knowledgeable sommelier, Vincent Feraud, offers to match each course with a different wine by the glass. On a recent visit he matched the seven-course tasting menu—it was a perfect example of the best kind of food and wine synergy. Notice that a white wine follows the red wine here—rules, after all, are made to be broken!

whelmingly sweet. Vin Santo, the Tuscan dessert wine, isn't usually very sweet, so it's served with biscotti, which are just a tiny bit sweet. Fruit tarts often work well for the same reason. For example, Sauternes is nice with an apple or pear *tarte tatin*. Chocolate, which coats your mouth and overwhelms other flavors, is a difficult match. A lot of people claim to like Cabernet Sauvignon with chocolate, but to me it tastes horrible. Port can work okay.

Some prefer to serve a dessert wine after the dessert.

"Wait!" you may be saying to yourself. At what temperature should I be serving these wines?

A big deal is often made about temperature, but I know you, and you're not about to stick a thermometer in a wine bottle. So let's dispense with the formality, and say anything sweet or

- Amuse-gueule: caviar and quail's-egg canapé, with Piper-Hiedsieck Cuvée Brut (Champagne)
- Fresh chestnut soup with stuffed squab legs and quenelle, with 1992 Château Cascadais, St. Laurent de la Cabrerisse (red Corbières)★
- Nage of seaweed macerated in sesame with Maine lobster and seaweed, with 1992 Riesling Bennwihr, Domaine Marcel Deiss (Alsace)
- Fresh duck foie gras with fresh quince, with 1985 Château Rieussec (Sauternes, *premier cru*)
- Rockfish fillet sautéed with fried onions and parsley with caviar butter, with 1992 Pouilly-Fumé, Hervé Seguin (Loire Valley)
- Milk-fed lamb roasted with herbs and seasonal root ragout, with 1992 Hautes Côtes de Nuits, Domaine Jayer Gilles (Red Burgundy)
- Little mandarine tart with mandarine sherbet, with 1990 Muscat de Beaumes-de-Venise, Jaboulet

sparkling should be served well chilled, and still, dry white wines a little less so. However, don't leave any wine in the refrigerator for more than a couple days, or it can go flat and dull. In general, the finer the white wine, the less cold it should be served. Colder temperatures hide flaws in wine, including too much sugar or acid.

Most of us have been taught that red wine should be served at room temperature. This is sort of true, but not exactly. The guy who made this rule probably lived in a drafty old stone castle in France, in which room temperature was quite a bit cooler than

---

★ Corbières is a region in the Languedoc, in southern France. The red wines from the region are made from Mourvèdre, Cinsault, Syrah, or Grenache.

what we consider comfortable today. Most red wines should be served at about 68°F or less. In most seasons, unless your house or apartment is overheated, room temperature should be fine. In the summer, however, homes without air-conditioning will probably be quite a bit warmer than this. If that's the case, you'll have to give your red wine a swirl in an ice bucket. Five or eight minutes in there should bring it to a good temperature, and you don't have to measure it; just feel it with your hand or taste it. The reason this is important is that if it's too warm, it'll just taste overly alcoholic ("hot") and any faults in the wine will be magnified. It should be sort of refreshing to be its most enjoy-

Speaking of Glasses

Speaking of glasses, make sure yours are impeccably clean, free of soap residue and chlorine smell, which will really interfere with your enjoyment of fine wines. If water in your area is heavily chlorinated, keep a bottle of distilled water on hand so you can give your glasses a quick final rinse.

Right or Wrong, Some Traditional Food and Wine Taboos

Red Bordeaux and Roquefort
Artichoke, anchovies, or asparagus with any wine
Vinegar with any wine
***Brut* champagne (or any dry wine) with dessert**

able.

There are also red wines, very young simple wines, such as Nouveau Beaujolais, which are served slightly chilled. Rosés are served well chilled. Dessert wines such as Sauternes or Alsatian Vendange Tardive are also chilled. Don't overchill really fine wines.

TIP FROM CABERNET FRANK

Don't make your guests pour their own wine: be attentive, making sure their glasses aren't empty. Pour for others before yourself, and *never* pour for yourself only—it's the height of rudeness!

IF YOU FORGET EVERYTHING ELSE YOU'VE READ IN CHAPTER ELEVEN, JUST REMEMBER THIS:

1. There are no hard-and-fast rules about matching wine and food.
2. If you like it, it's a match.
3. White wines before red.
4. Dry wines before sweet.
5. Young wines before old.
6. Don't forget sauces when considering matches.
7. Keep your guests' glasses filled.

Chapter Twelve

BUYING WINE FOR DRINKING AT HOME

Buying a bottle of wine in a shop, of course, is a much less complicated undertaking than choosing one off a restaurant's wine list. There are several different kinds of retail outlets, depending on where you live, in which to buy wine: supermarkets, specialty wineshops, liquor stores, and wine discounters. Wine may also be purchased through mail-order catalogs.

SUPERMARKETS
In most states across the U.S., except those with archaic "blue" laws, such as New York, supermarkets and grocery stores may sell wine. Depending on where you live, this may be anything from a few odd bottles to a wide selection taking up rows and rows of shelf space. For many people, this is a convenient way to pick up a bottle that will go nicely with that night's meal while they're doing their grocery shopping for dinner. Prices are often reasonable, though of course that depends on the store. Only two problems. One, the selection is often limited to the larger, more

commercial labels—don't look for buried treasure in a supermarket. And two, you can't ask the staff for guidance.

Specialty Wineshops

A trusted wine merchant can be the wine lover's best friend; the place to find one is the specialty wine shop. If you find a wine merchant with a good selection who can offer good advice, you'll return again and again. Such a wine merchant can learn your tastes and make suggestions with you particularly in mind.

But to do so, the merchant needs your help. Say you pick up a bottle of

> **TIP FROM CABERNET FRANK**
> **One notable exception to the drawbacks of buying wine in a grocery store: the famous Oakville Grocery in Napa Valley. The selection it offers is among the best in the area!**

Pinot Noir at Jane's Wineshop. A few days later when you come in again, you can say, "Gee, Jane. That Pinot was okay, but it was a little fruity for me. Do you have something in the same price range, but one that's more restrained?" Now Jane has the infor-

IT IS IMPORTANT TO DEVELOP A RELATIONSHIP WITH YOUR WINE MERCHANT

I'M NOT QUESTIONING THE VALUE OF A 10% CASE DISCOUNT, MR. PETERSON, I JUST THINK YOUR RELATIONSHIP WITH YOUR WINE MERCHANT BEARS FURTHER DISCUSSION.

mation she needs to guide you toward something else, and if she's a good wine merchant, she'll later remember that you don't like very fruity Pinots. She can even apply what she knows about your taste to other types of wine.

Another approach is to say, "Jane, we're having pasta with fresh tomatoes and basil for dinner. What can we have that will go nicely?"

A knowledgeable wine merchant can also guide you toward wines from regions you may not be familiar with, or varietals you haven't tried.

Often you'll find that a wineshop specializes in particular varietals or regions; this usually reflects the personal taste of the merchant. For example, in some shops you'll find a huge selection of Italian wines and only a few French bottles; in others mostly American wines, with a focus on California Cabernets, and not too many Zinfandels.

A specialty wineshop is also the place to go if you've read about a particular wine or type of wine and you can't find it anywhere. Even if your merchant doesn't stock it, he or she will often be able to order it specially for you.

Prices in specialty wineshops may not be the lowest you'll find, though in major metropolitan areas such as Los Angeles and New York City, they *can* be the lowest. I recently went shopping for a bottle of California sparkling wine in New York City. The price was $17.99 in one specialty wineshop. I happened to know the suggested retail was about $14, so I told them their price was ridiculous and that they ought to be ashamed of themselves. Eight blocks uptown, in a specialty wineshop known for its good prices, as well as good service, the same bottle was $10.99. 'Nuff said.

LIQUOR STORES
Stores that primarily sell liquor will often have a selection of wine, which can range from poor to excellent. Yet even if the prices are close to those of a specialty wineshop, you generally won't find the same level of knowledge on the part of the merchant.

WINE (OR WINE AND LIQUOR) DISCOUNTERS
Often large stores with wide selections, these discounters usually offer the best prices, though for the most part, the only way the stores can afford to do that is by offering the minimum of service. If you need a lot of questions answered ("Is this Crozes-Hermitage ready to drink, or should I put it away?"), this probably isn't the place you'll get it.

First-Growth Palate, Second-Label Pocket

In order to make wines of such a high quality that Bordeaux's various classified châteaux can release them, the winemakers must select meticulously from their best vats of wine and include only those in wines destined for fame. So what does a Château Latour do with batches of wine in each vintage that may be good, but not quite up to snuff? It makes a *second wine,* also known as a *second label,* and charges considerably less for it than the *grand vin.* If you're dying to try a *premier cru* Bordeaux, but can't quite afford it (not many people can!), you might like to try one of the second labels.

Crus and their Second Labels

Premier Cru	Second Label
Château Haut-Brion	Château Bahans Haut-Brion
Château Lafite-Rothschild	Moulins de Carruades
Château Latour	Les Forts de Latour
Château Margaux	Pavillon Rouge du Château Margaux

However, if you know exactly what you're looking for, or can recognize bottles you've read about or heard about when you see them, you may want to give a discounter a try.

BAIT 'N' WINE SHOPS

In rural and out-of-the-way places, you may have a tough time finding a good selection of wine. A number of years ago I visited an aunt and uncle of mine at their summer house in Wisconsin. One night I planned to prepare a nice dinner for them, with wine, of course. The supermarket in Luck, Wisconsin (the nearest town), didn't have any wine at all. Much to my surprise, there were no wineshops, or even liquor stores, anywhere. Finally, I found the only option. I think it was called Gus's Bait and Wine Shop. Between the worms and the leeches, I found three wine choices: two kinds of Manischewitz kosher wine and one bottle of some kind of commercial red table wine from California.

If you live in a place with this kind of selection, catalogs can be a good way for you to enjoy wine.

Several mail-order catalogs offer excellent prices, and your wine will be delivered to your door a few days or a couple weeks later, depending on how you have it shipped. Although it's not legal to ship wine to every state, this can be a great option. Certain catalogs, for instance the Wine Exchange, send out monthly newsletter-type mailings that are informative as well.

RETAIL PRICES

When I mention prices, take them with a major grain of salt. They can vary wildly depending on geography and the type of store, and can become out of date quickly. In any case, the *Wine Spectator* magazine regularly lists suggested retail prices. *Wine Spectator's Ultimate Guide to Buying Wine* is another useful guide.

WINE TO DRINK VS. WINE TO PUT AWAY

One of the main differences between serious wine geeks and regular people is the way each group makes its purchases. Serious wine types, you see, are in the habit of buying wines to stock their cellars, not wines that they'll drink that very night with dinner. This way, when they see something interesting, they buy it and put it away, without having to worry about whether it goes with some particular dish.

However, the majority of American wine purchases are made by people buying something to drink that very night.

The main difference between the two types of wine lovers is that buyers-for-the-moment have to pay more attention to the

Wine Catalogs

Here are a few reputable wine catalogs, and their phone numbers:

Wine Exchange: **a nice selection of wines from around the world from a well-known retailer in Orange County, California. Offers bottles at a wide range of prices from $5.99 bargains to several-hundred-dollar blockbusters. (714) 974-1792 or (800) 76-WINEX.**

Burgundy Wine Merchant: **offers almost exclusively Burgundies, sometimes American Pinot Noirs, and some very good deals and information. (212) 691-9092.**

Twenty Twenty: **a fat catalog full of higher-end stuff from the Bel-Air Wine Merchant in California. Specializes in wines from vintages past. (310) 447-2020.**

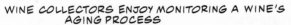

WINE COLLECTORS ENJOY MONITORING A WINE'S
AGING PROCESS

maturity of vintages. In other words, although 95 percent of the
wines of the world are ready to drink when released, some of
what you see in the shops will not be ready to drink tonight.

In particular, classed-growth Bordeaux, including Sauternes,
need some bottle age. If you feel like drinking one of these, see if
you can find one at least five years old. It won't be drinking its
best, but it will be starting to be mature. Simpler red Bordeaux,
such as *cru bourgeois* or just plain Appellation Bordeaux Contrôlée, drink much better young, so they shouldn't be a problem.

Red wines from the northern Rhône, such as Hermitage,
Crozes-Hermitage, Côte-Rôtie, etc., usually also need more bottle age, as do many Barolos.

Vintage ports usually need cellaring, though you may find
some that are ready (ask your merchant). Aged tawny ports are
ready upon release.

In terms of American wine, many California Cabernets will
benefit from some additional aging, though many are perfectly
drinkable on release. The fancier ones (twenty dollars and up),
however, often need at least several more years.

And that's it: just about anything else you buy will be ready to
drink right away. Spanish wines, for instance, aren't released until

they're ready because the *bodegas* do the cellaring for you. And the vast majority of wines are made to drink young.

ADOPTING A HOUSE WINE

If you find you're crazy about a particular wine, especially one that's not expensive, you may want to make it your "house wine." You'll be entitled to a case discount, usually 10 percent, from many retailers. (A case is twelve bottles, in case you were wondering.) You also won't have to run out to the wineshop every time you have dinner at home. Keeping a case of house wine makes it easy to enjoy wine with your dinner whenever you feel like it.

If you want, you can have a house white and a house red—even in the smallest dwellings, two boxes shouldn't be much of a problem. And if you get tired of it, and you feel like trying something new, it's fun to find another.

BRINGING WINE TO A DINNER PARTY

For some people, one of the rare occasions they'll walk into a wineshop and buy something occurs when they're invited to a dinner party. You've seen these folks, standing in front of a shelf, staring dumbly, with no idea where to begin. Aren't you glad you're not one of them?

Still, this can be a tricky decision. If you know what your friends plan to serve, the choice becomes much easier. But besides the food, you also need to take the rest of the company's taste into consideration. Are they wine lovers? If so, try to find something intriguing or interesting, which doesn't necessarily mean expensive. Wine lovers always enjoy trying something new, especially if it's from a region or producer they don't yet know.

Or perhaps you happen to know that they're fond of a particular region or a particular varietal—look for something in that realm. On the other hand, you may know that they can't stand a particular type of wine: California Chardonnays, for instance. Or white wine in general. That'll help narrow things down, too.

Dessert wines are a great idea. Often the hosts will have bought wine for the meal, but neglected dessert. By the same token, sparkling wines work well because everyone loves bubbles, and they make the perfect apéritif.

For people who don't give a damn about wine, or those who are vaguely interested but not gaga, you'll have a much easier time. If you have no idea what they're serving, yet you think they'll want to pour your wine at dinner, these are your best choices: a Sauvignon Blanc (from California, New Zealand, Chile, or the Loire Valley), a Riesling, a Pinot Noir, or a Beaujolais Cru. If you go with the Riesling, it can be from Alsace or Oregon, or a Kabinett from Germany. If you want to go red, Pinot Noir is a great choice because it goes with such a wide range of food. Look for something in the appropriate price range from California, Oregon, or Burgundy (if you can afford it or feel the need to impress at a superficial level). Or consider a Beaujolais-Villages Cru, such as Morgon, Fleurie, or Moulin-à-Vents, which will go with a wider range of food than a bigger red such as a Cabernet or Bordeaux.

While many hosts will serve the wine you bring, others will

have already chosen and bought the wines they want to serve. In that case, don't be offended if they acknowledge your kind gift and then enjoy it without you at some later date.

STORING YOUR WINE

Even if you don't want to start a cellar, you'll need to pay just a little attention to where you store a few bottles.

Wines to Bring to a Dinner Party

Impressive and interesting wines to bring to dinner that won't break the bank:

    Albariño from Spain
    Vin Santo from Italy
    Monbazillac
    Alsatian Riesling
    New Zealand Sauvignon Blanc
    Muscat de Beaumes-de-Venise
    Châteauneuf-du-Pape
    Crozes-Hermitage
    Ribera del Duero
    Single-*quinta* port

Or consider one of these particular bottles from California:

    Scharffenberger Brut, Blanc de Blanc, or Brut Rosé
    Domaine Chandon Etoile or Brut
    Mumm Napa Cuvée Napa
    Au Bon Climat Chardonnay
    Calera Pinot Noir
    Chalone Pinot Noir
    Bonny Doon Vin de Glacière
    Preston Muscat Brûlé

The worst things that can happen to wine are sudden changes of temperature, exposure to light, and vibrations. Unless you live under a roller coaster, like Woody Allen's family in *Annie Hall,* vibrations shouldn't be too much of a problem. Darkness can easily be provided in a closet. Which leaves the problem of temperature. Let me say right off the bat that I do know certain people who love wine, including one prominent wine writer, who store bottles in far-from-ideal conditions.

If you live in a centrally heated, centrally air-conditioned house, you're in luck. Otherwise, you'll just have to do your best to keep the temperature fairly stable. Do not put wine anywhere near a radiator, heater vent, oven, stove, refrigerator, or air conditioner. If you happen to live in a house with a cellar, that's fabulous, since cellars usually stay cool, even in very hot weather.

To keep your corks in good shape, you'll have to lay the wines on their side. If the corks dry out, the airtight seal will be destroyed, and your wines will oxidize. An inexpensive wine rack is helpful here.

GOOD STORAGE IS OF PARAMOUNT IMPORTANCE TO SERIOUS WINE DRINKERS

IT WORKED OUT WELL. WE SENT PHILLIP JR. HERE TO BOARDING SCHOOL AND CONVERTED HIS BEDROOM TO TEMPERATURE-CONTROLLED WINE-STORAGE SPACE.

WINE STORAGE, CONTINUED

OH, GOOD, I SEE FRANK'S GONE TO OUR CELLAR TO CHOOSE A BOTTLE FOR TONIGHT'S DINNER.

If you can't find a good place to keep your wine, don't fret; it just means you don't want to age it much more than a year or two after you buy it. Which brings us to the next question: what if you really do want to start a small wine cellar?

STARTING A CELLAR
It doesn't have to be as intimidating—or as expensive—as it sounds.

You can even start a wine cellar by accident. You pick up a bottle here and a bottle there; someone gives you something special as a gift, another bottle here and there, and before you know it, you have a collection.

You can also start with a small base and build on that. The great thing is that once you start collecting, friends and family members will always have a wonderful gift possibility for you, at any price level. And imagine having a collection to peruse each night at dinnertime!

Base Collections to Help You Start a Cellar

Low-Cost American Wines (Around $100 Total)

- 2 California Chardonnays, @ around $10 each (e.g., Acacia Carneros, Byron regular label, Chalone Gavilan, Sanford, Edna Valley)
- 2 California Sauvignon Blancs @ around $8 each (e.g., Murphy Goode, Preston, Mondavi Fumé)
- 2 California or Washington State Cabernets or Meritages @ around $10 each (e.g., Columbia Crest, Buehler, Franciscan, Mondavi Unfiltered Cabernet, Estancia, Rodney Strong, Benziger)
- 1 California Zinfandel or Washington State Merlot @ around $8 each (e.g., Zinfandels: Château Souverain, Deloach Estate, Preston. Merlots: Columbia Crest, Château Ste. Michelle)
- 1 Oregon or California Pinot Noir @ around $12 each (e.g., Acacia, Adelsheim, Byron, Calera, Robert Mondavi, Sokol Blosser)
- 2 Rhône Rangers @ around $7 to $14 each (e.g., Joseph Phelps Vin du Mistral Grenache Rose or Le Mistral, Preston Marsanne, Bonny Doon Le Cigare Volant)

See the box above for two starter cellars: a low-cost American cellar for only about one hundred dollars, and a low-cost international cellar for a mere two hundred. Remember, these are just suggestions.

Once you take the plunge, you'll have to figure out where to store the wine. Ideal cellar temperature is between 50° and 60°F, and if you don't have a cellar below your house, you can start out with a simple wine rack. The only advantage to one of these as

**Add the Following, and You'll Have an International
Starter Cellar for About $200**

- 2 red Bordeaux, Médoc Cru Bourgeois @ about $12
  each (e.g., Château Larose-Trintaudon, Château
  Greysac, Château Puy Blanquet, Château de
  Rochemoron)
- 2 Alsatian whites (1 Riesling and 1 Pinot Blanc) @
  about $8 each (e.g., Hugel Pinot Blanc, Domaine
  Schlumburger Riesling, Trimbach Riesling)
- 1 German Riesling (estate Kabinett or Spätlese) @
  about $10 each (e.g., Dr. Loosen, Kurt Darting, Schloss
  Schönborn, Staatsdomäne Niederhausen)
- 1 Beaujolais Cru @ about $8 each (e.g., Fleurie,
  Moulin-à-Vent, Morgon, etc.)
- 1 white Burgundy, such as Pouilly-Fuissé, @ about $10
  each (e.g., Louis Jadot, Labouré-Roi, etc.)
- 1 Châteauneuf-du-Pape or Gigondas @ about $14
  (Guigal, Vieux Télégraphe, etc.)
- 1 Côtes du Rhône-Village @ about $7 (Guigal, Brunel,
  etc.)
- 1 Chianti @ about $10 (Antinori, Ruffino, etc.)

opposed to a cardboard box is that you can pull out the bottles
more easily.

If the wine bug really bites you, you may wind up investing in
something a little more elaborate, such as a temperature- and hu-
midity-controlled wine cabinet or a special wine storage unit
that you can rent.

**IF YOU FORGET EVERYTHING ELSE
YOU'VE READ IN CHAPTER TWELVE,
JUST REMEMBER THIS:**

1. A trusted wine merchant can be your best friend.
2. Almost everything you find in a wineshop will be ready
   to drink right away except classed-growth Bordeaux,
   northern Rhône reds, and super-luxury California
   Cabernets.
3. If you live in the countryside, look into catalog sales.
4. Sauvignon Blanc, Riesling, Pinot Noir, and Beaujolais
   are the safest wines to bring to a dinner if you don't
   know what's cooking.
5. A base cellar needn't cost more than one hundred
   dollars.

Wines That Make an Impressive (If Expensive) House Gift

Jean Moreau Chablis Vaudesir
Zind-Humbrecht Riesling Alsace Herrenweig
Kistler Chardonnay
Domaine Drouhin Pinot Noir (Oregon)
La Pousse d'or Volnay Clos de la Bousse d'or
Peter Michael Les Pavots (Cabernet)
Caymus Cabernet Sauvignon Reserve
**Dunn Cabernet Sauvignon (Howell Mountain or
   Napa)**
Quilceda Creek Cabernet Sauvignon (Washington)
Château Lynch-Bages Pauillac
Domaine de Bonserine Côte-Rôtie
Château La Tour Blanche Sauternes
Taylor Fladgate Vintage Port Quinta de Vargellas

Chapter Thirteen

HOW TO LEARN MORE

Our little tale is drawing to a close, and now you can look wine squarely in the face. Hasn't a great burden lifted? Wasn't it painless?

But perhaps this book has done more than liberate you from fear of wine; perhaps it has whetted your appetite for more. If so, where do you turn from here?

Books and magazines are always a good place, and a list of options follows at the end of this chapter.

But I do need to say a word about the ubiquitous numerical rating systems you'll bump into in the *Wine Spectator* and other publications. Many of these systems are based on the collective judgment of a committee, and it's widely acknowledged that in blind tastings in which the various judges' scores are averaged, any unusual wine will suffer. Everything has a way of getting rounded out, not necessarily to the lowest common denominator, but certainly to a middle level of correctness. Robert Parker's guides and his magazine the *Wine Advocate* don't have that problem, since he's just one person. But that presents another

WINE CLASSES CAN HELP BUDDING WINE BUFFS
INCREASE THEIR WINE KNOWLEDGE

problem: Although he has a great palate and wide knowledge, it's only the palate and taste of one person. Yours might be different. Think of it this way: If a famous and well-respected food critic writes that your favorite dish, the pasta with wild mushrooms at Pietro's Restaurant, is ill-conceived and overseasoned, do you reconsider immediately? Or do you say to yourself, "Well, I guess we just have different taste"?

Another problem with assigning numerical ratings from 1 to 100 is that a numerical scale can sometimes become meaningless. Is a 100 the best possible wine in the world from the best possible vintage? For instance, the *Wine Spectator* gave a score of 100 to Château Latour 1990, a *premier cru* red Bordeaux that costs $145, and a score of 98 to a Yalumba Muscat Rutherglen Museum Show Reserve, non-vintage, a fortified dessert wine from Australia that costs $12 for a half bottle. Are they saying that the Yalumba is really almost as "good" a wine as the Château Latour? Or does it mean that the Yalumba is very close to an ideal fortified Muscat? Consider using a 1-to-100 scale to rate all foods. If a *chaud-froid de homard en gelée* at three-star L'Espérance in Véze-lay, France, is a 100, what would you give a perfect delicious hamburger? Since different wines attempt different things, a numerical scale is problematic.

That said, the information contained in these types of magazines, especially feature stories on particular wine regions, can be fascinating and informative.

There are also a number of other ways you can continue expanding your knowledge and experience of wine.

WINE COURSES

Depending on where you live, you may be able to enroll in a worthwhile wine course. Do check it out thoroughly, for a lot of what's out there are beginning mini-courses, and you may already know more than these have to offer. If the teacher is good, your time won't be wasted, since he or she will be able to teach you something about tasting anyway. But be forewarned that many teachers don't know that much themselves.

WINE WRITERS ARE ACCUSTOMED TO PRONOUNCING A WINE'S QUALITY WHILE IT IS STILL IN ITS INFANCY

I'M SORRY TO HAVE TO SAY THIS, MRS. MARTIN, BUT I JUST DON'T THINK HE'S IVY LEAGUE MATERIAL.

One way to find a good course in your area would be to ask your trusted wine merchant. Another would be to ask the sommelier or wine director of a restaurant in your area with a great wine list. Or, if you have a culinary school or winery in your area, that might be a good place to inquire. Or contact:

Society of Wine Educators
132 Shaker Road
East Longmeadow, MA 01028
(413) 567-8272

Some of the most serious courses in the country are given in New York City, at the International Wine Center. If one day you wanted to work your way toward becoming a Master of Wine (an ultraprestigious "degree" granted by the Wine and Spirits Education Trust in London), this is where you would start. Courses are given at all levels, as well as short-term seminars focusing on specific regions. Here's the address:

International Wine Center
231 West 29th Street
New York, NY 10001
(212) 268-7517

In the Los Angeles area, unconventional, unpretentious courses, such as "Escape from Chardonnay Hell" and "Life after Cabernet" are offered through Wine Expo, a merchant in Santa Monica:

Wine Expo
2933 Santa Monica Boulevard
Santa Monica, CA 90404
(310) 828-4428; (310) 828-2969 fax

In the San Francisco Bay Area, Joel Butler, a Master of Wine, offers courses in the East Bay. They are self-enclosed evenings,

Before

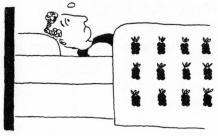

After

each of which covers a single topic such as "Value Wines for the Nineties," "Rhône Varietals," "South African Wines," and so forth.

The Bay Area Wine School
Joel P. Butler, M.W.
1 Northwood Drive, #2
Orinda, CA 94563
(510) 254-1686 (phone & fax)

TASTINGS

A painless and fun way to expand your knowledge is to attend formal or informal tastings.

A tutored tasting is one in which an expert explains each wine to you as you taste. This can be incredibly interesting, depending, of course, on the tutor.

No matter what kind of tasting you attend, you'll want to take notes. If you want, you can photocopy the box on page 292, and that way you'll just have to fill in the appropriate information and jot down your impressions.

Depending on the laws in your state, wine merchants in your area may offer informal tastings.

In New York City the laws were recently liberalized, so many of the finer wineshops are for the first time offering wines to sample.

Tastings are held every Saturday at:

Union Square Wines & Spirits
33 Union Square West
New York, NY 10003
(212) 675-8100; 675-8663 fax

In Los Angeles, many of the better wineshops offer tastings. Among them:

The Wine House
2311 Cotner
Los Angeles, CA 90064
(310) 479-3731 or (800) 626-WINE

The Wine Merchant
9710 South Santa Monica Boulevard
Beverly Hills, CA 90210
(310) 278-7322

In the San Francisco Bay Area:

Prima Trattoria
Negozio di Vini
1522 North Main Street
Walnut Creek, CA 94596

The American Institute of Wine and Food periodically spon-sors large, tutored tastings for its members. For information:

American Institute of Wine and Food
1550 Bryant Street, Suite 700
San Francisco, CA 94103
(800) 274-2493

Or contact the Tasters Guild, a nationwide organization that may have a local chapter that holds tastings in your area:

Tasters Guild
1451 West Cypress Creek Road
Suite #300
Fort Lauderdale, FL 33309
(305) 928-2823

AT-HOME TASTINGS

One great way to investigate a region or a varietal is to have a tasting at home, inviting a number of friends. You can do this one of several ways. In any case, there's enough in one bottle of wine for up to twelve people to taste.

One approach is to ask each friend to bring one bottle from a particular region, or one particular type. If everyone brings their own glasses (four or six apiece), you won't have to supply them all, and you'll only have to rinse them all once.

Or perhaps you'd like to exercise a little more control over the wines to be tasted. In that case you can go out and buy them all, and ask your friends to share in the cost.

Tasting Notes

WINE TASTED:
VINTAGE:
PRICE (if available):
REGION:
Where tasted:
Tasted with food?
APPEARANCE
Color:
Clear or opaque?
Weight (thin, viscous, etc.):
NOSE
Intense or faint?
Aromas:
PALATE
Flavors:
Texture/Body:
Balanced:
Finish and Length:
ASSESSMENT: Do I Like This Wine?

Either way, you can either taste blind or not blind. Not blind is easy—everyone knows what's being tasted at any given moment, and you can try to discover what you know about the characteristics of the type of wine you're tasting, as well as finding things you don't know or haven't read about.

Lots of wine aficionados like to have blind tastings. To do this, each person brings a bottle of wine, completely covered up. Some people wrap them completely in aluminum foil, but don't forget that doing so gives away the bottle shape. That's okay if you're tasting something like Bordeaux only; they'll all be in the same-shape bottle. But if you want to hide the shape, you might put the bottle in a paper bag, secured with a rubber band around the neck. Either way, each person should mark the bottle with his or her name.

Then start tasting. You'll have to play it by ear in terms of the order of the wines. But if, for instance, you're blind-tasting wines of the southern Rhône, those who brought white wines will have to remember to pour theirs first. If someone brought a Muscat de Beaumes-de-Venise, they'll have to serve it last, and so on.

Here's the way it goes: Whoever's going first opens their wine and passes it to be poured. Just an inch or so in the glass will do. Now she shuts up and everyone tastes and talks. The object, of course, is to guess the producer and the vintage, though that's very tough for beginners.

Try tackling vintage first. The color of the wine should give you a clue. White wines become deeper yellow as they age, and red

wines that start out purple in their youth become more brick red. Obvious fruit aromas fall away with age and turn into more complex bouquets. It will be difficult to name a year. But you may be able to say, "I think this wine is still fairly young, but not brand-new. Maybe it's four or five years old." Then you can count back, and hazard a guess. If you happen to know that 1990 was a great year for that region, but 1991 was lousy, the information will help.

Then try tackling the grape variety or the general region, based on what you know. If you smell blackberries in a deeply colored red wine, you might guess Cabernet Sauvignon or red Bordeaux. If someone nails the grape variety, the person who brought it should say, "Yes, that's it."

Once you know the grape variety or the general region, work on the exact region, zone, or AVA.

After you do this for some time, you'll be amazed at how much better you can get!

Of course, if one or two people at the tasting know a lot about wine and have good palates, they'll help everybody learn.

BLIND TASTING AT DINNER
Wine geeks will often engage in a meaner version of the same game. If they're invited somewhere for dinner, they'll bring a bottle of wine, disguise the bottle, and make everyone guess what it is. The reason it's mean is that they're never required to guess themselves! Still, if your friends are into it, this can be fun.

A PRACTICAL BLIND TASTING
While blind tastings can be done purely for pleasure, some people hold regular tastings to discover new wines to buy.

Each person brings one wine that is widely available in their area. All the wines are blind-tasted and rated from 1 to 10. The votes are then tallied and the wines ranked.

The number-one choice of the group will often be something expensive, usually over twenty-five dollars. But invariably, the number-two choice will be something very inexpensive, surprising everybody. Everyone will then rush out and buy a case of this great value.

Ideas for Tastings at Home

Oregon Pinot Noirs
Washington Merlots and Cabernets
Wines of the Pacific Northwest
California Cabernets and Meritages
California Zinfandels
American Dessert Wines
Rhône Rangers
Italian Varietals and Blends from California
Red Bordeaux
White Bordeaux
White Burgundies
Loire Valley Whites
German Kabinetts
German Rieslings
Sparkling Wines That Aren't Champagne
California Whites That Aren't Chardonnay
Sauvignon Blancs from Around the World
Spanish Reds
Tuscan Reds (Chianti, Brunello, etc.)
Reds from Piedmont (Barbaresco, Barolo, Dolcetto, etc.)
Rhône Valley (north and south, red and white)

WINE ON-LINE

If you're comfortable behind the wheel of your computer on the information superhighway, you'll have fun with wine forums on the various on-line services. But beware: Wine geeks thrive in cyberspace. Here's where to go:

Compuserve: CIS: food, then GO Wine Forum

America Online: Key Word: wine

BOOKS AND MAGAZINES

Finally, here are a few books and magazines I recommend if you want to learn more.

Some easy, enjoyable reading to take you to the next step:

The Simon & Schuster Beginner's Guide to Understanding Wine, by Michael Schuster (Simon & Schuster). Great on tasting techniques.

Hugh Johnson's How to Enjoy Wine, by Hugh Johnson (Simon & Schuster). Also especially good on tasting techniques.

Oz Clarke's Wine Advisor, by Oz Clarke (Fireside). An excellent pocket-sized reference to take to wineshops or restaurants, published annually.

Windows on the World Complete Wine Course, by Kevin Zraly (Dell). You already know a lot of the stuff in here, but it provides some technical information you might find interesting. Zraly was the wine director of Windows on the World Restaurant, famous for its incredible cellar.

For fledgling wine geeks who want to invest in some great general reference books:

The Oxford Companion to Wine, Jancis Robinson, editor (Oxford University Press). A mammoth of a reference. Pick it up, and it's tough to stop reading; great photos, too. Great gift for a wine lover.

Parker's Wine Buyer's Guide, by Robert M. Parker, Jr. (Simon & Schuster). An excellent reference, incredibly comprehensive, including extensive vintage charts. It doesn't list prices, but Parker's tasting notes are really fun to read, as is his introduction.

Académie du Vin Guide to French Wines, by Steven Spurrier (Macmillan). Provides descriptions of every wine region in France and just about every single wine.

New Signet Book of Wine, by Alexis Bespaloff (Signet). A good general guide, better on France than California.

Wine Spectator Magazine's Ultimate Guide to Buying Wine (Wine Spectator Press). Basically, this is just information compiled annually from the magazine. Useful for price information and vintage charts, but doesn't necessarily cover every region thoroughly.

Books on specific regions:

Bordeaux, by Robert M. Parker, Jr. (Simon & Schuster). The definitive guide on the subject.

Wine Atlas of California, by James Halliday (Viking). A gorgeous and very informative book.

Guide to the Best Wineries of North America (André Gayot/Gault Millau). This guide, presented by the American Automobile Association, is a huge help if you want to visit wineries; it gives interesting information about each one.

French Country Wines, by Rosemary George (Faber and Faber). Like the whole Faber and Faber wine series, this is serious and thorough, but not obnoxious.

German Wines, by Ian Jamieson (Faber and Faber).

Italian Wines, by Philip Dallas (Faber and Faber).

> **TIP FROM CABERNET FRANK**
> If you want a fun way to learn about the different wine regions of France, as well as sharpening your food-and-wine-matching skills, check out a board game called "The Wines of France" from the Brandywine Game Company.

Italy's Noble Red Wines, by Sheldon and Pauline Wasserman (Sterling). The definitive guide to the great red wines of Italy.

Italian Wine, by Victor Hazan (Knopf). A walk through the subject, starting with tasting. Wines are organized by style.

Making Sense of Burgundy, by Matt Kramer (William Morrow). The best way into the convoluted Burgundy region by a guy who's crazy about it.

Sherry, by Julian Jeffs (Faber and Faber).

Investigative books about wine:

Napa, by James Conaway (Avon Books). A captivating history of the Napa Valley and its wineries, with lots of juicy stuff about personalities who are still there.

Wine Snobbery: An Exposé, by Andrew Barr (Simon & Schuster). The title is a little misleading; it's really more a real inside look at wine and the wine industry. Fascinating reading.

Magazines:

Wine Spectator. An attractive and fun-to-read magazine, with good features about different regions, in-depth looks at particular wines, and interesting columns.

Gourmet magazine. Gerald Asher's wine columns are well written and often interesting.

Decanter. A look at the world of wine from a well-known British magazine.

AND JUST WHEN YOU THINK IT'S ALL BEGINNING TO MAKE SENSE, CONSIDER THIS:

1. HALF OF ALL VINHO VERDE OR "GREEN WINE" PRODUCED IN PORTUGAL IS RED.
2. "VINO de TAVOLO" (TABLE WINE) IS THE CATEGORY FOR BOTH SOME OF THE BEST AND WORST WINES IN ITALY.
3. WHITE ZINFANDEL IS NEITHER WHITE NOR ENTIRELY ZINFANDEL.
4. THE FIRST OFFICIALLY DESIGNATED "AVA," AMERICAN VITICULTURAL AREA, WAS AUGUSTA, MISSOURI.

Index